RIDING THE ELEPHANT

Unraveling the Mystery of My Childhood Trauma

A Memoir

By Philip A. March

OVERCOME
— PRESS —

Published by Overcome Press

ISBN: 979-8-218-51181-4

Library of Congress Control Number: 2024919570

This is a work of nonfiction. Some names and identifying details have been changed to protect the privacy of individuals. Composite characters and altered details are used to enhance narrative coherence while maintaining the truth of the experiences described.

Edited by Lisa Manterfield and Molly Spain

Cover design by Julie Ahn

Printed in the United States of America

For more information, visit: www.philipmarchbooks.com

Follow Philip on social media:

Twitter: @PhilipMarchBooks

Instagram: @PhilipMarchBooks

LinkedIn: Linkedin.com/in/philmarch/

10 9 8 7 6 5 4 3 2 1

For Kathy. Your unwavering love and support have been my anchor through the storms of life. This book is a testament to your strength, patience, and belief in me. Thank you for being my rock, my inspiration, and my love.

Author's Note

The following events are true. Some names have been changed to protect identities. Some characters are composite and partially fictionalized to preserve privacy. Some survivor group names have been changed to preserve anonymity. Some family members have been fabricated for similar reasons. Some facts have been altered inadvertently due to incomplete recollection of events. As time does not pass linearly in the subconscious—in fact time doesn't pass at all—the events in this memoir are not ordered chronologically in all cases.

"While most societies have maintained a sense of taboo regarding incest, in point of fact, the sense of taboo has not been in committing incest, but rather in talking about incest, especially by those who have experienced it."

— Anonymous survivors' group

Table of Contents

PROLOGUE

Serenity in the Storm

1995

I rode the crest of a formidable swell, adrenaline coursing through my veins, as I sailed two miles offshore in the San Francisco Bay. With each exhilarating surge forward, I felt alive, invincible.

Until everything changed.

I soared forward at thirty miles per hour, the force of the sail propelling me toward the trough of the wave. I sensed, only vaguely amidst my state of ecstasy, my weight tipping precariously beyond the equilibrium of my board. Then, in a surreal slow-motion dance, life paused, suspended in midair.

With a sudden jolt, reality crashed down around me. The sail, still tethered to my harness, slammed into the water and halted abruptly, sending me hurtling headfirst into its unforgiving grasp. My head hit with a force so fierce that it punched through the very fabric that had been my impetus. As shockwaves reverberated through my body, the rush of wind and water transformed instantly into a deafening silence. As the world went dark, the sun's warmth vanished, replaced by emptiness.

* * *

Three hours earlier, I sat in my boss's office, the air thick with congratulations combined with a tension fueled by increased expectations.

"Well, that's at least good news," said English-Ian. "Whilst I know it's a challenge managing this third-party product, you've still built up awareness and let the account team know what it can and can't do. The numbers are great. I don't know if you're aware of this but our flagship automation product is late to market. We desperately need the revenue. Your product is saving our bacon right now. Keep up the good work!"

I left my boss's office with mixed emotions. I was working at Tencor, a Bay Area semiconductor manufacturing equipment company. The product I managed was doing well. I was thirty-five and was engaged to be married the following year, my MBA almost finished. Yet it had been a stressful few weeks and my constant pushing against the current with an outside-the-box product was starting to take its toll.

I needed some sort of stress relief. Something to get my mind completely off the work pressure. Something that would push me to the limits, generate some excitement deep inside my core, and focus my mind acutely on the moment. I stepped outside and called the San Francisco Airport automated weather recording. It was 2:00 p.m. and the robotic voice said: "Wind: two-eight-zero at one-niner." It was already blowing nineteen knots from the west northwest. Perfect conditions for an exhilarating afternoon of windsurfing on the bay.

An hour later I drove into the parking lot at Third Avenue. I had timed it perfectly. The sun was shining, the wind had picked up to twenty knots, and the tide was ebbing—a good thing. I shuttled my eight-foot-four windsurf board to the setup area, then rigged my 4.7-meter sail. Fifteen minutes later I was on the water.

After tearing across the two-mile stretch of chop, I arrived at the edge of the channel and immediately spotted Joe and three other friends on the water. This was where all the magic happened. The wind flowing over a long fetch of water created large waves that welled up against the sandbar along the edge of the channel near the marker. The trick was to get on the wave, luff the sail, and surf downwind.

The sensation of the strong winds propelling my board across the water was electrifying. My body was doing something it was meant to do: balancing, twisting, edging . . . shifting my weight as I carved down wave after wave. And the more intense the conditions became, the more focused I was and the less distressed I was about my hardships. Everything else faded away. There was no time or mental energy to think about day-to-day stress. The waves and strong winds required every ounce of mental energy I had to offer.

As I surfed down a large section of wind swell near the far edge of the channel, I felt my boom line hook back into my harness, causing the force of the sail to pull me forward and down. My feet floated off the board as my body began to catapult, pivoting headfirst toward the trough of the wave.

The sail stopped abruptly as my body hurled toward it. I saw the bulk of the sail moving toward me at breakneck speed as my ears registered a loud crash. Everything went dark. No light or sound penetrated the frigid water to brighten my senses.

I thought I was dead.

I lay there in the darkness, the weight of the water pressing in around me. Time seemed to stand still as I struggled to make sense of what had just happened. Each passing moment felt like an eternity, the silence broken only by the rhythmic beating of my heart.

Following what seemed like an eternity, I began, slowly, to sense the cold water on my face. The icy chill on my hands, feet, and neck. Over seconds, as I began to panic, gasping for air, it dawned on me slowly that I was underneath my sail. Somehow I had magically transitioned from above my sail to being underneath it while still being tethered to the boom. My hands searched frantically for the lynchpin that would undo the twisted knot pinning me under the sail.

As my hands blindly tried to make sense of the enigma that comprised my harness, hook, boom, and cable, I came upon the precise location where my harness connected to the cable. I reached for the line and firmly pulled it down, but it didn't budge. I tried again. It was then that I realized the cable was twisted around my harness hook. In a final herculean effort, I pushed my waist toward the rig while pivoting my body in hopes that this motion would undo the fatal twist that had locked my harness to the boom.

In an instant, the cable came free of my harness, and I swam out from under the sail. As my head breached the surface, I glanced around trying to locate my windsurf rig. Catching it in my peripheral vision, I began to swim over toward it. It was at that point I realized something was terribly wrong. Parts of the sail that should have been in one solid section were flapping back and forth as the waves rolled through. Relief that I hadn't broken my neck was quickly replaced by fear that I was in the middle of the tumultuous channel two miles offshore with waves and high winds, but without a functional sail.

It wasn't just a matter of lacking directional control. My board had a tendency to submerge. Without the propulsive force of the sail to lift it onto the surface, the board would swiftly descend under my weight, disappearing beneath the water's surface until only my thighs remained visible. In fact, absent sail propulsion, even mounting the board would prove futile without the necessary lift to boost myself onto its surface.

I would have to swim back—a three-hour proposition. And with the wind blowing me toward the San Mateo Bridge, this likely meant sliding through the span to a much less hospitable landing and an exhausting, treacherous walk through thigh-deep bay mud . . . that was if I made it back at all.

I berated myself for being out there in such perilous conditions. Why in God's name was I sailing in high winds and huge swell with no life vest, no helmet, no radio, and no means of propulsion without a working sail? What had driven me to this point in the first place?

I made all kinds of deals with whatever higher power— God, the Universe, my Creator—I could conceive of at the time. If I made it back, I'd never take risks again. I'd be more careful. I wouldn't be so obsessed with sailing and spend more time with my family. Whatever it took.

At that moment, consumed by fear and desperation, my usual lack of religious belief and absence of morning prayer were quickly replaced by an urgent sense of needing assistance. A belief that there must be something or someone out there watching over me, ready to judge whether I had lived a righteous life worthy of survival.

In my peripheral vision I caught sight of another sailor. My good friend Joe had jibed after seeing me down in the water and headed back in my direction. He sheeted out and came off a plane, sinking down into the water next to me.

"You OK?" he shouted over the sound of the roaring wind and crashing waves.

"I blew out my sail."

"Shit," he said. "Do you think it's sailable?"

He and I discussed the best next course of action. I was

convinced the sail was either completely useless or that if I tried to water start, whatever was left of it would disintegrate. Joe suggested I fly it up out of the water and we'd take a look.

I pulled the mast up and into the wind and flew the sail, exposing the full extent of the damage. The entire panel above the boom—the largest and most important part of the sail—was completely gone. It looked like a wall when a cartoon character blows through it, leaving shrapnel and cracks radiating outward around a hole shaped like the character itself.

But there was a glimmer of hope in what I saw.

"It looks like the trailing edge is intact," Joe said.

The trailing edge—a narrow, quarter-inch strip of stitched material that ran up the leech of the sail—was still in place and hadn't ruptured. This was fortuitous because the rest of the sail above the blown-out panel was still holding its shape. It seemed incredibly fragile, and I was convinced that as soon as I loaded it this quarter-inch strip of Dacron would rip, and I'd be holding a flag instead of a sail.

"Worth a try," I said to Joe.

I swung the sail across my body by gripping the mast with my right hand. Then I grabbed the aft portion of the boom with my left and shifted my right hand to the boom. Placing my right heel on the board, I gingerly sheeted in to lift myself onto the tail of the board. The fragile sail barely held together, and I knew if the quarter-inch fabric border on the trailing edge gave way, I'd be facing a long swim in twenty-five-knot winds and head-high waves.

I gave the sail a few very delicate pumps. To my astonishment, the board transitioned from bogging and began to plane, porpoising playfully under me. After a few seconds I was moving at twenty-five mph back toward the launch site. The high winds that had caused me to be overpowered before the crash were now powering my 4.7-meter sail—turned 4.0—onto a plane.

Joe sailed behind me, holding vigil. Within a few minutes I was back to shore.

Back at launch, I set my broken rig down in the rigging area. A crowd gathered around as friends gawked at the blown-out sail. One guy handed me a beer as if I was walking into a frat party.

"Dude, where did you break down?" frat boy asked me.

"The far side of the channel," I said, with a slight sense of pride.

"Holy shit . . . how did you get back?"

"The leech held together," I said. "Fortunately! It could have been bad,"

"Shit, yeah!" he said.

My fear-induced adrenaline had transformed into something else.

Bravado.

We exchanged stories of crashes and close calls. Even tales of those who had died out here before us.

This was, in more sense than one, survival for me. The tumultuous wind and water—even the close call—took me from feeling empty and flat to living an exciting life with moments of ecstasy combined with sheer terror. These extreme experiences were something that I craved. I had to get out into the storm. Into the tumultuous waves and the menacing wind. I had to put myself squarely in the eye of the hurricane. Because only then would my mind calm. Only then—when I was solely focused on negotiating the violent wind and waves—was I truly present and living in the moment. Only then did I stop thinking about . . .

They say what you don't know can't hurt you. I believe the exact opposite. What one doesn't know—especially about oneself—can and will hurt them. It will rule their life, perhaps secretly, but nevertheless completely, until they square up to face their demons and accept that human beings, even loved ones, can be incredibly cruel.

If I could have finished that sentence and understood what I was avoiding, I might have saved myself decades of pain. I could have circumvented twenty-five years of building up my life, only to tear it down again. If I could have faced what was broken inside me and stopped denying it, I might have moved forward instead of being constantly triggered and reacting negatively to power, authority, and perceived bad motives. Of fighting vehemently against outside powers which were actually manifestations of my own inner turmoil.

But I couldn't finish the sentence—at least not then. So instead, I spent the next twenty-five years searching for answers, trying to piece together what it was I really needed to be whole.

Act I:
In the Beginning

CHAPTER ONE

Apology

"I really think you two should come to Monterey," he said.

A month after my windsurfing mishap, my eldest brother, Holly, called me on the phone. I hadn't seen him in over five years. I worshiped him as a child. He was the oldest in the family, a rebel and a rock star. The firstborn and the moral leader of our family. He was tall, confident, with lengthy auburn hair and a scruffy reddish beard. He meant everything to me. But we had gotten out of touch during the late eighties as he pursued romantic relationships and his love for sailing—and moved a couple of hours away.

He seemed adamant that my younger brother and I come down and meet with him in Monterey. It wasn't just a routine gathering of siblings. He seemed to want to delve deep into topics of a profound nature.

Pete and I agreed to make the drive to Monterey. We met in the office of his therapist, Judith Wolfe. It was pleasant and smartly decorated, which was in stark contrast to most of Holly's environments—his pawn shop, his boat, his shack up the hill.

Though it wasn't his environment, Holly took charge. "First off I want to thank you both for coming," he said in a confident, yet compassionate way.

He seemed different these days. From the druggy, alcohol-laden days of the sixties and seventies, to the cocaine-filled eighties, we had never known him to be fully responsible or present. He was always seeking a thrill—motorcycles, booze, drugs, the open ocean, surfing.

But here in this office he was thoughtful, compassionate, and empathetic. He seemed to want to tell us something. To demonstrate that something had changed in him.

We began to talk about family dynamics. About growing up together. About pressures and disappointments. Holly brought up his concerns about Pete not wanting to maintain a relationship.

"You seemed uninterested in hanging out," Holly said.

He recounted having reached out to Pete more than once and Pete having always been too busy to connect. He shifted the tone slightly to imply that Pete seemed *above* the idea of staying connected with Holly. That he was *too good* for that.

As Holly articulated his sense of hurt at being rejected, Pete jumped in and talked about his own family dynamics. He teared up as he talked about his commitment to his wife, Katy, and the feelings of pressure, even burden, at trying to spread his attention too thin, away from his cherished family. He began to weep openly as he said it.

I glanced at Holly and Judith and noticed an immediate shift in their demeanors, a softening. They leaned in as a combination of endearment and compassion came over their faces. Holly and Pete apologized to each other and eventually hugged.

Now Holly turned his attention to me. The dignity and importance of his diction were palpable. He indicated he had given up drugs and alcohol and had turned his life around in earnest. His speech and demeanor were in striking contrast to anything I had seen in previous years.

"How about you, Phil . . . how are you doing these days?" he said. It felt to me a little like a setup. He was going somewhere but I couldn't discern where.

"I'm OK. It's been a while since I've seen you. Thanks for getting us together," I replied superficially, all the while searching for clues as to exactly what was happening.

"Yeah, I agree," Holly continued. "Thanks for making the drive down here . . . I know that's a long way to come, and I appreciate it."

The small talk was killing me because I sensed there might be something bigger to come. My propensity for efficiency would typically have motivated me to steer the conversation toward a rapid conclusion, but it felt daunting to cut to the chase.

"So do you feel OK these days? I've thought over the years that you might have some things under the surface that are bugging you." Holly edged into a topic I didn't expect. In an even bigger surprise, Judith jumped in.

"I think what Holly is getting at is that you seem on the outside very controlled . . . very put together. Yet there is a tension underneath that might imply perhaps you're overcontrolling things to compensate for something else. Like you may be holding something back."

The words sent a shock wave through me. I hadn't thought of myself as being necessarily tense or overcontrolling. And I certainly didn't think I was covering up anything.

At the same time, something in her words resonated deep in my subliminal mind. Maybe it was the tone. Maybe it was my propensity to defer to people with power. Whatever the case, my self-assuredness was stayed for the moment as her words lingered.

It galvanized in me a feeling of discomfort . . . as if I was being scrutinized. It was reminiscent of sitting on the family room sofa as a young child and having my father come over and put his hand on my shoulder, in response to my constant tic—a shoulder twitch I'd had since I was a young child.

Controlling, but not seeing me.

Who was this therapist to assess me? We had only just met, yet she was speaking as if she had known me for years.

Suddenly, Holly jumped in with another surprise topic. "One thing I've wanted to say to you . . . for a while . . . was about that go-kart episode on La Barranca when you were really young."

I scanned my mind for the episode but there was nothing there.

"I just remember telling you to get into the kart and you didn't want to. I just wanted to say I'm sorry about that. I shouldn't have forced you and I apologize."

Still nothing but a blank screen.

"I . . . don't even remember that," I confessed, still racking my brain trying to come up with the event.

"Really?" Holly replied. He and Judith glanced at each other with inquisitive, knowing expressions as if lab scientists saying, "Ah . . . now this is interesting." Their demeanors made me feel like an outsider, an alien. Like a lab subject. As if there were certain behaviors a normal person should engage in, but I wasn't reacting that way, and for that, I was abnormal.

While I was still reeling from the go-kart story, Judith shocked me back to the present.

"I think you should try some somatic work."

"Somatic what . . .?"

Holly jumped in like the second half of a two-person infomercial. "They're exercises you can do that help bring the mind and body together." He explained one form of somatic exercise called bioenergetics where one moves the body—doing things like pounding pillows or punching bags—while thinking about traumatic events. It lets the subconscious brain come together with the body to work through difficult, even repressed, memories.

"Hmmm," I said, still feeling off-balance. "I'll look into that."

I was still bewildered about what, exactly, Holly and Judith were trying to get at. There seemed to be some sort of buried agenda. Something under the surface.

Toward the end of the session, Holly thanked us both for coming and reiterated that I should explore somatic things like bioenergetics. It seemed like more than a passing suggestion the way he said it. He seemed to be saying this was something important for me, something I needed to understand, in order for me to go on and live my life in a productive and happy way.

It was invasive and pushy, and I didn't want to hear it. I was already a productive, achieving member of society with a budding technology career and an MBA on the way. I didn't need to be more productive.

I thought more about the somatic comments. What had prompted those anyway? Was it my tic? Was it something Holly knew had happened to me as a child?

Over time I would think of this experience a little differently. Like maybe it wasn't so much about the go-kart but something bigger. Like he was making amends for something, or someone, but he was doing it in code.

My mind was reeling, trying to put the pieces together. But they just wouldn't fit. That evening my mind wandered in and out of my few childhood memories. Back to third grade, a time when I struggled to fit in.

No, scratch that. A time when I clearly stood out, yet

without understanding why.

I was a slight kid in third grade, under four feet tall and weighing about forty-six pounds. Some adults called me shy at the time but I was really just scared . . . of everything and everyone.

Despite my desire not to be seen or noticed, I had begun to dress loudly and flamboyantly. To make things worse I had developed a pronounced tic where I would shrug one shoulder and twist my elbow outward as if nudging some invisible friend. (Or, as my father interpreted it, pushing someone away.) Kids began to mock me by doing the same motion, glancing at each other, then laughing hilariously. The combination of flamboyant dress, the tic, and my incongruously shy, reserved demeanor created a perfect storm.

It's not even evident to me why I chose to dress that way in the first place. It was 1968 so the bell bottoms and vests were a thing for older kids, like Holly, but not for kids my age. I admired Holly, even worshiped him, so it made some logical sense that I imitated his dress.

One morning in October, as I lined up for kickball, I had on a leather vest with tassels, reminiscent of the Berkeley hippie culture that was growing rapidly at the time, and a brightly colored bandana fastened with a gold clasp around my neck. It was a loud ensemble and I stood out like a sore thumb.

"Hey Apache," one classmate jeered, as he passed by.

"Hey hippie," another kid mocked, poking me in the arm.

As I walked up to the plate, I twitched my shoulder and elbow again. A few of the infielders snickered.

The pitcher asked how I wanted the ball.

"Soft with a low bounce," I replied obsequiously.

As the ball approached, I ran down the asphalt embankment and swung my right leg wildly, jerking my head up to look at where the ball should have gone. But it careened off my shin and went left into foul territory. I heard a gasp or two, a few faint chuckles, and some faint boos from the outfield.

On the second try I sent the ball right into foul territory.

On the third try I struck the ball with my toe, then it ricocheted off my shin, bouncing awkwardly toward the small gap between the pitcher and first base. The first baseman easily scooped up the ball and ran back to the base, tagging me out.

I tried to put together this memory with the therapy session and Holly's apology. Was the bioenergetics suggestion a response to seeing me isolated and dysfunctional as a child? Was it about my twitch? Was it about seeing me as a loner kid who was shy, yet drew attention to himself as if on purpose? About dressing like a hippie as an eight-year-old?

And what about the apology? Was the go-kart episode real? Or was it a proxy for something else? Had this event happened earlier in my life . . . before the flamboyant dress and pronounced tic even started? Maybe it had been too early for me to remember?

The conversation sat in my subconscious for a while, concerning me enough to schedule a few therapy appointments of my own. But nothing came of it. I eventually passed it off as commentary from an overly zealous, born-again Californian evangelizing his newly discovered enlightenment. The way people talk about fasting, taking up yoga, and doing a colonic cleanse.

CHAPTER TWO

The Fall

The sales organization had a propensity to choose lavish, haughty locations for their meetings—boondoggles as we called them—and this one was the ultimate. It was scheduled for Stowe, Vermont, at the peak of leaf season. This made it desirable to many corporate personnel so I knew I would have my work cut out to get onto the agenda. I would be fighting the perception that I was just yet another marketing guy who wanted to jump on the bandwagon.

Two years had passed since the bizarre meeting in Monterey. I was still managing the third-party semiconductor testing product. We'd merged with our competitor and the newly formed KLA-Tencor sales organization was going through a massive retooling as the product lines merged. My product had developed a kind of redheaded stepchild connotation with the newly assembled sales team. Still, it was a good product and filled a gap we had in our semiconductor test product line. And it was my job to continue driving its success through our sales team.

I reached out to Jared, my longtime friend and business school colleague. We had met in marketing class at Santa Clara University while pursuing MBAs and became instant friends. He was slim with attractive features, a slightly receding hairline, and very fair skin. He also had a supercharged sense of humor that I could only vaguely attempt to keep up with. We would sometimes get riffing on a subject using puns and go on for ten minutes, each one trying to one-up the other. I felt like he "got me" and, since we had been through so much of life together, it was probably true.

Jared would have ideas about how to get included in the upcoming sales meeting. He was typically diplomatic, but he could also be blunt and focused on his own interests—though in a funny and compassionate way, one that made you like him even if he was saying what you didn't want to hear.

"I need to drive this microscope product and get it adopted through the sales organization," I explained, almost pleading with him. "I was hoping to get onto the agenda for—"

"Dude, it's not really on my radar screen," he said.

Goddammit! Not you too.

I had hoped for something more helpful. Something that would help steer me in the right direction. But he was under no obligation to solve it. And I knew as a sales manager he had bigger fish to fry.

"Lunch tomorrow?" I asked.

"Absolutely!"

"Later, Scooter."

"Later, Sparky."

I backpedaled and decided to go a different route. I knew my product had to be represented in this meeting, but I hadn't been invited. I realized I would have to push my way into it. I reached out to Dan, the director who ran the Portsmouth office. He was the alpha, the one in charge, and the exec who had founded the event.

Dan was a former military guy and would be a tough nut to crack. I hadn't prepared a lot before the call as I was afraid any overpreparation would cause delay and that would lead to procrastination. The meeting was only three weeks away.

I asked the receptionist to transfer me to Dan's line. Once Dan got on the call I jumped the gun out of nervousness and began making a pitch about how my product should be part of the agenda, and could we somehow work it in?

"Would you introduce yourself?" he said coldly.

I stopped, took a breath, and reset for a moment.

"I'm Phil March. I work here in Mountain View with Jared Smith, and I work closely with Mark Fishbaugh in your organization; I'm the product manager for the confocal review station."

"Well . . ." he paused, loosening up slightly, but still maintaining his dominant tone. "There are a lot of corporate guys trying to jump on the bandwagon. I've got to maintain control and we don't want to drive up costs or pad the agenda just for the sake of giving the corporate marketing guys a vacation in Stowe."

"I totally understand." I had learned that matching aggression with assuredness and confidence was the only way to survive. "My goal isn't to jump on this for the sake of fun. This product has a lot of potential, and one of your own guys, Mark, is actively pursuing it. I think the team needs to know what it can do and when it's appropriate to sell it. It's not for all situations but it's another tool in the kit. If they don't know what its capabilities are they may either oversell it—cannibalizing other more lucrative KLA-Tencor products—or miss an opportunity and lose out to our competitor."

Silence on the other end of the line. Ten seconds passed.

"Hmmm. OK . . . I get your point." Then, in a distinctly

softer tone, "Yeah, it probably makes sense to include you. Alright, here's what you do: contact Jan and tell her I approved you to attend. She can set you up with the hotel and timing. Burns is handling the agenda. Send him an email with your proposed topics and copy me; and I'll instruct him to fit you in."

And just like that I was in the meeting.

Three weeks later I was sitting in the bar just off the lobby of the Stowe, Vermont, hotel, talking to Mark Fishbaugh.

Mark was a doughy, fair-haired guy with a quick wit. He was one of the top account managers in the company and could be abrupt, even glib, when making a statement, causing one to suddenly stop and think about what he had just said. I felt a sense of validation, even comfort, that he had taken time on the night before the meeting to hang out with me. My scope of influence had been fairly limited up to that point.

Mark asked me, in his probing way, how I was doing. He asked in a way that didn't seem invasive and solicited an honest, even vulnerable answer; it conveyed that I could trust him.

"Well, it's been kind of a tough road," I said, explaining how I had struggled with legitimacy as the product manager for a third-party product causing me to have to force my way into deals. That my product was often not accepted, so I had to justify many of my engagements with the sales organization as they wrestled to understand it. This was not a product we manufactured and there was a fair amount of "not invented here" mentality running through the organization.

Just then Dan came up to the bar and sat next to Mark. Mark introduced me and we shook hands. Dan was fairly tall—around six-foot-two—and sturdily built. He was an ex-military man turned business executive who lifted weights to keep himself in shape and maintain his imposing stature. The power shift was palpable as he sat down and joined us.

"Did you hear that?" Mark asked Dan.

"Hear what?"

Mark paraphrased my concerns about legitimacy and discomfort about pushing a product that many people were lukewarm about, despite its clear efficacy.

Dan paused for a moment, considering my comment.

"Pussy!"

Mark burst out in laughter. Instinctively, I laughed also—an obligatory laugh—yet I wanted to deck him. What an asshole. I was offering some candid honesty and he met it with the demeanor of a twelve-year old: taunting and bullying.

Dan, the same executive who had at first objected to my attending the meeting but then decided it was imperative that I participate, had just flung a childish insult my way, playing to his underling, Mark. And now both of them were having a laugh at my expense.

Instantly I felt both embarrassed and disconnected. Dan was the leader, the top dog. I had just been rebuffed by him and I felt diminished, demeaned.

We engaged in small talk and while Mark and Dan mostly conversed, I was a distant third player. Then we wrapped up the evening and went to our rooms.

Once back in my hotel room, I felt a strange combination of emotions. On one hand, I was glad to have made it into the event and gotten onto the agenda. That was a clear win.

Tucked beneath this was a negative feeling—one of disconnection, of being an outsider. It was exacerbated by the encounter with Dan. But in my heart, I knew it wasn't brand-new. I had struggled with negative feelings in the context of corporate events where aggressive alpha-dog behavior was exhibited—and this was true for many of the sales meetings I had attended. There were always people jockeying for position, for power, for control, often acting juvenile. Men one-upping each other, trying to make the strongest impression with the more powerful—and almost always male—executives.

But there was also something else—a third feeling that I couldn't fully identify. Arousal, but not what I was used to. I was typically attracted to women and the female form was alluring to me. That had been true since junior high school. And that attraction would manifest with certain physical sensations.

But this arousal felt different. It started in the back of my neck and ran down my back to my tailbone. It was as if some ancient memory had been awakened by being in the midst of this aggressive behavior.

I didn't know if it meant something about my sexuality or if this was just a case of experimenting to find pleasure wherever it could be found.

Twenty minutes later I stood looking down at the bedsheets. It resembled a crime scene. Dark wet spots, but also brown and beige stains: mucous, semen, some blood.

Shame welled up inside me. Embarrassment joined the fray. As if my mature self was observing, like a judgmental parent, something my juvenile self had done and was disgusted.

Thoughts raced through my mind: *Why had these feelings arisen in the presence of powerful men? Not just powerful, but men I looked up to and admired?*

I felt like my body was no longer mine. I had muscled my way into the agenda, wanting to be strong and powerful. Yet at that moment, I was overcome by a sense of weakness, vulnerability, and lack of control.

The feeling of frailty and insecurity washed over me, sending me back to the therapy session years earlier when Holly and Judith had tried to communicate something very personal to me. That I was overcontrolling in order to suppress something. That this tension underlying my confident, bold outer demeanor was an indicator of something deeper.

I felt I knew supremely who I was. Yet there was this homoerotic tendency showing up when I least expected it: in the presence of powerful, boisterous men. I hadn't believed Holly and Judith at the time, but maybe they had been onto something after all.

CHAPTER THREE

Hospitalized Christian Scientist

"Oh my God!" my sister's urgent cry pierced the air, jolting my father from his unresponsive state. A week after my return from Stowe, Cindy, my next-eldest sister, burst into our father's room at 12865 La Barranca. The room, cluttered with every item our mother had banished from the house, lay shrouded in dust. Our father, once lively and vibrant, now appeared depressed, immobile, practically comatose. I had been too preoccupied with my own life—marriage, kids, career—to notice the deterioration happening right under my parents' roof.

Cindy had discovered a massive wound on the bottom of his left foot and implored him to get medical attention. My dad objected, his unwavering commitment to Christian Science and prayer—instead of doctors—for healing ever present. But in his dire state, some survival mechanism must have kicked in just enough to override his Christian Science dogma and he agreed to go.

Ninety minutes later I walked into the hospital lobby to see Holly approaching me. The environment was disorienting. Most of our get-togethers had been at family events, typically in a comfortable, relaxed setting with no specific agenda. The unusual Monterey therapy session had been an anomaly. The present venue—with families talking in muted, serious voices, names being announced from the front desk, occasional emotional outbursts—was in stark contrast to our usual gatherings.

As he approached me, his expression conveyed both warmth and a sense of resolute determination. I sensed the shift in tone from our typical cordial exchanges to something more solemn and momentous.

After a brief embrace, we delved into the task at hand. Holly assumed the role of leader with a clear agenda, dictating our course of action. My role was to execute those directives. Oddly enough, I didn't feel pressured; it seemed entirely natural to comply with his requests, almost as if it were my inherent duty as his next-youngest brother. We were partners in crime, despite seeing each other only occasionally.

After a briefing from the medical team, my father's diabetes complications became clear. He had a blood sugar of over 400—we had no idea for how long—and a foot wound which had become infected, borderline gangrenous.

The doctors recommended surgery to remove the wounded portion of his foot—part tissue, part metatarsal bone. My father refused. Whether it was because of his commitment to the Christian Science faith, or something more existential—that they would start chiseling away at him, piece by piece, and eventually might recommend a complete leg amputation—wasn't clear.

To complicate things further, his sister flew into town from the East Coast to help out on day three of his stay. Aunt Shirley was also a staunch Christian Scientist, and a fairly controlling woman. She immediately began influencing him and the medical team by injecting her opinions wherever she could.

While Shirley and my father were against medical

intervention, Holly and I swung into action to get his condition attended to. Over the course of his weeklong hospital stay, we took turns visiting him, covering all briefings with the medical team, and keeping close communication with the attending doctor.

Holly felt strongly we needed to mitigate Shirley from intervening and to keep her out of the process. My wife and I had agreed to let her stay with us in our Mountain View home while in town.

"Would you find a way to keep her out of the hospital?" Holly said on one particular morning. "Even if you have to take her keys away to keep her out of there, just do it."

It seemed like a fairly extreme measure, especially given that I tended to exhibit deference and politeness to relatives I didn't know well, especially elders. I hesitated for a moment, knowing it might cause significant family friction. But that hesitation was quickly overcome by a sense of camaraderie and kindred spirits. Holly and I were a team. He knew best and I was his right-hand man. We worked well together; it was as if we were in the military and Holly was my sergeant—but a wise, benevolent one. He was the leader, now that Dad was laid up in the hospital.

While Shirley was in the bathroom getting ready, I went into her purse and grabbed her keys, hiding them in an obscure cabinet elsewhere in our home. A few minutes later Shirley came into the kitchen with a somewhat bewildered look on her face.

"Have you . . . seen my keys?" she asked slowly, incredulously.

I explained to her politely, but in no uncertain terms, that she shouldn't go to the hospital anymore and that it would probably be best if she left town. Shirley's expression shifted from bewilderment to shock. Then after what seemed like just a moment—perhaps too brief a one—it transitioned to acceptance. It was as if she knew she had been meddling and I'd caught her, shattering her alibi. To my surprise, she complied, leaving town later the same day after a brief phone call with my father.

My dad's refusal of surgery had prompted his doctor to inspect the wound and clean it as best he could without actually performing surgery. This translated into using a cotton-tipped swab as a makeshift scalpel. On the afternoon of day four I stood to the side, just behind the curtain while the doctor tried fastidiously to clean the rotten flesh out of his foot. I leaned over just a little too far, trying to ascertain just how bad the wound was and if it was getting better or—

"Phil, would you please not watch while the doctor is looking at my foot," he scolded.

"I'm just getting a sense about how serious the wound—"

"PHIL, I SAID NO!" he shouted.

There was that familiar feeling of being controlled by my father. Of not being seen. Of him governing, even owning me. I walked away feeling belittled, like a dog with its tail between its legs. His reprimand made me feel small, judged, and powerless. Emasculated.

At the end of day six, I'd had enough of the hospital. Instead of going straight home, I decided to visit the home of my childhood at 12865 La Barranca.

CHAPTER FOUR

Shirleys

"You OK?" I asked. My mother was sitting at the kitchen table, trying hard not to seem shaken.

"Fine, fine," she said. "I'm really just trying to stay out of this whole thing." It was clear she was referring to the unwelcome combination of her husband being in the hospital and her sister-in-law meddling in the decision-making.

In her younger years my mother was a beautiful woman with light brown hair, usually done up in a modified beehive hairstyle. Her skin was perfect, her eyes blue, and she had a slight, slender build. She had a cute, somewhat sassy, style about her and people who met her on the street took a second look. She had aged well and now at sixty-seven years old she was still lean, active, vibrant. Her hair was now white instead of brown, coiffed in a bob: ethereal, yet attractive. Her given name was Shirley, but she went by "Shan," a contraction of Shirley Ann.

After a long pause, I got up the nerve to broach the subject of my father and their complicated relationship.

"I know you guys have been living in separate rooms for a long time," I said. "It just seems like he's wasting away in there these days."

"Well, it's not my fault he was there with a foot wound," my mother said, defensively. "He wants to be in there. You realize he won't let me or the housekeeper go in there, don't you?"

That line of questioning had quickly come to an impasse. I decided to pivot.

"Aunt Shirley is a handful. Holly and I are having to work our tails off to keep her from controlling things."

"I try to stay away from her these days." My mother said this with an obsequious smile.

"So . . . what is the beef you guys have, anyway?"

"Well . . . it's a long, long story . . . it could take hours," she said.

"I've got time," I said.

She thought for a minute or two.

"Well, when we visited the East Coast back in 1970, Shirley was terrible to me."

"What do you mean?"

She explained how Cindy—my next-eldest sibling—got her period for the first time while we were visiting Shirley's family on the East Coast. My mother had directed her to stay out of the water while the rest of us went into the river for a swim. Aunt Shirley usurped my mother's authority and told Cindy it would be fine if she swam, essentially pulling the rug out from under my mom, infringing on her motherhood.

My mother paused for a while, collecting her thoughts.

"And then there was the sexual experimentation between her and your father."

"Experimentation?" I felt a nauseating feeling in my stomach.

"Well . . ." my mother paused. She seemed to be trying to formulate the thought in a way that would be least offensive. After careful consideration, she proceeded to recount an eerie story about my father and his sister.

"Your Aunt Shirley told me just after we were married that they played around naked together when they were teenagers. That . . . Well . . . they wanted to see if it would fit."

I was stunned. This news about the two of them experimenting sexually was disturbing to say the least. But it was downright shocking to think that the teenage boy in the story was my father—my mom's husband.

"She told me," my mother continued as her voice intensified, "in a very blithe tone that it was fine—that they had a 'healthy curiosity about body parts.'" My mother punched this last sentence with a forceful exhale of air that came out as a combination of an incredulous chuckle and a scoff.

Apparently when Aunt Shirley told my mother about this my mother was consumed by resentment and jealousy. She already disliked Shirley for being controlling and meddling. But hearing about her and my father's sexual experimentation put her over the edge. She never let it go and hated Shirley ever after that. It probably didn't help that Shirley had recounted it so nonchalantly and justified it as normal, healthy curiosity.

After hearing this story of incest, I wondered if it was Shirley or my father who had been the ringleader. Holly's comments in the therapy session years prior still lingered on my mind. I began to wonder if what Holly had alluded to in his pseudo-apology was related to something my father had done within the family . . . and possibly to me.

CHAPTER FIVE

Rising Star

I never got to find out, because six months after my father's hospital stay he passed away. Sepsis from his untreated foot wound caused by unchecked diabetes. My mother had transferred him to a Christian Science nursing facility on day seven of his hospital stay, just after I had pressured his sister to leave town. I had thought I was helping the situation by clearing my aunt out of town. But in the end, my mother had made an even more abrupt decision, moving him out of the hospital into what was essentially hospice care but without the medication. No doctors. No drugs. No medical treatment. Just basic hygienic care and prayer.

My suspicions about my father intensified just after his death. But as the months progressed, this began to fade—not ever disappearing completely but draining from the forefront of my consciousness. I got on with the business of advancing my career and raising our daughter, Rebecca, born the same year my father passed.

Time accelerated. Three years flew by.

By the spring of 2000, our second child was born: a son

named Brandon. Something in my genetic code clicked and I immediately began sinking more energy into my career. I had to be a shining example of what a man could be to my newborn son.

I felt underutilized at KLA-Tencor, and I was less productive than I wanted to be. I was bored and wanted to make a bigger difference. No one ever got famous in semiconductor processing. But networking and the internet: that was the big league. Everyone needed networking gear. The internet was booming. And it was something you could talk about at cocktail parties.

I began scouting opportunities.

A short while later, I made the move to Cisco, diving headfirst into the acquisition integration process. "Reach out to Scott in the acquisition integration team," my new boss said. "He needs help looking at how the PixStream devices get integrated, now that we've acquired the company."

"I'm on it."

The next day I sat in a conference room in Building Nine across from a heavyset man with fair skin and light, curly hair with a soft-spoken style. He looked like a big koala bear mixed with the demeanor of a mouse. Big Mouse.

We were one building away from John Chambers, Cisco's CEO and revered leader. I had spent the first few months on the job engaged in an executive training program implemented by an elite consulting firm called The Layne Group. It was very different from any corporate training I'd ever had before. This group focused on how organizations communicate and work together in an efficient way to meet the high-level objectives of the executive team. To close in on what they cared about. FSOW was the unassuming acronym. *For the Sake of What?* Yet in that small phrase was encapsulated an elaborate strategy that aligned the organization from top to bottom. And it was about people's intentions, not about amorphous organizations' goals.

If someone at a high level asked you to do something, there was a reason. It was imperative to know that reason. To succeed as an organization meant dialing in on that underlying intention, whether it was improving partner profitability around Cisco gear or cutting costs around deployment of large solutions. I learned to reject phrases like "Finance wants me to do this." There were no groups or walls, only people with influence trying to achieve something. What was that thing they were trying to achieve? And more importantly, why were they pursuing it?

I pulled out my Layne Group techniques with Big Mouse and we were soon talking about the acquisition integration process and his goals and criteria for success. I learned that Bug Mouse was responsible for the first six months of the integration. After that, it transitioned over to the respective business unit. It was fascinating and I felt like I was suddenly playing a high-stakes game. It also told me that my focus needed to be the first six months and not what happened after that—this is how I would satisfy my stakeholder, Big Mouse.

A few days later I was on a plane to Toronto, Canada. I caught a cab out to a suburb northwest of Toronto and stayed in a hotel. The next morning, I caught a cab to the PixStream facility. I met up with the head of engineering and we briefly discussed my goals. I did my best to downplay the process and appear disarming. I was there to understand the deployment process so that there would be no blind spots for Cisco as we took on the business.

I thought I was being honest and transparent—at least to the best of my knowledge. Yet in the back of my mind was a question mark: perhaps this could go a different direction . . .?

The head of engineering introduced me to the deployment lead, and we got about the business of documenting the process. I created a spreadsheet and projected it onto the front wall of the conference room so everyone could see what was being captured. I figured I had nothing to hide and if everyone knew what I was capturing—and could request modification at will—there would be less anxiety. The process was fully transparent—a search for the truth.

After half a day we had a pretty good snapshot of how this device was to be deployed. It was a complicated, expensive machine that converted radio-frequency signals to internet protocol and back again as part of a cable headend system.

I called a number of different experts into the conference room to help fill in blank spots as we encountered them. By the end of the day, we had a solid view of the deployment steps and the time and tools needed for each step. The process of calling on various team members and having them come into the room and question them while at the same time disarming them, made me feel productive and useful—important, even.

At the end of the day, I was done and ready to head back to San Jose. By 10:00 the next morning I was on a plane, armed with the information I set out to get. I'd accomplished the goal and was feeling good.

The following morning, back on the ground, I met with Big Mouse and went through the data. He winced as he first looked over the spreadsheet with the summary I compiled. Then a knowing look came across his face.

"Yeah, this isn't economically feasible," he said. "There's no way we can put in this kind of time and money to deploy these things."

My mind reeled momentarily but I forced myself to stay present in the conversation. "Did I . . . screw up?" I sheepishly asked Big Mouse.

"Not at all! On the contrary, this was exactly what we needed to know. You've done a stellar job. This will save Cisco five million dollars over the couple of years."

Two weeks later I read the company-wide

announcement from Big Mouse's manager that PixStream was being shut down. The company was being mothballed and those personnel deemed critical would be rolled into Cisco. It was a classic acquisition, shutdown, and subsumption of personnel. It's how Cisco, as I came to find out, acquired a lot of its personnel in these competitive times.

It's a scary feeling having that kind of power over other people's careers. I wondered if the PixStream employees saw it coming, whether they felt I had been honest about the process. Still, I had a job to do, and I did it.

After my first year at Cisco, I was awarded three Cisco Achievement Program awards and had a top "X" rating. It was a coveted designation, given only to the top two percent of employees. I was forming close connections with high-level people in the Customer Advocacy organization.

I felt good about my work at Cisco and continuously heard the rush of progress in my ears which sounded like an ocean wave breaking. I spent the next four years building my career. I jumped on a strategic project that had a direct line to Chambers himself. I began leading a team.

On one impulsive Friday evening, over a bottle of red wine, my wife and I decided to move to El Dorado Hills, 150 miles to the northeast. A lot of Bay Area tech workers had moved to the burgeoning community in the foothills of the Sierra Mountains just east of Sacramento. It was better for raising a family and had a lower cost of living. I'd work remotely and still have my high-paying Cisco job. But we'd have more to show for it.

I was only remotely aware that I was throwing away what had become a primary stress outlet for me: windsurfing. There was virtually none of that in the El Dorado Hills region. I passed it off at the time as a trend toward being a family man. I was maturing. I no longer needed the frenzy associated with heavy winds and chaotic waves. And I'd find other activities to do—

perhaps ones less dysfunctional than windsurfing.

My career was on the upswing. I was more productive than I had ever been. A rising star!

Damned be Holly's comments from therapy years prior. Whatever happened between me and my father died with him.

CHAPTER SIX

Sudden Death

"He's dead," Pete said.

Shock ran through my body like an electrical current and my gut tightened as if gripped by a boa constrictor. I stood there with the phone to my ear and an empty, dumbfounded expression on my face. An evening that started as a fun gathering of friends and reminiscences of old times had come to a sudden halt.

* * *

Four hours earlier my wife, Nancee, and I were preparing to host our former neighbors from Mountain View. Steve and Martha were coming to visit, and we wanted to make a good impression.

Nancee and I had met at my high-school buddy's wedding. I found her intoxicating: long, flowing red hair and slim, long legs that she used to prance and sway to the music of the B-52s. Early on we engaged in dinners, wine, and romance. Then, when I almost broke it off after two weeks of dating, she adamantly pointed out that we had gotten in a rut and not done anything active together that didn't involve dining or sex. We tried a few outside activities and quickly found a connection. A few months later we had become active partners together, rollerblading, skiing, windsurfing, and running. Lust had transformed to kinship, soul mates.

Nancee and I were both busy preparing the meal and sipping wine in the process. We had planned a sleepover for Rebecca and Brandon at a friend's house, so the preparations felt easy and unencumbered.

"Martha Stewart says the way to be relaxed while entertaining is to have the first glass before your guests arrive," Nancee said with a giggle.

The doorbell rang. Steve and Martha had arrived. We had wine chilling in the fifty-bottle fridge and a bottle of red at room temperature to follow that. We cracked open some Chardonnay and began touring them through the house.

Steve and Martha performed the perfunctory "oohs" and "aahs." These reactions were followed by quick glances toward each other and knowing smiles. They lived in the Bay Area, and we had moved from there. Our trappings were very lavish compared to Bay Area homes that were older and densely compact. We had a two-story home on a hill with a stone facade, a manicured lawn, and a small grove of redwood trees along the lower edge of the property. We showed them the upstairs primary bathroom with its built-in jacuzzi tub and 270-degree view of the mountains.

When we got to the kitchen Martha's eyes got big and she let out a gasp as she covered her mouth. It was a large open room with granite counters and a granite-slab island, including an integrated gas stove and oven. Behind the stove was a retractable vent that elevated when in use. There was a large brushed-stainless fridge and a window view of the large backyard with its pool and built-in waterfall. For most couples this was something unattainable in the Bay Area.

I commented about the wine we were drinking, playing

armchair sommelier. "This is from a winery we visited in Napa. It's heavy in the malolactic fermentation category with a creamy, even buttery finish."

I pulled the tri-tip off the barbecue and tented it with foil to let it rest. I opened a bottle of Gundlach Bundschu Zinfandel; it was the perfect wine to go with the rich flavorful marinated cut of beef. It had deep, earthy flavors of black cherry and pepper but with a smooth, rich finish.

We sat down to dinner in the formal dining room, its walls painted the color of Cabernet. We ate and talked and reminisced about old times; of kids' birthday parties in the neighborhood, quick catch-ups over the back fence, and windsurfing.

As the phone rang, I swiftly retrieved the cordless handset from the kitchen counter, well within the view of Nancee and our guests. On the other end of the line was my brother.

"Phil, it's Pete," he said in a voice uncharacteristically curt and serious. An urgency tinted his voice, sending a sudden tightness to my throat.

"Something's happened to Holly . . . he's been in an accident and . . . well, he's not OK."

There was a pause as Pete collected himself. And then—

"He's dead."

Some events can catapult a person out of the present moment and into a completely different realm in a mere heartbeat. Thoughts swarmed my mind. What had transpired? How had he passed? Was it a result of recklessness or perilous actions? Had his girlfriend met the same fate? Whose responsibility was it?

Nancee looked at me trying to sort out the meaning of the shocked expression on my face.

Pete explained that Holly had been out on the bay on his tender—the small craft moored to his sailboat—with his girlfriend. They had apparently gotten into a collision with another boat, and he had been killed instantly. His girlfriend was next to him in the boat, but somehow she had come out of the event unscathed, save for emotional shock.

A thousand thoughts and images flashed through my mind. I recalled the month prior when I had visited him on his boat, contemplating a spin on his small Boston Whaler but we'd decided against it due to the lateness of my arrival. Then my mind wandered to his visit to our home two months earlier, when we collaborated on repainting the south wall and repairing the central vacuum.

I hung up the phone. By that time all three people at the table—Nancee, Steve, and Martha—were staring at me in shock.

"My brother just died in a boating accident."

The expressions on their faces moved from shock to concern to . . . something else. Something akin to pity.

"Oh no, Phil . . . I'm so sorry," Martha said.

"Oh my God, that's terrible," Steve echoed.

Nancee came near and tried to provide some comfort. She was cautious, circumspect. She placed a hand on my elbow, the other on my shoulder. She inched closer. She seemed afraid, unsure of how I would react.

* * *

It's been said that what we don't know about ourselves guides us from our subconscious. Like a human riding atop an elephant, our conscious mind often believes it's in control, but it's the subconscious that truly steers the course. Something inside me switched on at that moment. It was as if I was standing in front of a movie projector and the bright image projected onto my visage was completely different than the previous version of me, causing me to appear nothing like my former self.

That night, as I lay in bed, my mind began to drift. I felt an unfamiliar heaviness, as if my thoughts were sinking into deeper, darker waters. And then, the dream came—a dream unlike any other. It was thick, weighty, as if tethered by a huge, massive wrecking ball that hung off it on a long chain and swung very slowly with the rhythm of the earth itself.

I was in a huge, lavish house with spacious bedrooms and bathrooms with ornate, exquisite faucets. There were beautiful women hanging out in different rooms of the house. In one there was a bunk bed—a very large one— with four women gathered on the top bunk, talking. I climbed the ladder. They were friendly and gave amorous glances toward me as we conversed. Back downstairs in the living room—really a huge courtyard with lawns and a gazebo—there was another beautiful woman.

It seemed each woman was more attractive than the previous one but in their own unique way. One had short blond hair and a slender, sleek athletic build reminiscent of Daryl Hannah in Blade Runner. Another—the one in the living room—had long dark hair and looked like a taller version of Natalie Portman in No Strings Attached. I desperately wanted to talk with Natalie.

She seemed in need of emotional support. I found her incredibly alluring. Yet at the same time she was eerily reminiscent of someone from my childhood. As she began to walk into one of the doors, I walked past her and said "Hey, could I talk to you for a minute; maybe it's best if we do it over here." I motioned to an alcove between the gazebo and cabana. We talked intimately. She leaned in—

Instantly, I was back upstairs in the primary bedroom. Staring at the sink, I suddenly realized it drained into a chute which ran directly onto the guest bed downstairs. I looked further and there was no plumbing to drain water from the sinks anywhere in the house. Water cascading down between walls and through crawl spaces.

As I inspected further, I saw that mold and bugs had

formed in many of these damp areas. In an adjacent wall, I peered through a hole and saw a number of small egg-like structures about the size of acorns. Upon closer inspection I saw they were cysts encasing the embryos of aggressive types of pests including roaches, huge spiders, and slugs. As I surveyed the scene I noticed more of these—hundreds of them—just waiting for the right time to hatch. It would be Armageddon.

The house was not as I had perceived it. All the beauty, both of the structure and the women that inhabited it, had transformed into rot, decay, and death.

CHAPTER SEVEN

Eulogy

I woke up from the dream with a feeling I've never had before. The residue of ancient childhood lingered like a fossil of what had been decades prior. I'd had thousands of dreams before this. But this one—and the ones that followed—had a different tone. I knew they were important, because of their huge momentum. They were thicker, more massive than others. They felt real, tangible.

This dream seemed to cast a different light on things I thought had been beautiful and happy in my younger years. The home felt to be that of my childhood, yet it was not the idyllic setting I had remembered. It was rotten and decayed beneath its gorgeous superficial facade.

The inhabitants of this dream house seemed somehow related to my own childhood as well. Daryl Hannah could have been my sister, Cindy. Nathalie Portman could have been the Friedman daughter, Anne. Yet they were purely sexual caricatures of what should have been complete human beings. The feeling of familial incest resonated with my mother's story about my father and his sister.

Just as Holly, during that bizarre therapy session, had

cast a shadow on my happy, carefree childhood, this dream took people and events I thought were good and wholesome, and recast them as dark and corrupt. The home was devoid of order and sanity. Attractive on the outside, yet with no caretaker or moral leader, it had transformed into ruin. It was as though, with Holly gone, there was no longer anyone there to care for it and protect it.

I jotted down the dream in my journal and got a cup of coffee.

I began thinking about Holly's memorial service which was planned for the following weekend. As I worked on my eulogy, I recalled the story of when Holly left home after the argument between him and my father back in 1970. The shouting, the grief. The anger. The negative authority exhibited by my father in the instant when my dad cruelly kicked Holly out of the house. When he left our home for good, I felt alone and crushed. I knew Holly was important to me and I loved him. No, I *adored* him.

The phone rang, signaling my scheduled 9:00 a.m. call with my friend Jared, his name echoing through my home as caller identification announced him. I recounted the haunting details of the dream that still plagued me from the night before.

"Dude," his voice came through the receiver, laced with compassion, "I know it sounds cliché but I can empathize with the pain you're feeling."

"Thanks man," I managed, appreciating his empathy. Jared had experienced a similar loss a few years earlier when his own brother passed. "It's strange, isn't it? How our lives have taken such parallel paths: marriage, kids, the loss of a brother . . ."

"Yeah, it's surreal," he replied, a hint of laughter in his voice tempered by the weight of shared grief.

As the memorial service was a week away, I was feeling the pressure of formulating something that was both profound but also captured, honestly, how I felt.

I read Jared an excerpt from a poem titled "Funeral Blues" by W. H. Auden:

He was my North, my South, my East and West,

My working week and my Sunday rest,

My noon, my midnight, my talk, my song;

I thought that love would last forever: I was wrong.

"Wow, that is intense," Jared responded in a tone combining surprise with a level of reverence.

"Yeah . . . I guess it is," I said, reviewing the poem, a sense of awkwardness sweeping over me.

"But I get it," he continued. "I felt the same way about my brother when he died."

My sense of awkwardness subsided as his words sank in. "I just felt like he and I were a team. Like we had a strong relationship. I really felt like I knew him. It seemed like we had a bond. With him gone, everything seems different."

"Yeah, it's life-changing," Jared replied, his voice a soothing balm in the midst of my anguish. "When someone that close to you dies, it seems like it takes the foundation out from under you."

"Exactly," I agreed, grateful for his understanding. "And this dream . . ." I continued, trailing off as I contemplated its implications. "It's unsettling, Jared. It's as if my childhood home is portrayed in an ugly light, tainted to its core."

In that moment, I realized how fortunate I was to have Jared on my side, even 150 miles away. He was a source of solace and understanding in the darkness of uncertainty.

CHAPTER EIGHT

The Fight

Over the course of the next few months, as I obsessed over the missing memories and the prospect of something bad happening to me as a child, my concentration at work lapsed. I took my eye off the ball and became less aware of the political environment surrounding the mission-critical project I had been managing.

Four months after the funeral I sat in my boss's office in one of Cisco's many buildings on Tasman Drive in San Jose. Our discussions over the past year had centered around preparing me to manage the group as Cliff, my boss, transitioned to another role. It wasn't just one event but a whole plan he and I had discussed. But as the stature of my winning initiative began to wane, I remained oblivious. I had kept on doggedly, doing what I thought was "God's work." I was the faithful lieutenant doing what my boss told me to do.

"There's been a shift in priorities in the department," Cliff said. "I know we talked about growth for you this year, but it's not going to happen. It looks like the opportunity that I was expecting to have for myself isn't panning out, and that means your growth opportunity goes away." His detached and brusque demeanor in this afternoon's conversation had a very different tone to it than in the past. It was quick, short . . . almost flippant.

On the way back to El Dorado Hills, my head still reeling as I circumnavigated East-Bay traffic on a Thursday evening, I stopped at a small Italian restaurant in Walnut Creek to have some food and a glass or two of wine and to collect my thoughts. I felt an emptiness in my soul, one that I wanted to fill with the warmth of rich red wine. As I sipped the soothing liquid, I started to rethink the many conversations Cliff and I had had over the last year. I began to wonder if Cliff had been disingenuous the whole time. Had his promises just been a ploy to both appease me and simultaneously get me to work harder? I felt used. Pushed to do something against my will by a force more powerful than me.

I ordered another glass and contemplated what I would tell Nancee. We had experienced friction recently. It had started back in the Bay Area. Two kids, higher stakes. We clashed over how the kids should be raised, each having our own ideas about what was important in raising happy, healthy children and what our respective roles should be. But after moving, things felt better—at least so it seemed. We developed the sense that all was well. Roles were clearer. I was the breadwinner, and she was the stay-at-home mom.

But there was friction under the surface. We fought once on vacation. I wanted to cut it short and get home to prepare better for the coming work week and she felt let down, like I was marginalizing family time. We got into an argument on the way home and were verbally mean toward each other. Another time we fought over the cable guy. He came into our home and told us how he'd route the cable to our new TV—and charge us an arm and a leg in the process. I knew I could handle the job myself. It was my home, and he was invading my space and convincing Nancee this was a job for a professional. I'd left the house in a huff and gone down to Town Center for a drink and to cool off.

Friction aside, I had to tell her the truth, even though it would probably upset her. I finished eating and ordered a third glass. As I continued to sip the rich red liquid, I felt the juxtaposition of two opposing forces. Stress on one hand about my job situation and what it would mean to my marriage. On the other hand, a growing feeling of numbness and calmness as the alcohol began to work its way through my system.

I left the restaurant and continued the drive back to El Dorado Hills. I remembered I had told her about the promotion plans months earlier. Based on that, she had probably developed expectations that I would be taking on more responsibility and getting a higher salary. Nancee liked the image of a successful career-pathed husband. I had built up this image of myself and it was going to suddenly be whisked out from under her.

I hoped Nancee could not only understand but also provide at least some support and comfort in my moment of reckoning. I didn't realize at the time how unrealistic this was. I was asking her to put aside her fear and provide emotional comfort to me. In my fearful, myopic mindset that evening, that was what I wanted—what I needed. That wasn't what I got.

"That's . . . that's awful," Nancee said over the phone. After a short pause she said, "Well, I know this is a tough situation, but we need to talk about this refinance thing that Jean is handling. We have to revolve our Visa balance this month to pay the fees of the refinance."

My head was starting to spin. "Listen, Nance'," I said, using her nickname, "could we just talk about that tomorrow? I've had a pretty rough day and can't deal with that right now. Let's talk more when I get home, OK?"

Ninety minutes later, at home in El Dorado Hills, there was an urgency . . . a tension in the house. I was still deeply shaken about the career setback and Nancee was nervous about the money situation. No doubt my career setback only amplified her fears. She came into my home office where I was putting work items away.

"We really need to talk about this financial situation."

"I told you; I don't want to talk about it tonight. . . . . It's been a really rough day," I said.

I could feel my already raw nerves becoming more frayed. Her words felt like burlap bags filled with lead piling up on me one by one. My gut tightened and my jaw clenched involuntarily.

And as the wine wore off, my feeling of rawness and exposure intensified.

"We need to deal with this," she persisted. "We are finally in a position to pay off some debts and get control. . . . You can't just avoid this. Your family and I need you to help."

Then she shifted, almost in an instant.

"OK, fine, you just can't support your family. I'll do it myself."

I did not react well. I felt emasculated and dismissed, inadequate as a man. I began to shout and she shouted back. The language devolved to insults and some four-letter words.

At one point I faintly heard Rebecca shout from the next room over: "WHAT'S GOING ON?" as she began to sob out loud uncontrollably.

I went into her bedroom to console her. She was in tears, sitting up in her bed. I tried to soothe her with a calming voice and my hand on her back. But as Nancee came into the room, my focus immediately shifted from consoling my daughter to the tension between my wife and me. The conflict was too much and, as I realized I couldn't be in the same room with her and keep myself regulated, I got up and left the house.

* * *

That evening I had another dream. The second of a new generation of dreams that were massive and disorienting. They seemed to be trying to communicate something to me in some sort of cryptic code.

I was in the midst of a war zone gun battle with a bunker to my left and insurgents down the hill to my right. Those in the bunker (the good guys) were shooting constantly but not very effectively.

One insurgent—the evil one—stood out in the open wearing a tux and a black top hat. He strutted in a self-assured, arrogant, cocky manner.

He walked slowly around the path up the hill circling back toward the bunker. He needed to be taken out. But the sniper was having trouble getting the shot off. The cocky insurgent strutted closer, as the sniper, played by Bradley Cooper, with long, rock-star hair and a closely cropped beard, tried again to aim and pull the trigger, but the rifle didn't fire. The cocky insurgent was going to win—I could just feel it.

I screamed at Bradley Cooper: "Take the shot, TAKE THE SHOT!" The insurgent was now a few feet away and pulled out a pistol while walking, now just five feet away, toward Bradley Cooper.

Bradly Cooper froze for an instant. The insurgent pulled the trigger and shot a hole in his forehead . . . and he fell to the ground, dead. The insurgent then turned toward the rest of us in the bunker, glancing at me with a sinister smile.

CHAPTER NINE

Family Unties

The taste of the dream inflicted a deep seemingly permanent sadness in my heart. My partner was gone. Killed by a wealthy, arrogant man in a top hat.

But who was whom? Bradley Cooper had long-ish hair and a short beard that had a hint of red in it. He and I were military comrades. The only man in my life who came close to this description was Holly, who, in his teens, had a closely cropped beard and long hair. And the military camaraderie was reminiscent of my relationship with him in the hospital.

The insurgent was arrogant and wore a top hat. He appeared powerful and imposing. There was a sense of aristocracy and a hint of the Monopoly man. Wealth, combined with arrogance and power. The only man in my childhood who fit this description was my father. He made the money in the family. And he sometimes wore a fedora around town thinking it was a smart, sharp look. It was as though Holly, my comrade and partner, had been killed by my father and that was the end of him and our relationship.

These realizations left me feeling alienated from those around me. No one was safe. Unfortunately, that included my wife with whom communications had devolved beyond recognition. Trust had evaporated. We experienced chronic friction in the form of arguments. Our marriage was crumbling, and I began to view her as the enemy.

* * *

Nancee and I got divorced quicker than any couple I've ever known. I never truly discerned whether I was driving the process, if it was her, or perhaps some other unseen force neither of us acknowledged. Some couples take over five years to do it. Some rush through it in eighteen months. Our divorce was completed six months after we separated. By the end of December that year it was final.

On the Monday after Christmas vacation as I dropped the kids at school, I glanced up to see a large clump of balloons floating upward from a house in the Marina Woods neighborhood. A birthday party decoration from over the weekend had somehow freed itself and was drifting up toward the stratosphere. In my mind's eye, rather than perceiving it as a happy moment, representing a party with fun and games it manifested to me as a bad omen, a symbol of something lost. It seemed, at that moment, like those balloons represented the innocence of my kids. As they drifted up and rapidly out of sight, my own kids' innocence and happiness was drifting away with them.

My children would not have the childhood that others in the community had. They wouldn't have the innocence and security to which other children were entitled. They wouldn't have two parents in their home. Their fate would be different. In that moment of ascension, their innocence and lighthearted happiness was drifting up, away, out of this world and was to be gone forever. My heart became incredibly heavy with the sadness of this omen. There was nothing I could do about it. Their fate had been decided.

The year Holly died, 2004, was baffling and chaotic, yet transformative. I didn't fully understand exactly how his death affected me. All I knew is that my life changed forever when he died. It was not like when my father had passed a few years earlier. At that time, I became numb and felt nothing, at least not anything positive or heartfelt.

But Holly's death was monumental. I had felt so close to Holly and admired him, worshiped him. I felt as though we were soul mates.

Once he passed, my entire foundation shifted. I can't articulate exactly how or for what reason, just that the basis of my very being was disrupted and pulverized to sand as if from a violent seven-point-eight earthquake. It felt as though my safety net had disintegrated. I was exposed and the world was raw and calloused now that he was gone.

Something inside me was brewing. It was angry and unraveling. Yet I could never get far enough away from the mirror that was my own self-awareness to see its reflection. It was running my life. But I had no idea what *it* was. I was really just trying to hold on, to survive.

The world was burning, as if in the aftermath of a nuclear holocaust. But the person next to me in the bunker was playing the radio too loud. They had to be stopped. I couldn't think straight. All of my anger, anxiety, and frustration became focused on nearby infractions. The straw on the camel's back.

I vented on those closest to me and Nancee became the enemy. I had lost my brother, my soul mate. The foundation of my childhood was gone. In my marriage, I knew I wasn't happy. I told myself if I got out of the marriage, everything would be better, would be fixed.

I would learn differently.

Act II:
Wandering the Desert

CHAPTER TEN

Powerhouse Pub

In the aftermath of my divorce, I found myself adrift, grappling with the daunting reality of single fatherhood and the sudden need to find a new place to call home. My brother's wife, sensing my discomfort, introduced me to Jeff—a tall, athletic, and disarmingly handsome man who was part of a small community of divorcees in town.

After a brief phone conversation, Jeff agreed to rent me two rooms in his house. One for me, and one for my kids to share half of the time.

Jeff introduced me to the rest of his posse: Deb and Tracy, both divorced with two kids. The weekend after my move, the two women came over to the house. We mixed drinks and sat out on the deck telling war stories about relationships and divorce. Immediately the stigma of being separated with kids started to fade. I sensed that there actually was life after a split. It felt like, at least for now, I had found my people.

But as the smoke from the move cleared, the unsettled feelings that had followed Holly's death returned. Thoughts about my childhood and what my father represented in my life continued to rattle through my brain on a daily, if not hourly, basis. Something was brewing deep in my soul. But it refused to reveal itself outright. It would only appear, briefly, when I least expected it.

Jeff, Debbie, Tracy, and I became a regular institution at the Powerhouse Pub in Folsom. On Friday or Saturday nights when the local eighties tribute band was playing, we were there. It always started with a drink or two to get "warmed up" before we left. On these nights I drank freely. It was a way to forget myself, at least momentarily, and escape my troubles.

One Saturday evening we headed there in Debbie's SUV, piling into one car so as to limit the number of drivers and reduce the potential for a DUI. We didn't have a designated driver, per se, rather the idea was that one of us would just drink a little less. And if we did get pulled over, only one of us would risk a DUI. But sometimes this plan changed spontaneously without much discussion about it.

Inside, the band was powering up. They started their usual lineup: "Push It," "Pour Some Sugar on Me," "Tainted Love; then segued into Devo's "Whip It." The crowd was riled up, hot, and sweaty, jumping and reeling with the music. No one seemed to mind the wet floor laced with pieces of broken beer bottles.

My intent had usually been to bring someone as I hated to ask strangers to dance. I didn't have a lot of luck, being relatively shy. And I struggled to dress the part. But this time was different. I had gone shopping the week before at Nordstrom and asked the sales assistant to essentially dress me. She had obliged with Lucky jeans that fit perfectly and a bold striped shirt with the colors of the American flag.

As I bounded on the dance floor sporting my pricey snug-fitting jeans and bold shirt, I got a few glances from women that seemed to say "OK . . . well that's interesting . . . who are you?" My confidence began to swell.

Amidst the grinding and dancing there was a slim blond woman a few feet in front of me and four bodies away. I could feel the gravity, the seduction. It seemed that she was the one everyone wanted to be close to, to touch. She was like a prize, a sculpture, an expensive work of art that was off-limits.

Her mystique tugged at me, luring me in. While I was sure I didn't have a chance with her, after minutes of glances and reeling and pulsing upon the dance floor, she maneuvered slowly over and backed up against me. The next thing I knew, we were brushing our bodies against each other, surging with the rhythm. She leaned her head back on my shoulder as her long, silky blond hair draped across my chest.

"My name's Phil," I shouted as I reached my hands around her waist, caressing her belly.

"I'm Jessica," she said, somehow managing to sound seductive, even over the din of the crowd.

"So . . . what do you do?"

"I'm a nurse."

A nurse! Jeff's words from the week before echoed through my brain. Nurses are the best—very attentive and comfortable being physical.

The excitement was building. It had been years since I'd been on a date. Yet there I was, having some semblance of success and it felt good to have someone, especially an attractive blond woman, show interest in me.

Suddenly the woman to our left lurched sideways and fell to the floor, disappearing amongst the hundred, or so, pulsing bodies. Jessica immediately swung into action, helping her back up, and the two of us brought her across the floor to the hallway that led to the restrooms. The woman had a large gash on her bare foot.

You were dancing barefoot . . . amongst broken beer bottles? What were you thinking? You may have just blown my chances. I tried to quell my inner resentment.

Jessica stopped the bleeding long enough for the bouncer to come by with some bandages. We were a little shaken—probably I more than she. But we'd also bonded over the act of helping someone else.

We went out on the patio to get some fresh air.

Suddenly, we were kissing.

"Want to get out of here?" I asked. It was like a line from a Hollywood movie. The booze had heightened my confidence. I was pulling off my best Daniel Craig impression. Maybe it was my feigned confidence or maybe just the heat of the moment.

But she went with it.

Ten minutes later we were back at my place, kissing and caressing each other. It was as if I did this all the time. Of course, I didn't, but I wasn't letting this opportunity escape. She wanted me and I wanted her.

We took our clothes off and got in bed. Her body felt electric. My heart started beating faster, almost pounding. I wondered what I'd done to deserve her. A brief doubt flickered through my mind: would something get in the way and stop this exciting encounter?

But we kept going because that's what normal people do. The sensation was deeply erotic, the scent intoxicating.

Then, out of nowhere, something changed. I felt a shock wave as if an electromagnetic pulse had just surged through the bedroom. I no longer recognized my body. Parts of me weren't mine any more. It was as if they were someone else's, responding to someone else's desires and intentions. Doing another's bidding. It was as if I no longer had sovereignty over myself, looking down on the two of us as my body followed some other person's narrative.

Then, a kind of absence, a void. All the excitement, the sensuality burst. It was as if I was holding a sandbag that was open on one end. The sand spilled out. The weight was gone until there was nothing but an empty bag. The import, the momentum . . . where had it gone? The excitement, the lust, the wanting—all of it evaporated. Nothing was left but shock.

Her eyes fixed on mine for a split second. Was it fear? Surprise? Disappointment?

Was she concerned about me? Or afraid this moment said something about herself?

She communicated all this in one ten-millisecond glance.

"Everything OK?" she asked, in a circumspect voice.

This woman. This beautiful specimen. I'm with an alluring, nubile female who wants me. Yet I'm emasculated. I'm not the man she sees on the outside. It's just a disguise. On the inside I'm something else. Maybe I'm just trying to act like a normal, heterosexual person.

I looked off to the side and sank down. I rolled off of her onto the bed, feeling like an awkward child engaging in something he shouldn't.

"It's . . . been a while since I've really been with anyone," I mustered. It was true, but not really the issue.

All this time I'd felt attracted to women. Lustful, even. Yet in my moment of truth, when that attraction should have translated into action, it switched . . . to something else.

Alicnation.

Maybe it was a sign from my subconscious. Maybe I'd been fooling myself this whole time. Perhaps, really, deep down, I was putting on an act.

And the truth was, I'm gay.

"I guess I'm just nervous," I lied. "I'm attracted to you . . . I mean I don't want you to think it's that. Maybe I just want you too much."

Another lie.

We made small talk. She told me it was OK; this happens. But I knew it really wasn't. I felt like a fool. What was I thinking? That I could be like other people? Something was different about me. Something set me apart from other humans. Like a thick plexiglass wall separating people and animals in the zoo.

There was something under the surface driving me that I didn't recognize. Something that made me do or think things that I didn't expect or even want. It was almost impossible for me to identify it, only arising when I least anticipated it, then disappearing during moments of self-reflection.

And it often arose in situations that were important to me. When the stakes were high and I wanted, *needed,* something.

Twenty minutes later she left, and I was again alone with my thoughts.

CHAPTER ELEVEN

Dr. Carol

After the disturbing encounter with Jessica and the lingering unrest about my childhood years, I decided to engage in some therapy. I sat in Carol's office in Cameron Park on a Tuesday afternoon. As far as I could surmise, she was a fairly middle-of-the road LMFT. Not what I would call a particularly exciting woman. If brash or audacious was on one end of the spectrum, she was on the exact opposite end.

She was a heavyset woman, standing roughly five-foot-two. She had very fair skin, giving the impression of someone who spent most of her life indoors. She had a kind, almost motherly demeanor about her. As if, were you in need of solace, she could envelop you with such warmth that your sorrows would dissipate in an instant.

At first, I found myself concerned about her appearance. I worried that perhaps she wouldn't be able to effectively address the issues I needed help with. However, after some consideration, I realized that her intelligence and the fact that she accepted my insurance were more important factors. Still, the initial worry lingered in the back of my mind.

She asked about my relationship with my mother. I responded that it was good. My siblings? Mostly normal with the caveat that my family had been steeped in a dogmatic cult religion. She asked about girlfriends. I told her, reluctantly, about my sexual dysfunction.

"Well, that's all the time we have today," she said abruptly. "We'll dig deeper into your female relationships in the coming weeks." I glanced at the clock. One fifty on the dot. I got up to leave, feeling demoralized. I'd hoped for some insight and hadn't gotten it.

The next three sessions were roughly the same. She would ask me questions about my family and past relationships. I would respond with fairly unremarkable accounts of my childhood, save for some lingering fatherly resentment. Then I'd write a check at the end of each session. Resentment built up over the course of weeks for paying someone to listen to, but not provide any insight on, my story. It was deeply demoralizing to feel unrest deep down in my soul yet have no clarity as to what was causing it.

CHAPTER TWELVE

Aly

As I watched Aly approach the door, I immediately recognized her from her profile. I was intrigued, not just by her appearance but by the energy she radiated. Her demeanor showed a warmth, accentuated by a smile that blended humility with confidence. Seeing her in person, I was struck by her poise and understated elegance. She had expressive eyes and a welcoming smile that complemented her natural grace.

After a month or two of casual dating, I wanted a deeper emotional connection. I felt the urge to find someone with qualities distinct from Nancee's. I wanted someone more compassionate, sensitive, and less likely to unsettle me with their demands for attention. I sought compatibility above all. My doctor had prescribed a small blue pill to alleviate challenges around physical intimacy. And despite the setback at Cisco, I retained my job and my confidence as a professional. I decided to register with Match.com and found a woman in nearby Cameron Park who caught my interest.

"You must be Aly," I said, feeling a slight sense of pride

in my boldness.

"You must be Phil," she responded sweetly.

"You look just like your profile picture," I said with a hint of surprise in my voice. "Only prettier," I added.

She laughed. "Well, thank you," she responded in a decidedly modest tone.

We talked about nothing for a few minutes. I knew at the outset I wanted to move to the next step. I had passed off the previous encounter as a fluke. I knew I found women attractive—at least I always had in the past. And I wasn't about to change my sexual orientation based on one odd experience.

But I had been cautioned by Jeff not to seem overly eager. I felt like a teenager learning to date all over again.

"I teach second grade at Folsom Elementary School," she said.

"I think teaching is the noblest profession."

"I'm glad you said that." She paused for a moment. "A lot of people don't get that," she continued, exhibiting the faintest hint of melancholy in her voice.

"So, what do you do?" she asked.

"I work in business development at Cisco."

Her eyes brightened just a little. Her engaging smile told me that there was a good chance she was interested. But then again, I was out of practice and didn't trust my instincts particularly well at that point.

I asked in a circumspect manner if she wanted to get dinner. She paused for what seemed like an hour.

"I think that would be lovely," she said.

A wave of relief washed over me, sweeping away the stress, anxiety, and self-doubt that had haunted me. In their place, a comfort settled inside me, akin to finally returning home after an arduous journey. Though we had only just met, her presence exuded a gentle warmth, as if she held the innate ability to quell the turmoil inside me.

CHAPTER THIRTEEN

Cisco Surprise

A couple of days later, as I sat at my desk, thinking about my encounter with Aly, a disturbing phone call interrupted my calm state. My office, in the living room of the home I had hesitated to purchase for so long, became the setting for an unexpected conversation with my new Cisco boss. Her sharp inquiry about my private engagements pierced through my meditative state, sending a tingling sensation down the scoop of my neck.

"I couldn't help but notice, Phil, you have a number of private engagements on your calendar," Elise said suspiciously. "What are those?"

Don't jump to conclusions, I thought. I tried to breathe and let the tension subside. Elise had taken over the group from Cliff. A feisty, bold Australian woman who had just transitioned from Cisco's Sydney office, she was having her moment and rising through the ranks. I'd set aside time for legal appointments while working through the messy details of the custody arrangements. I didn't want to advertise it to my colleagues, given our "open calendar" work style—something Elise had insisted on. So

I had cloaked them using the privacy feature in the calendar app.

"Well, I've had some legal appointments relating to the divorce and I didn't want to advertise these within the group, so I marked them private," I replied. It seemed like a reasonable response. I didn't want my colleagues snooping around and jumping to conclusions.

"Well, given this situation," she said in her quaint Sydney accent, "I think you really need to think about if you're in a position to continue leading your team."

The bristling turned to shock . . . then embarrassment . . . and then to full-on defensiveness. She was attacking me for an issue that had surfaced in my personal life. And she was intimating that I should step down as the leader of my team.

"Wait . . . so, why do you say that?" I asked. "I'm completing all my work and managing my employees well. I'm never out of touch for any length of time. What are you saying is wrong with my work?"

"Phil," she said in a parental tone, "you have to think about these things realistically. I've had employees go through personal issues, divorce, even a death in the family. These things happen and sometimes you just need help and that's the time I bring in HR and we talk about it."

While I wasn't absolutely sure, my experience told me that there was a ninety percent likelihood that she was not here to help me. Rather, this was just one more tactic she was using to get her group torn down to a flat level. And that meant no more senior managers like me.

I tried to maintain my composure but could feel the defensiveness growing in my gut. I was only subliminally aware, in that moment, of a deeper sense of victimization building inside me. A connection that a hidden part of my brain was making while my conscious brain continued to engage in the conversation.

Something about Elise's demeanor and tone transported me to a completely different place and time. A woman significantly more powerful than me working at cross purposes to my physical and emotional safety. It was as if someone with no interest in me as a human being controlled my fate.

If I allowed this to happen I would be handing over my sovereignty to her. I would endure not only powerlessness, but humiliation, and emasculation.

In actual fact, Elise wasn't really humiliating or emasculating me. Yes, she was taking a vulnerable, even tragic moment in my life and twisting it around to serve her own purposes. But she wasn't shaming me or corrupting my manhood. She was trying to get her needs met and I was in the way.

But in my very distorted mental state, she was going to overpower and obliterate me. She was fighting against the forces of good and embracing the forces of darkness. If I allowed her to succeed, then evil would triumph and I would be destroyed. It would be decades before I would even begin to uncover the source of this disturbance. And years more to separate the victimized part of me from modern day.

But in that moment, all I could think of was finding a defense. I searched my mind frantically for something to say. A phrase or insinuation that would somehow endow me with enough power to protect myself. I fired a warning shot in her direction.

As I hung up the phone, something seemed amiss. A daunting feeling came over me. She had pushed me aggressively, and I had reacted quickly and impulsively.

From that point forward, she dropped the issue, never again bringing up the divorce or questioning the entries on my calendar.

* * *

As my work in Elise's group progressed and my sense

of job security waned, I began to feel a growing sense of alienation. I decided it was time to move on—and it would behoove me to do it quickly. I eventually found a position in the HP Strategic Alliances team working for a director named Mike. Elise had even helped connect me with the group and had been kind enough to put in a positive reference with the VP of alliances. For the next few months I worked fastidiously marketing and promoting joint Cisco-HP solutions around IP Telephony.

Three months after transitioning to his group, I sat across the desk from Mike in his office. He had called a meeting to issue my performance review. I was certain this would be yet another top rating, just as I had received in my first four years at Cisco.

But his expression was more stoic than usual. And his demeanor bordered on pugnacious.

"This shouldn't be a surprise," he said.

Something clamped down hard on my chest. I had heard about this language. It had never happened to me personally, but people in the industry knew that this was a foreshadowing of bad news to come. It was a way for executives to not only soften the blow, but to actually shift the onus onto the employee. *You should have seen this coming,* the phrase signaled. If it was a surprise, it was on you, not the manager. And how could you be so naive, anyway?

"Your performance hasn't been up to expectations," he continued.

"What . . . why?" was all I could muster. "The business is solid, Mike. I don't understand—"

"Phil you're just not meeting expectations," he shot back curtly. He said a number of words and phrases, none of which seemed to register with my conscious brain. I was in complete shock, and I had no idea it was coming. Just as I was leaving his office, Mike offered a small consolation. A three-month severance package if I agreed to quit.

Over the next few days, as I contemplated resigning, I racked my brain, trying to figure out what had gone wrong. Was I truly a bad employee and a terrible worker? Was I just lazy, yet unaware of my shortcomings?

The events of the previous months seeped into my mind over the course of the next few days. The Australian. The moniker she used for the men in the group. I had called her out on it. I had threatened her, overreacting in a manner that was significantly more serious than the threat itself. And I had fallen under the naive impression that it had all blown over.

Regardless, my time at Cisco was over.

CHAPTER FOURTEEN

Crossroads and Conversations

"Remember that new boss at Cisco, Elise?" I asked Jared.

"You mean the feisty Australian who was a bull in a china shop?"

We sat on the deck at the El Dorado Saloon, a week after the upheaval at my job. He'd come to visit for the weekend in solidarity. We sat sipping our beers as the ancient, tall oak trees around us seemed to eavesdrop on our conversation, the dry warmth of the Sierra surrounding us.

"Yeah, I remember her," Jared continued. "The one with the black belt in corporate politics, right? What about her?" Jared's interest was piqued, his tone laced with a hint of irony.

"Get this—she calls me up one day, all serious, questioning my private calendar entries. Like she's a police detective and I'm suddenly under scrutiny because, God forbid, I had some personal stuff to sort out." My frustration bubbled up as I recounted the episode.

"Jeez, she made a drama out of your schedule?" Jared's flippant comment cut through the tension.

"Totally. She zeroed in on those private entries. I explained they were just mundane legal appointments, but then she hits me with this veiled threat about my fitness for the job. Like suddenly my personal life's on trial."

"No way! She didn't take the hint that maybe, just maybe, you wanted to keep your private life, well, private?" Jared's disbelief was evident, his voice rising almost an octave in solidarity.

"Nope. So I'm there, trying to keep cool, explaining it's just some boring legal stuff, and she goes all 'corporate police' on me, suggesting I rethink my role. Like my divorce is some kind of corporate espionage!"

"Jeez, sounds like she'd put her own mother on trial!" Jared's mockery was a welcome comic relief.

"Right? Then, in what I thought was a moment of genius, I hit back. She had this habit of calling all the guys 'Doll.'"

"'Doll'? Seriously? Did she think she was in a 1950s sitcom?"

"Yeah, well, it always felt condescending and a tad sexist. So, I told her to knock it off."

"Wait, what? You didn't. You actually played that card out at that moment?" Jared looked astonished, his expression mirroring someone who'd just witnessed a friend making a high-stakes gamble.

"I thought I was standing up for myself," I continued, somewhat defensively. "Asserting some control. I mean, you're always talking about setting boundaries."

"Yeah, but timing is everything, Phil. You've got to pick your moments. And 'Doll'? That's a risky hill to climb," Jared refuted, his tone a mix of amusement and concern.

"Well, that would explain her reaction: dead silence,

then a curt, 'You should have mentioned this sooner.' I shot back with *'I'm telling you now!'* Felt like dialogue from an action thriller."

"Oooooh, Phil! Bet that really smoothed things over!" Jared couldn't help but laugh, shaking his head.

"Not so much. But then, everything just . . . froze. She backed off, never mentioned the divorce or calendar again. I thought I'd dodged a bullet. But man, the plot thickens. Fast forward, and there I am with my new boss, Mike, with the HP Alliance Team, expecting kudos. But instead, he slaps me with the 'not meeting expectations' line."

"They hit you with the 'it's not us, it's you' spiel?" said Jared, his tone incredulous yet unsurprised.

"Exactly," I responded, unable to suppress a chuckle. "Offered me a golden parachute to just vanish. Like I was being handed a bag of hush money to disappear."

"You think Elise had a long memory?" Jared posited, his analytical side kicking in.

"Must've. She played nice—even helped me transition to the new group—but probably set me up from the moment I challenged her."

"That's cold, man. Sounds like a power play, straight out of a corporate thriller." Jared's voice carried a note of empathy mixed with fascination at the unfolding drama. After a brief pause, he continued, his tone more measured. "So, Phil, you're my friend, and you know I don't judge you, right?"

"Most of the time," I quipped.

"So what made you react to Elise that way in the first place?"

"Well," I began, suddenly feeling a wave of vulnerability wash over me, "that initial phone call . . . it felt like more than a job threat, Jared. Like my whole identity was under attack. It was like being teleported to an alternate reality where she held all the cards. Then, after being canned, the dreams started . . ." My voice trailed off, the memory of those vivid nightmares flashing before my eyes.

"Dreams? What, like you showed up naked at work and then it turned into a circus?" Jared chuckled, attempting to lighten the mood.

"Worse. They were about John Chambers, of all people. My brain kept casting him in this recurring nightmare where he's dissing me, in front of coworkers, saying I just don't fit the Cisco *Top Gun* vibe. Over and over, like my brain was on a loop. I guess my subconscious decided it wasn't enough to live it by day; I had to be haunted by John Chambers at night!"

"Chambers? The big man himself? Dude, that's like being rejected by tech royalty. Wow, your subconscious is really punishing you! It's like you're haunted by the ghost of Cisco past." Jared's attempt at humor barely masked the seriousness of the situation.

"Tell me about it. It started off now and then but ramped up to a full-blown nightly festival of humiliation. Like I'm stuck in this cycle of replaying my worst fears."

Jared paused for a moment before his face brightened as if he'd landed a brilliant idea. "Maybe it's your mind's way of telling you that you've outgrown them, you know? Too cool for the Cisco school," he said, trying to implore me with his tone to shift to the brighter side.

"You are so . . . precious," I said with a hint of sarcasm. "You always have a way of making things seem better, even when they are absolutely awful."

"Brutal, buddy. But hey, they say you've got to face your demons, even if they show up as tech moguls in your sleep."

"Is that what they say? Sounds pretty specific," I quipped as Jared chuckled. "But hey, here's to breaking free from that, right?" I continued, taking up Jared's optimism.

"Yes, here's to new beginnings, Phil. May your next chapter be free of corporate overlords and full of career success," Jared toasted, a smile finally breaking through the heaviness of our conversation.

I raised my glass, a gesture of hope amid the uncertainty. Clinking his glass, I welcomed the camaraderie surrounding us like the warm evening air. "Here's to that, my friend. And to conquering whatever corporate bullies come our way."

CHAPTER FIFTEEN

Profiling

Back in Dr. Carol's office the following week, I told her about the recent job loss and the longstanding tension I had toward my father. How I often felt misunderstood by him. I shared with her the shame I felt about my own sexuality, particularly with regard to impotence, despite having temporarily solved the problem with erectile dysfunction pills, I felt there was something wrong with me for needing them in the first place. My discontent with my present situation was exacerbated by the realization that, despite five weeks of therapy, I still hadn't gotten any answers. I needed something. I didn't want to continue being reactive and confused while still having no idea about the cause.

"So . . . what is going on with me?" I said in a very pointed, measured tone. Something that couldn't be misconstrued. I knew I was putting her on the spot and it was unlikely she'd have an answer. But the time had come.

She stared back at me and said, slowly and confidently, without even pausing: "Well, it's pretty clear something negative happened to you. Based on my experience I'd say you fit the profile of a sexual-abuse victim," she said, nodding, an assured expression on her face.

"What? Why?" I was shocked. Speechless. I could feel the adrenaline coursing through my veins.

"Well, the sexual dysfunction, negative feelings about male power. The triggering at work." She paused briefly, staring at the wall behind me. "You know, being triggered is a type of trauma response," she continued. "These things all lead me to believe that some kind of sexual trauma happened to you as a child."

"But if that happened, wouldn't I remember it?" I protested.

"Not necessarily. The brain is a very complex organism. We think it retains all important information. But often the brain shuts out traumatic events."

"But why would it do that?" I said in a more argumentative tone than I intended. "If something important or . . . monumental happened I would think it would be etched in my brain and never forgotten."

"It's about survival," she said, again without a pause. "The brain reacts to the trauma when we get into a similar situation. That has allowed us to steer clear of trouble during about a million years of evolution. But the rest of the time we can't constantly be fearing for our lives because we wouldn't be able to function. Organisms need to feed, reproduce, and create shelter. If we had this trauma in our conscious brains we couldn't function. So the brain pushes it down into the subconscious where it lies, waiting for the moment when we need it to protect us. The problem is, in today's world of more complex human interactions, it doesn't suit us anymore."

I don't recall leaving the appointment. I only remember being outside, walking along the sidewalk next to the professional building toward my car, feeling dazed, as if floating above my body. There was something that had been residing inside me for years that needed to be addressed. And now that she had put a name to it, I had to understand it.

I had no choice but to confront my family about it. They hadn't said anything up to now—I wasn't sure why. Then again, I hadn't specifically asked the question. Maybe they had kept it under wraps to protect me. Or perhaps it was self-preservation on their part. Whatever the reason, it was time for the truth to come out.

And there were a number of family members who were old enough and in positions to be aware. Cindy was just a couple of years older, yet she might have seen something. Pam was six years older and would certainly be able to remember. Holly had passed away, so, unfortunately, he couldn't bear witness to it. My mother was there and, as an adult, would remember. As would my father, unless he was part of the abuse. This activity can't happen without a parent or sibling witnessing it.

I set out about the daunting task of confronting my family with the raw truth of what had happened to me.

CHAPTER SIXTEEN

Pam's Denial

"How's the new house working out?" Pam asked, her voice carrying a subtle edge that hinted at hidden agendas. With her turbulent past of drugs and wanderlust, Pam had always operated on the fringes of conventionality. From teenage rebellion to a career as a helicopter pilot ferrying rough longshoremen to oil rigs in the Gulf, she had an untamed spirit that belied her age of fifty-five. Yet beneath her veneer of worldly experience were layers of mystery, causing me to wonder what secrets she might be hiding. Pam had been a teenager when I was just a child, possibly privy to events that had escaped my understanding.

"Good," I responded, continuing the casual chitchat. "It's a lot better than renting a couple of rooms out of a friend's home. Now the kids have their own bedrooms when they're with me. We're in Crown Village, just about a mile from the kids' school."

"Well, that sounds like a better environment, for sure," Pam responded with ostensible empathy.

"Yeah, it wasn't an easy move," I said. "Buying a house

kind of made me feel like the divorce was more . . . permanent. But I just felt like it was time."

"Oh . . . right. Yeah, that makes sense," she replied, her tone continuing with a hint of exaggerated empathy.

I needed to bring up the topic. Knowing Pam's straightforward nature, I anticipated that broaching the topic wouldn't require a lot of preamble.

"So I kind of wanted to talk to you about something serious," I said, attempting to ease my way into it.

"Uh . . . OK . . ." she said in a decidedly suspicious tone.

"Well, I've come to the realization lately . . . that I went through some kind of sexual abuse when I was young."

"Hmmm . . . what made you come to that conclusion?" She responded in a very measured, almost mechanical tone.

"I'm seeing a therapist," I explained, feeling a strong sense of vulnerability wash over me. "She said I fit the profile of a sexual abuse victim. And it rings true to me . . . some of the reactions I have these days."

"Well, I have my own view of therapists," she said in a perfunctory tone. "But anyway, how can I help?"

"Well, I'm wondering what you saw," I said in as steady a tone as I could muster while feeling my power slide rapidly away.

"Like what?" she said flatly

"Well . . . you were six years older than me," I began, starting with an obvious fact in hopes of regaining my sense of control. "So you probably know more than I do. Did you see anything either in the family or with relatives or neigh—"

"No, I didn't see anything," Pam said emphatically but with a somewhat haunting, almost hollow, tone.

I tried to collect myself. There must have been signs. Some sort of indication that she would have witnessed.

The phone remained silent. No comforting words. No statements of validation. No answers. After collecting my thoughts, I continued.

"My therapist was very confident—"

"You know, Phil, sometimes therapists plant that stuff in people's minds," she retorted.

"Really? I don't think this therapist is doing that. . . . I mean what does she have to gain—"

"There have been court cases," she continued, her tone more urgent. "One businessman whose daughter accused him of molesting her as a child. It turned out all that stuff was planted there by her therapist. I think you should be really careful about what this person tells you."

It would be an understatement to say I felt empty inside. A feeling of hopelessness began to overcome me. I didn't want to be the abuse victim. Yet something in Carol's words rang true. And Pam was in a position to know.

Yet she purported to see nothing and, in fact, seemed convinced that this whole thing was complete fabrication, an artifact placed in my consciousness by my therapist.

CHAPTER SEVENTEEN

Jared Therapy

Settling into a quiet corner of my home, I dialed Jared, eager to catch up and unburden some of the thoughts swirling in my mind.

"How's Aly these days?" he asked, always diligent in keeping track of my life's changes.

"You know, Jared, things with Aly got pretty serious," I began, my voice tinged with a mixture of fondness and unease. "There was this connection, like she could really see into me, more than most have ever done."

"Sounds intense, man. Good intense or bad intense?" Jared said, his tone a mix of curiosity and concern.

I paused, reflecting. "Well, it's hard to pinpoint. It started off comforting, but then it shifted, felt almost invasive. She was seeing things in me that, well, maybe I wasn't ready to face."

"Sounds unsettling. Anything specific that might have set off that feeling?" Jared coaxed, urging me to continue.

I recounted the incidents that had unsettled me, each one a thread in the unraveling tapestry of our relationship. "Like this one time on a double date—I was pretty tanked—I started eating off our neighbor's plate. Aly brought it up later, and man, the embarrassment hit me hard."

Jared chuckled sympathetically. "Oh, dude, that's awkward. But come on, we've all been there." His optimistic tone shifted over to doubt about his assertion.

"You're being way too generous. I don't think most people have been *there*," I said with a reluctant chuckle. "But there's more," I confessed. "There was this bed and breakfast mix-up in Nevada City. Booked the same place I'd been with my ex, Nancee. Realized it last minute and just couldn't go through with it. The drive back was painfully silent."

"That's rough, man," Jared empathized, his voice soft. "Past memories can really sting."

"And the last straw," I continued, "was the boating incident. Got carried away with the guys, drinking beer and hanging out on the lake. Completely forgot to call Aly."

Jared's response was measured. "Sometimes we lose track of time, man. It happens."

I shook my head trying to grasp the internal struggle. "But it's more than that. She was holding up a mirror to my flaws, and I hated the reflection. It felt like she was exposing parts of me that I didn't want to face."

"That's a heavy realization. Nobody wants to feel that way," Jared agreed, his voice a comforting baritone. "So did you break it off?"

"It all piled up," I admitted, a heavy sigh escaping me. "I felt controlled, unseen, and it brought back that isolation I felt in my marriage. I had to end it, told her over the phone. Said it was about us drifting apart, but . . ."

"But what? There's more to it, isn't there?" Jared prodded.

"Well . . . it's more than that, Jared. I'm wrestling with

this shame, maybe from something way back in my past that's haunting me, making me act recklessly."

Jared listened intently, his presence a steady anchor. "Facing that kind of shadow is brutal, Phil. But recognizing it, that's the first step." His voice was soft but firm.

I nodded to my good friend 150 miles away. "I hope so. It's like I'm on the edge, trying to figure out who I really am beneath all this."

"You're brave to confront it, Phil. Takes guts to look inward like that."

There was a momentary pause, a brief interlude of silence that seemed to bridge the distance between us. It was as if Jared was right there, in the room, offering a silent nod of understanding before shifting the topic gently.

"So . . . on a related topic, what happened after your therapy appointment? Your therapist made a fairly bold assertion a while ago. Weren't you going to ask your family about that?"

"Yes to both. But they said there was nothing," I said in a forlorn tone, feeling both demoralized and hopeless. "I thought that one of them might give a hint that might substantiate the abuse. But, nope, nothing. They all denied it."

"So let me understand this," he said. "Your therapist says that you probably went through sexual abuse as a child, but your family says they didn't see anything?"

"That's pretty much the scenario. I even tried to reach out to Sally, my third sister," I said, my voice trailing off in contemplation.

"Wait . . . third sister? I thought you only had two—"

"It's a long story. None of us have seen or talked to her in years," I interjected, not wanting to get derailed. "Anyway, they all said they saw nothing."

"Dude, I'm sorry, that sounds really invalidating, to say the least." He paused for some time, contemplating. "Have you talked to anyone else in the neighborhood? Maybe they saw something your family didn't. Or maybe your family doesn't want to talk about it, but someone else outside the family might?" He said this last word like a question—as if he was grasping at straws.

"Yeah, I called Chase from the La Barranca neighborhood. He was the older brother across the street. He and Holly were buddies. I remember him being kind of a sixties rebel. He was a bully . . . kind of a kingpin in the neighborhood. We all kind of feared him."

"And you called him? That must have been scary."

"Yeah...well, he's grown and married now. I just figured those days are over."

"Still, that's pretty brave," Jared responded. "What did he say?"

"Well, he said there was no abuse."

"Really? That seems like a pretty bold statement."

"Yeah, he even said he would never have allowed that to happen."

Jared jumped in, his tone incredulous. "Never have—"

"He seemed confident," I continued. "They all did."

"Hmm, are there any other possibilities?"

"Well, I don't know where else to look. Who knows . . . maybe something in the church? It's all very frustrating and demoralizing."

"I'm sorry."

"This makes me feel like I've got something buried deep down inside that's bad. That needs to be fixed. Like a cancer that's eating away at me, but I can't get at it."

"That's rough, man." Jared was silent for a minute as he tried to formulate an encouraging comment. "But hey, look at the bright side: you've got a new job, right?"

"Yeah, and it's local. No more commuting to the Bay Area. Which is good and bad. Kind of a bummer that you and I won't be face-to-face as much."

"Yeah, we'll stay in touch by phone," he said reassuringly.

"I hope so!"

CHAPTER EIGHTEEN

Colonoscopy

I spent the rest of the week in a haze, trying to make sense of it all. By the time Sunday morning rolled around, I was tired of thinking about my childhood. My thoughts drifted to a procedure I had scheduled for the following morning.

I reached under the sink and pulled out a half gallon of liquid. It was the day before my colonoscopy and I'd been prescribed a prep kit consisting of sixty-four ounces of Colyte. I was supposed to consume its entirety over the course of the afternoon. I began, dutifully, to drink the disgusting liquid—or at least as much as I could stomach.

Sitting in my home, sipping on Colyte just wasn't doing it for me. I decided to go next door to Tony's house for some companionship and perhaps a distraction— something Tony had always been exceptional at. I knocked on his door and walked in, bottle in hand. Tony was a gregarious, rotund man of Italian heritage, standing six feet, four inches tall, weighing about three hundred pounds. He had a shock of dark, curly hair on the top of his head. Three of them, actually: two on either side of his crown and one smaller, fading one in the middle. His appearance was reminiscent of the manager in the *Dilbert* cartoon, but with slightly more hair.

He was just back from a San Diego bridge construction job in which he worked as a site manager. Normally he was a womanizer in the evenings and weekends. His primary stated goal was turning women to the dark side, a reference to some promiscuous sexual activities he often engaged in, some of which were team oriented. But this weekend he was solo, as was I.

"Colonoscopy tomorrow," I said as I sat down at his kitchen bar.

"Uh oh," he said. "That sounds like a shit-ton of fun." He continued rummaging through the cupboards looking for just the right snack.

"I'm supposed to drink only clear liquids."

"Want some chicken broth?" he said.

"Uh . . . OK."

I had stopped consuming real food at 8:00 a.m. that morning and was feeling pretty anxious. And hungry.

Then I got a really great idea. "Hey . . . alcohol is a clear liquid, right?

"Yeah, I guess," he chuckled. "Want a drink?"

A drink was just what I needed to get my mind off food.

"I thought you'd never ask," I quipped. "How about a gin and tonic?"

Tony pulled out a glass.

"Nah, not a tumbler," I said carelessly. "The tall one. You know—there's going to be ice and a bunch of tonic. Might as well save some time and go with the big one."

Tony got out a pint glass and put some ice in it, glancing at me out of the side of his eye, flashing a wry smile. He poured it two-thirds full of tonic water, then topped it off with a generous amount of Bombay Sapphire gin. Then stirred it with his finger.

I took a couple of big sips of the cold, tangy liquid. After the initial burn, I began to feel a warm, calming sensation.

"I'm not looking forward to it," I said after a few moments. "I don't like people going up in there."

"I get it, man," he said, looking away.

For the next two hours I continued to alternate between gulping the Colyte and drinking gin and tonics.

As the evening approached, I recall walking into Tony's hall bathroom with a fairly nauseated sensation. The next thing I knew, I got on my knees and began heaving into his toilet.

Then things went black.

* * *

I woke up and looked around. The room didn't make sense. The bathroom should have been down the left hallway but instead it was down the right. The bed and the room were unrecognizable to me. I noticed there were no posts on the bed.

Was I on a business trip? Did I go out drinking last night at a bar and wake up in someone's home? I got up and immediately sensed a throbbing headache coming on. My eyes felt dry and crusty. My nose felt like I had been breathing hot desert air for hours. My mouth felt like cotton soaked with stomach acid.

As I walked down the hall I heard a voice boom: "THERE HE IS!"

I walked into the kitchen to see Tony making eggs.

"What happened?"

"You got shitfaced and then got into my bed!"

"Seriously?"

"Yeah. I'm going to call you Goldilocks from now on. . . . Apparently my bed was just right."

"Where did you sleep?" I asked, fearing the answer.

I knew the things he did with women and some of the group behaviors he was into but had no idea what his propensity was for engaging with other men. He was a tall, large man who, by his own admission, had fairly loose morals. I had climbed into his bed. Maybe even while he was in it. Was this a subliminal act?

I contemplated the events of the previous night, as my peripheral vision caught a glimpse of the half-full bottle of Colyte on the kitchen counter. It seemed like this entire episode was triggered by something deeper. Maybe the colonoscopy itself had created some disturbance inside me: the prospect of being violated. Perhaps instead of a nameless, faceless doctor doing the deed, I wanted someone else, someone closer to me. A familiar party, as if to create the illusion I was in control.

I needed to hear his answer, even though I dreaded what it might imply about me.

"In the guest bedroom," he said flatly.

The evening following my colonoscopy, I had a dream that intensified my concerns about my sexual orientation. More than that, it struck at the very core of my sexual identity.

I was going through changes as an eight-year-old child. When I looked in the mirror, I saw I had transitioned my appearance to look like a blond girl with short hair. Somewhat tomboy-ish, but attractive. A little like Inga, my high-school sweetheart, with her Dutch-boy haircut.

My family acted as if everything was normal. I still had my "junk," but I had modified my appearance to look like a pretty blond girl. To them I was just "me" and they paid no attention.

I awoke from the dream, startled and disturbed. It had the heavy, apocalyptic feel of the other dreams following Holly's death.

I hadn't had many androgynous dreams over the years. At least not ones about myself. This one struck me as odd. Not just because I was the woman in the dream but because of the blond theme. I had dated a couple of blond women. Inga, who had a similar haircut to my persona in the dream. Aly was blond. Within my own family, my sister, Cindy was the only true blond with long, silky, eye-catching hair. And she was very pretty as a teenager. A cheerleader and homecoming queen, she was highly coveted at Gunn High School. Boys lusted after her.

But in this case, it was I who was blond. Was this dream trying to communicate to me subliminally that I wanted to be attractive to other men, like she was?

CHAPTER NINETEEN

Sexual Roulette

"I'm worried I might be gay," I told Dr. Carol the following week. The dream and the awkward night with Tony seemed to be pointing to something. Something I didn't want to admit. Did I have a thing for men? And for large men, at that? Did I want to be desired by them?

In my conscious brain, I didn't find them attractive. Yet I found myself physically drawn to them as the moon is drawn to the earth. It doesn't lust after the earth, rather it's just drawn toward it by natural laws.

"Well why do you think that?" she asked matter-of-factly.

I explained about being provoked by, and even drawn to, large, tall men.

"Why are you worried about it?" she asked.

"Well . . . I don't want to be gay," I said.

"Why?"

I thought about it for a moment, contemplating how the gay population is sometimes marginalized. How acceptance, though on the rise, is still less than ubiquitous. And how being gay would mean a lot of changes to my own life; and there would be people close to me that would have a hard time accepting it.

And then there were my own views about it that stemmed from my religious upbringing. I had been a dedicated student of the Bible growing up. In the scripture, being homosexual was considered an abomination. In Christian Science you prayed away the gay. I had long since abandoned these beliefs. Yet I could feel their subtle influence decades later.

"Well . . . I think being gay can be a hard lifestyle," I said finally.

"Well," she said after a deep sigh, "it sounds like you have a lot of judgments around this that might have built up from outside social pressures. Let's say, for the sake of argument, you are gay. What's the worst that can happen?"

I thought hard about it. After a minute or two I told her bluntly the worst thing I could think of happening. "The worst thing would be that I am gay. That I have sex with other gay men. I get AIDS . . . then I die."

"OK, well that's interesting . . ." she paused. Then after a minute or two she continued. "We're all going to die eventually. There's no sense worrying about something like that without even knowing one way or the other."

* * *

A week later, after I'd had some time to digest the discussion, I decided I needed to explore the issue scientifically, without making any assumptions. I got on Match.com and looked up *men seeking men*. It was worth a try, and if I never explored the issue then I would never really know for sure.

I found the profile of a man with dark hair and a goatee who lived in Sacramento. He was a decent-looking guy whose profile said: "Sacramento's not so bad, give it a try." He had a kind, compassionate expression in his photo. He seemed approachable.

I reached out and we made contact.

The following week, while visiting my mother in Los Altos Hills, I texted him and arranged to meet at a coffee shop in East Sacramento near the medical center. I would meet him on the way back from the Bay Area. This would give me some distraction along the two-and-a-half-hour trip as well as help keep me from stressing out at home while getting ready for this very unusual date.

The next afternoon I hit the freeway around 4:30. I had a sense of both excitement and fear as I headed east. By 7:30 the Sacramento skyline rose up from the farmland as I approached from the west on I-80. I took the Stockton Street exit and found the coffee shop.

I walked in to see him sitting at a table against the wall. He looked over at me with a sense of recognition. He was about my height. He had an easygoing, kind demeanor about him.

"Hey, how you doing?" I said as we shook hands.

We made small talk as we got our coffee and sat at a secluded table along the wall. Then in a moment of nervousness—

"I really have no idea if I'm straight or gay," I blurted out.

"Oh . . . OK, "he said. Then after a pause, he asked, "Well . . . what is it about men that you find attractive?"

This question cut me to the quick. I didn't really know the answer. I paused for some time, trying to formulate the thought.

"Well . . . I think that's part of what I'm trying to figure out," I said finally. "I don't necessarily know that I find specific things attractive as much as I'm drawn to some men, in a kind of subconscious way."

I was struck at that moment that this seemed incredibly

late in life for me to be finding out about my true sexuality. And for reasons that were not entirely apparent to me.

"I was raised in Christian Science," I told him, as if this would explain things. Then I realized how many dots had been left unconnected.

"What I'm saying is we didn't talk about sex or sexuality.... There was a lot of repression. At least for the three younger kids." I explained how I never took sex education, and we didn't talk about sex at all—whether heterosexual or homosexual—so I had no experience with which to even broach the gay topic. I went on to explain to him as best I could that I was living a life I thought I was supposed to live rather than necessarily the one I wanted. Now, on my own and unattached, I was finally free to explore.

The sudden import of this admission hit me. I wondered in that moment if I had gotten ahead of myself. Perhaps jumped in too deep.

"I realize age fifty-five is pretty late in life to start on this exploration journey," I added with a hint of self-consciousness.

Despite my vague answer to his question combined with my conversational unraveling, he still seemed interested in continuing the meeting. We talked about various different lifestyles.

At one point he mentioned that some men who were heterosexual liked to hook up with gay men in a clandestine way.

"It's called being on the down-low," he said with a precocious expression.

"But doesn't that make them gay or at least bi?" I asked incredulously.

"No, because they're usually married, sometimes with kids, but they just like to have encounters with men, on the down-low," he said.

This seemed foreign to me. Men who liked men—at least in my myopic thinking—were either gay or bi. But I had sworn off black-and-white thinking. I was here to open my mind, rather than make judgments. Maybe there was a whole way of acting, a whole set of behaviors, that wasn't dictated by societal norms or religious principles. Behaviors that were stimulated by wants and desires. Ones that were free and couldn't be categorized into a specific bucket.

I felt I would know more about my own sexuality if we could be in private, away from public scrutiny. That if we could explore some kind of physical interaction, it would inform me more about who I was.

"Can we take a walk?" I asked

"Sure," he said.

We walked out the back door and around the parking lot of the strip mall making small, talk.

"Maybe we should kiss," I said abruptly, immediately feeling a sense of embarrassment.

At that moment he became circumspect. I had thought he was out as a gay man, but it seemed like there was something keeping him from operating out in the open. He suggested we go back to his place.

He gave me brief directions and suggested I follow him. After a short ten-minute drive, we arrived at his home in a residential neighborhood somewhere near Oak Park.

Inside it was small and darkly lit. He had Catholic imagery and figurines all over his living room. The tension was thick—at least for me.

After a few minutes of idle conversation, we approached each other. I really wasn't sure if I was the one who took the initiative or if he was. But this seemed like the moment.

We embraced each other and—

CHAPTER TWENTY

Sodom's Gate

There is a line in the movie *The Sure Thing* in which John Cusack is about to have an encounter with the object of his sexual desire. In his moment of truth, he suddenly becomes introspective:

> *Thoughts raced through his mind. Did she really want him? What had he done to deserve this bounty? Does God exist? Who invented liquid soap and why?*

In my John Cusack moment, I had my own racing thoughts: *Who am I? Do I like men? Am I leading him on? Will this change my life? If I do like men, will my conscious brain override those base urges and send me back into denial? Do I even like what's happening? Will I —*

Eeeeesh!

The feeling of kissing this man was not at all what I expected. Instead of excitement or arousal, I felt an odd, reminiscent feeling as if I was kissing my father. It was rough. It was abrasive. It was off-putting. It bordered on revolting.

At that moment I felt naive and stupid, as though I had inadvertently led him on in a way that wasn't fair. I felt a sense of pressure invading my chest. I struggled to find words to express what I was feeling. All I could think of to say was:

"Hey, I'm really sorry to say this but . . . would you mind if I left?" I wasn't sure if he would be angry, or disappointed, or something else. But instead, he showed a moment of grace.

"No, you're good," he said. "It's no problem."

I felt an incredible sense of relief. We said our goodbyes and I thanked him for getting together. I apologized again.

As I left his home and drove out of the neighborhood, I felt relief, combined with a twinge of guilt for the unfairness of it all. I had tried to be transparent about my mental state from the beginning. But had I really led him on? My head was spinning, wondering what it all meant. I had given it a fair shot. It wasn't what I expected. But I had my answer.

As I navigated the familiar streets back to my home in Crown Village, the introspection from my unsettling experience mingled with an emerging sense of apprehension about my professional life. The encounter had been a journey into the depths of my own identity, leaving me with more questions than answers, but also a clearer understanding of who I was—and wasn't.

Yet, as the comfort of home enveloped me, the solace it offered was fleeting. The tranquility of the oak-lined streets and the sight of my house, a symbol of stability, stood in stark contrast to the growing turmoil I sensed at work. The relief of resolving a personal dilemma was now overshadowed by the daunting challenges of my professional life.

CHAPTER TWENTY-ONE

Trish

"We promised them," Trish said. "We don't have a choice."

After the bizarre date and exploring the question of my own sexual orientation, I began to settle down. I'd faced my doubts and figured out who I was. I had grappled with my identity and emerged on the other side.

Yet, despite this personal clarity, my position at Micron as product manager began to feel increasingly precarious. I had full reign over a series of memory chip products—at least in theory. But I sensed my control slipping away. Trish, a prominent and powerful figure in the sales department, challenged my decisions. Her demeanor combined a commanding professional presence with an underlying charisma that was both intriguing and intimidating. To me, she embodied a blend of allure and unattainability, reminiscent of Anne Friedman, the enigmatic older girl from my childhood neighborhood. Trish didn't just exert organizational influence; she possessed an intangible personal magnetism, subtly exuding a kind of sexual power.

Nevertheless, I was the product manager, which meant I should control business decisions around product development and profitability, not her. Trish was encroaching on my professional sovereignty. I felt like not only was my position at stake but my very essence was also under threat. The situation felt existential, as if her triumph might lead to my own erasure, as if I would somehow vanish if she succeeded.

"Trish, the ROI numbers say this isn't good business for Micron. I know the customer is Cisco, but—"

"Well, it's too late now. We've already committed to them."

"Who committed to—"

"Phil, we have to do it!"

She had thrown down the gauntlet. There was no room for discussion or negotiation. She had declared how it would be.

I felt cornered. Something was very wrong. She was usurping my authority. She hadn't gotten the necessary approvals. She hadn't even involved me. Yet she had made a decision that not only affected my job, it also affected, so it seemed, my humanity.

The feeling of dismissal loomed again in my consciousness. I felt as though I was being put in a box. Controlled by a powerful female who was charismatic and influential, yet didn't care about me or my role in the organization. I couldn't endure this—not again.

I wrote up a lengthy email discussing why we shouldn't proceed with the Cisco special project. I copied my manager and other key people in the organization.

The next morning, I got a call from my boss, Scott. He was not happy.

"What you did was the wrong approach," he said. "You shouldn't have reacted that way and copied the other managers." I recall him using the word "unprofessional." But then, seconds later he softened. "It's not . . . I mean it's not like it's a huge problem."

Once I got off the phone, I thought about the whole interaction. About Trish. About the power she had. Her confidence. Her dismissive nature. Treating me as irrelevant in the larger scheme of things. Almost like I was a child to her adult persona. The incident took me back to a time during my childhood days . . . and brought a feeling of sheer terror.

For the time being, things seemed fine at the office, as if it would all blow over. Just after the holidays things appeared to be going reasonably well. I was working harder, having more projects put on my plate. I was working my fingers to the bone, delivering on commitments for two managers at that point, Scott and his boss, Kevin.

I received a meeting invitation from our HR manager to meet the next morning at nine o'clock. As I headed toward the meeting, I sensed a slight tingling on the scoop of my neck. Once in the conference room, the tingling turned to shock. Across the desk sat our HR rep along with Scott. In front of him was a pile of papers.

"This shouldn't be a surprise," Scott said.

* * *

Walking out of the Micron building for the last time, the finality of being fired wrapped around me like a surreal fog. The moment my feet hit the parking lot, my connection to the Micron intranet was cut off—a digital severance that mirrored my abrupt physical exit. In an instant, all of the professional and personal contacts I had nurtured and relied upon that were hosted within the company's network became inaccessible, vanishing as if they had never existed. The impact of this disconnection jolted me to the core. It was more than just losing a job; it felt as though a vital part of my identity, built over countless hours, meetings, and projects, was erased, leaving a void where once there was a rich network of colleagues and collaborators.

Driving away, the building shrinking in my rearview mirror, the magnitude of what I had lost began to sink in—not just a job, but a window to relationships and opportunities, now gone.

CHAPTER TWENTY-TWO

Purple Place

"What the hell is going on?" I vented to Jared over the phone, still stunned after being fired from Micron. My mind was in turmoil, stirred up by my therapist's insights, leading me to confront my family about past abuse, which they outright denied. I'd delved into my sexuality and concluded I wasn't gay. Yet here I was, jobless again, twice in two short years.

"Dude, you're not lacking in smarts or skills. You've got the whole package—top-notch education, solid experience. A great user interface," Jared quipped, trying to lighten the mood.

"So why the heck do I keep getting the boot?" My plea for answers was raw and unguarded.

"What went down with Micron?" Jared probed, his curiosity piquing.

"It was Trish. Her aggressiveness, her overstepping. It was like she was trying to be the product manager instead of me," I explained, frustration lacing my words.

"Yeah, but what specifically about that got under your skin?" Jared nudged, his tone softening, almost therapeutic.

"Come on, that would irk anyone, right?" I argued, feeling the weight of the injustice.

"Sure, but tough personalities are a dime a dozen in the corporate world. I mean, Phil, I'm dealing with my own 'Trish' at the moment," he chuckled, his laughter not quite masking the gravity of our discussion.

I paused, lost in thought. "It's her influence, her power . . . even her charm. It felt like she had control over me," I admitted, my voice trailing off into silence.

Jared's empathy was palpable. "That's rough, I get it. You felt sidelined, unheard."

"That's just it," I sighed, the confusion clear in my tone. "I couldn't find my footing. She dazzled everyone, her word was law, and I was just...there, voiceless. But it was more than that. She had this charisma, this magnetic draw, all the while working at cross-purposes toward me.

"Let's think this through," Jared suggested, his analytical side kicking in. "Both your Micron and Cisco experiences have a common theme—strong women making executive calls that sidelined you. Sounds like these encounters are more than just bad luck; like they're triggering something deeper."

"Triggering?" I echoed, the concept resonating uncomfortably with me.

"Yeah, like those movie scenes where the protagonist gets hurled back into a past trauma," Jared explained, always quick to draw cinematic parallels.

"That . . . sounds accurate," I acknowledged, a sense of clarity beginning to emerge.

"So, what memories are these situations dredging up?" he prodded gently.

I hesitated, then shared, "It's like the chaos in our family when I was young. The turmoil. My mother's domineering decisions . . . it's all resurfacing."

"Could it be," Jared interjected thoughtfully, "that these workplace dynamics are echoing your family's past, maybe even hinting at your mother's role in your deeper issues?"

The suggestion hung heavily in the air. It was a stretch, yet the parallels were unsettling. My mother, the epitome of virtue in my eyes, was now cast in a dubious light by my current predicaments with formidable women at work.

While some clarity seemed to be emerging, it felt uncomfortably close to home. Too raw to handle. I had to break free from the suffocating pressure and somehow shift my mood. I needed an escape.

I hung up the phone bolted out the door to meet Tony at the Purple Place, our local hangout that still held onto its gritty past amid its polished present. His knowing grin and the cold beers awaiting on the table as I walked into the bar acted as a welcome comfort to my frayed nerves. Tonight was about escapism, not introspection.

* * *

Waking up the next morning, I was momentarily buoyed by an undefinable lightness, a stark contrast to the previous day's turmoil. However, the fleeting calm was soon shattered by the encroaching reality of a pounding headache and building anxiety as I grasped for memories of the night's escapades. The last thing I could remember was heading from the Purple Place over to the El Dorado Saloon . . . but the rest was blank.

I looked out in the garage and the driveway to see if I had driven home. My car wasn't there.

Somehow, I had either mustered the judgment not to drive amidst my drunken activities or I just couldn't find my car when I left the bar; either way, at least I hadn't compounded the situation with a drunken crash or worse.

But how did I get home? And where on earth was my car? The feeling of dread spread through my body like cold, clammy brown liquid dripping from a rusty shower head. Then it slowly shifted to anxiety and a tingling in my chest—a combination of heartburn and some sort of fear that was closer to my very soul.

Then the realization that I'd lost another job sank in. I had nowhere to go. Nothing to do. And along with that, no source of income.

As the morning progressed, the combined headache and anxiety quickly worsened until I realized this was untenable.

I mixed up a large batch of Bloody Marys and began to sip. As I finished the first and moved onto the second, the headache and anxiety began to lessen, replaced with a welcome level of calmness.

By late morning the calmness had been again replaced by a growing level of anxiety. I took an Uber back to the Saloon and found my car parked right there in front of the venue. I got in and turned the key. But it wouldn't start. I kept trying, but despite the starter turning over, the engine wouldn't run. I cashed in one of my AAA services and had the car towed to a shop in Folsom.

I knew something was wrong. Yet I couldn't seem to figure out the source of the unrest deep in my soul. All I knew was that after a drink or two I felt better and the angst that typically filled my soul faded away.

An hour later the mechanic called. "Did someone put diesel fuel in your tank?"

CHAPTER TWENTY-THREE

Captain Morgan

We were on Captain Morgan's cruise ship—no relation to the liquor company, just a boat owner named Morgan—which set out from Brentwood California. Brentwood was not a coastal town by any means and not a place you would normally associate with setting sail. As we floated along the slough in the west end of California's Central Valley Delta we could see small bits of vegetation mixed with rotting pieces of driftwood along the banks, the water a silty dark brown. The occasional tree was visible in the distance but mostly the terrain was flat, indistinguishable in all directions. Yet here we were, on a four-hour corporate team-building cruise.

After getting fired from Micron I landed a job with a small marketing agency called Precision Marketing. It was a tiny firm consisting of a husband and wife who ran the place and some fifteen or so employees, one of which was now me. It was a remote position, which meant I didn't have to report into an office. This was perfect for the occasional afternoon beer or, if needed, an occasional Bloody Mary to ward off particularly bad hangovers—hair of the dog.

My boss, Susan, a fluffy, gregarious blond woman, was also co-owner of the agency along with her husband. On this particular event—I'd been there a couple of months by then—Susan was relaxed and easygoing. This was in stark contrast to the work environment when she tended to micromanage her employees. I often got calls from her at 4:59 p.m. on a weekday with no particular agenda to speak of. After a number of these calls, I realized she was just checking in to make sure I was still on the clock up to the committed 5:00 p.m. quitting time.

We floated along between the rock banks. In places where the levee dipped low enough, we could just see the surrounding cornfields. Every now and then the captain would point out a place of interest. At one point he stopped at a bridge over the waterway comprising a railroad crossing. He announced that on some days, at certain times, a train would come over the bridge and it was "quite the site." Huge, imposing, magnificent.

But not today. Today, the bridge was quiet. Maybe next time.

He also mentioned that, on occasion one could see a coyote scuttling along the levee, scavenging for food.

But again, not today.

He pointed out a small dirty beach where water skiers typically pulled up their boats for a lunch break or to wait it out between sessions. Today being a weekday, the beach was empty.

As we cruised along the delta waterways, I couldn't decide if I was happy or horrified. I had a job, true. But it was a far cry from where I had been years earlier. A long way from Stowe, Vermont. And I was making thirty percent less than I had earlier in my career. This meant that after the mortgage, groceries, gas, booze, and other necessities, I had little left over for entertainment. Or for a decent car.

My buddy Jared was a VP at a semiconductor intellectual property company composed mostly of lawyers. They made immense amounts of money and had some of the most lavish off-site events known to mankind: a ten-course tasting menu with wine pairings in Napa and trips to Cancun to discuss the upcoming strategic plan.

In contrast to all of that, I found myself floating amongst the cornfields in a glorified houseboat along a body of water fifty yards wide, a view of the man-made rock levees on either side.

I had traveled here in my newly acquired 2001 Camry with a very worn, silver paint job and blown shocks. After the diesel incident following my Purple Place binge the previous month, my 4Runner had exhibited some catalytic converter issues that were generating error codes. Further investigation revealed the converters were shot and it had a blown head gasket. The car was totaled. I made a deal with the mechanic to trade in what was left of my 4Runner for a very old Camry. Apparently that car had, in turn, been traded in by another unfortunate soul who couldn't afford its repairs.

The shocks were so worn, the car would bounce when going over the slightest bump. The roads from Stockton to Brentwood, being in the Central Valley, were mostly flat and geometrically straight. Yet, because of the water content of the soil, the roads undulated slightly like ribbons of pavement. One couldn't see the waves. But you could feel them. Each time my car went over one of these undulations it would lumber up, then down, then oscillate for seconds afterward.

Things had shifted over the last fifteen years. There was no glamor in my job. There were no expensive trips. The roar of progress had faded from my ears. Now, it was just me and this fifteen-person agency, and a very controlling, overbearing boss. As we motored obsequiously along the waterways, I decided I had effectively worked my way down the ladder of success. This job had no frills, no perks, no opportunity for advancement. Just a sad little agency floating on the delta waterways that were constructed for the purposes of irrigating crops.

Driving back home I thought hard about how I had gotten here. I had been fired from Micron due to a clash with a powerful, assertive woman who prioritized her own interests, often working in cross-purposes with me and my role at the company. I had felt marginalized, not just in my job but as a human being. Like if she won, I would be destroyed. And she would fool all the people around me into thinking she was right and *I* was the crazy one.

I wanted to interpret this as an isolated case. As if there weren't many people like Trish in the world. But then thoughts of Cisco and Elise came flooding back into my brain. Another powerful female working at cross-purposes to me and my role in the organization, not acting in my best interests. I had overreacted to this behavior, and the result had been the same.

And then there was the drinking. Was that the problem? While I didn't typically spend my whole workday drinking alcohol, there was the occasional afternoon beer or the morning Bloody Marys after a rough night of drinking. Did my employers somehow know what was going on? Did it come through over the phone? Was I slurring my speech and not realizing it?

Quitting drinking didn't seem like a good option. Drinking made me feel better. I worried less. I could function. It was like a mental reset each time I imbibed.

Yet, the better I felt in the evenings by letting loose, the worse my interactions during the day at work got. The more I cloaked myself with alcohol, the more reactive I was to the injustices of authority figures on the job, and the more resentful I got toward those who had power over me.

When I arrived back in El Dorado Hills, the sun was still shining and the evening was young. The agency hadn't fed us dinner, so I needed to get something to eat. I didn't want to sit at home alone. I wanted to be out where the happy people were.

After a quick change, I got back in my rundown Camry and drove to the El Dorado Saloon. After a drink or two I turned from sullen, shy Phil into a confident socialite. I met a pretty brunette sitting at the bar and we began talking. It was exciting. The place was bustling and crowded.

I did my best job of listening and empathizing. I really wanted to connect with her. Her husband had just died of cancer, and she had nursed him through the final six months of his life as his body deteriorated—a gut-wrenching story. It must have been—

Then moments later we were up and dancing on the makeshift concrete dance floor. There was a band playing in the corner. Or maybe it was house music coming over the PA system. I was in no state to notice these things.

I had an oversized glass of gin and tonic in my hand as I twirled and bounced like a drunken idiot. In one swift move the condensation on the glass caused it to slip through my hands downward and onto the floor, shattering. Ice, broken glass, and booze flew everywhere.

Inexplicably, she remained interested in me.

Despite my drunken blunder, the bartender passed it off: "I'm guessing the condensation on the glass made it slippery and that's what happened, right?" He handed me another drink, this one in a plastic cup. I barely noticed as I continued acting the dancing fool, the alcohol making me bold, confident, invincible.

I held her hand, twirling her to the music. Then looked deep into her eyes . . .

Fade to black.

CHAPTER TWENTY-FOUR

Wine Country Klonopin

I woke up hungover and anxious the next morning. I couldn't recall exactly how much I'd had to drink the previous night and under what circumstances. This continual cycle of introspection, regret, and ephemeral escapism couldn't sustain me forever. As the mayhem of the previous night gave way to the quiet, yet painful, introspection of the morning, I recognized the need for a change from this self-destructive orbit.

At least for a brief period.

Unfortunately, the acute pain of alcohol withdrawal quickly superseded my moment of awareness. *I am not going through this again,* I thought. I had been through severe withdrawal hangovers before and used the hair-of-the-dog trick in order to function. But this instance called for something stronger. I rifled through my medicine cabinet and found a bottle of Klonopin. I had been prescribed tranquilizers after the divorce to get through the "rough spots," as my psychiatrist had called them. At one point he had prescribed around-the-clock Xanax, every four to six hours. But after I lost one of my jobs, I had decided taking it every day was imprudent and I weaned off the med. But every now and then, when I needed some comfort, as I did in this moment, I would take a pill or two. And Klonopin was longer acting than Xanax and therefore less addictive, or so my thinking went.

I decided to take a soak in the hot tub. My mood began to improve as the medicine found its way into my bloodstream. Champagne sounded like just the right complement to this carefree Sunday morning in which I had nothing to do and nowhere to be. Moments later, a flute full of sparkling wine in my hand, I was feeling good—even better than normal. Euphoric.

My fourteen-year-old son walked out onto the deck to see me relaxing in the hot tub with a glass of champagne in my hand on a Sunday morning. If he was in any way shocked by the scene, he didn't show it.

"Can you take me to Town Center?"

"Well, hmmm . . ." In my uninhibited state I got an idea. Suddenly, the allure of wine tasting on a serene Sunday morning beckoned—a chance to find escape in the tranquil beauty of the vineyards. "I'm going to head over to meet some friends for wine tasting. I can take you there on the way." It was mostly true. I had, moments prior, contemplated going to the wine country. But I hadn't arranged to meet any friends.

"Cool."

I got dressed and we both got into my well-beaten Camry. It was a beautiful late summer day with a clear-blue California sky, not a cloud nor a concern within sight. My feelings of hope were heightened by a growing sense of anticipation.

I dropped Brandon in town. Forty-five minutes later I walked into Bella Piazza winery near Fair Play. It was the first winery along the El Dorado County wine-tasting route.

After a couple of tastes I found myself talking in fluent French to a gregarious, heavyset woman. She was animated and laughing, happy to be talking in her native tongue. The two ladies to my left noticed. One was young and pretty, with beautiful red hair. The other was older—as in my age—and with sandy-blonde hair. She was also attractive, but in a more mature, experienced sense.

I was instinctively drawn to the redhead. The three of us began to talk. I suggested we take our wine out to the patio. We began sipping wine together outside, and at one point, the older one went to the restroom.

The young redhead and I began talking and flirting. Then, in an act which seemed completely natural, I leaned toward her. She leaned in—at least in my mind she did.

I kissed her. Passionately! It felt exciting, sensual!

"We need to go!"

Her friend had just returned and wanted to leave. It seemed I'd been caught in a terrible act between two girlfriends. Yet I was surrounded, protected by the alcohol buzz mixed with Klonopin armor. I was invincible. As they left, I shook it off and decided it was time to call it an afternoon, despite the half-bottle of wine in front of me.

So naturally, I drove over to the Di Arie winery, which was just around the corner. I was already pretty inebriated, but I was in the mood to keep going. As long as the adventure continued, I was immune from self-reflection.

I tasted a series of wines. I bought a glass or two or maybe it was a bottle. I had a vague recollection of being frowned at in the tasting room. I went out to the picnic table next to the pond and drank my wine. It was lovely, cultured. There were turtles sitting on a rock in the pond. It was beautiful, like a painting. It was—

An instant later, I was driving my Camry, heading along a winding road toward Latrobe. I headed around a sharp left turn and swung wide. I grazed a small bush standing just off the shoulder and felt a large jolt.

I sluggishly glanced in the rearview mirror. The foliage had been laid bare to expose a thick trunk and branches of a small but stout tree. It had gouged the right side of my car.

I didn't make too much of it. I'd take a look later, when I got home.

I was having trouble keeping my eyes open. Heading northwest on Latrobe, I had a vague awareness of the out-of-gas light on my dash illuminating. Then a fuzzy recollection of driving to Town Center. Of rolling over curbs. Arriving at the gas station. Pumping gas . . . or at least trying to. Was this a dream or was it actually happening?

* * *

I woke up and looked at my phone. It was 8:30 p.m. Slowly some of the events of the afternoon began to soak into my consciousness. I looked around and saw the inside of my bedroom.

Where's my son?

I panicked, jumping out of bed. I ran down the hall to his room. He wasn't there.

I ran into the kitchen. Nothing. I breathed hard. Sweat ran down my forehead.

Then, to the left of the kitchen, I saw something out of the corner of my eye. My son was on the sofa holding a video-game controller, playing Grand Theft Auto.

Thank God.

Hangovers were starting to become commonplace. I knew I needed to do something about my drinking. I had tried quitting before. I had quit for months, even as long as a year. But I eventually always started up again. I don't know if it was boredom, or I thought I was cured, or I just wanted to be like other normal people. Inevitably I'd begin drinking again.

CHAPTER TWENTY-FIVE

Sac County

After the latest string of chaotic evenings and the glaring mistakes that seemed to multiply with each passing day, I found myself at a crossroads. What little self-reflection I could muster began to tell a story I could no longer ignore. The nights blurred into mornings, with the aftermath always seeming to outweigh the short-lived joy of intoxication. It was clear: the drinking had to stop. I was teetering on the edge of losing much more than just my dignity or a few productive hours; I was risking everything that truly mattered.

With a newfound resolve, I reached out to my friends, determined to prove to them, and myself, that I could be the life of the party without the crutch of alcohol. Inviting them out on my boat seemed like the perfect setting—a day of sun, water, and good company, where the focus would be on the laughter and stories shared, not on the drinks consumed. I envisioned it as a testament to my willpower, a declaration that I was taking control back.

The day was picturesque, the kind that postcards are made of, with the gentle lull of the waves and the warmth of the sun creating the perfect setting. My friends, unaware of my inner pledge, brought along their usual array of wine, beer, and hard liquor. The atmosphere was infectious, and as the early afternoon hours slipped by, my resolve began to waver. The clink of ice, the pop of beer caps, the glint of liquid amber, and the carefree abandon of my friends began to wear on me.

In a moment that felt as inevitable as the afternoon sun, I reached for a drink. The familiar, comforting burn of the alcohol as it slid down my throat felt like a long-lost friend, welcoming me back with open arms. Laughter came easier, the stories grew more animated, and the weight of my earlier resolve faded into the background, replaced by the old, reckless joy of letting go.

Six hours later, as the sun began to dip below the Folsom Dam, we navigated back to the marina and hauled the boat out of the water. Desperately not wanting the blissful moment to come to an end, I suggested we continue the evening with some wine tasting and dinner. I glanced at my buddy, hoping for a moment of solidarity, which he readily provided.

We drove around the lake to the Granite Bay side, boat in tow. There, we found a tiny liquor store in a little strip mall. The small shop—like a lot of flagging businesses—was trying to reinvent itself and shift its image to a more upscale operation. They carried fine wines and were offering tastings on Friday and Saturday nights.

We descended on the place. The Indian woman who owned the store greeted us with a smile and pointed toward the tasting section—a couple of aisles that had been converted into a bar-style configuration with table cloths to give a fancier feel. Our small group of six people overwhelmed the place.

She poured us generous tastes of white, then red wines for our evaluation. After eight or ten different wines we left and walked around the corner to an Italian restaurant for dinner.

More wine!

I felt a little woozy. "I think it would be wise to walk around a little," I said to one of my friends. We did a couple of laps around the strip-mall parking lot. The sky was clear, the moon shone bright, and the warm Granite Bay air felt relaxing.

After twenty minutes of walking, I felt clearer and slightly steadier; and decided it was time to get on my way.

I drove back over the bridge to the Folsom side, heading toward El Dorado Hills. Nearing Blue Ravine I entered the double left turn lane. The stoplight was green but, just as I approached the light, it turned yellow. I slammed on the brakes, bringing the car and boat to a stop. The front wheels of the car stopped a few feet over the limit line, but at least I hadn't dangled the boat through the intersection on an aging yellow light.

Once the light turned green, I headed up Blue Ravine toward El Dorado Hills. It was a pleasant drive, and the night was easy and laid back. I would be home in a few minutes.

Just as I approached the Purple Place, flashing red and white lights appeared immediately behind me!

I wasn't sure what the problem was, but I felt a slight sense of dread. Yet it was mostly covered up by the warm, secure blanket of alcohol.

I pulled over. Wanting to be proactive and responsible, I grabbed my driver's license and got out of the car, walking around the trailer toward the police car. The officer approached me with a flashlight in his hand.

"You came up to that stoplight awfully fast," the officer said.

I explained articulately how I didn't want to go through the yellow light towing a boat as that would be dangerous. Having the trailer behind me, I had done the right thing. I knew this would be a routine stop and he would let me go on my way.

"Have you been drinking this evening?" he asked.

"Yes . . . just a few," I said. Honesty is always the best policy.

"How much have you had to drink?" he continued.

"Well . . . let's see. We had some wine out on the boat, then a gin and tonic, then some wine tasting in Granite Bay . . ." I had nothing to hide. "Then a couple of glasses over dinner." The words came out sounding different than I expected. Slightly more excessive.

"I'd like to run you through a few tests," the officer said. "I want you to walk an imaginary line, with your hands down at your side, heel-to-toe."

Despite walking a perfect straight line, hands by my side, his tone shifted abruptly, and he shouted:

"PUT YOUR HANDS DOWN!"

Why so angry?

* * *

I sat in a holding tank with thirty other people. It was spacious enough. New faces would show up every now and then. People were friendly and relaxed, recounting stories about how they had been arrested on a Saturday evening.

"I had been smoking pot," one guy said.

"They arrested you for that?"

"Well, I was unresponsive when they came to my car."

Oh, OK . . . now I get it.

Then we were moved into a small room with an open-air toilet. It smelled like human waste and there were liquids on the concrete floor. There was enough room to stand but not enough for everyone to lie down—and who would want to anyway?

After about thirty minutes, I laid down on the concrete

floor using a filthy, wadded-up orange jumpsuit as a pillow. I awoke a few hours later with a splitting headache and a raw, shocking feeling of disorientation. It was still nighttime and mostly dark in the holding tank. Not only had the alcohol worn off, but my anxiety meds had also drained from my system, leaving me in a stark, frightened, raw state of anxiety, as if I were being lowered into a pool of ice-water, all the while my head was being clamped by a vise. I lifted my head off the dirty orange jumpsuit. Feeling a vibrating sensation, I lifted my right hand up into my field of view and I saw it trembling uncontrollably.

I tried to recall the events of the night before. Where were my kids? I was a responsible father . . . or at least I had been. Shame welled up inside me. I focused beyond my trembling hand to see the open stall of the toilet come into view with a lean, half-clothed Hispanic man sitting on it. Just then he clenched his elbows against his ribs and emptied his bowels in an explosive blast of diarrhea, tiny drops of brown water spraying out the gaps between his thighs and the seat. Seconds later the stench overwhelmed my nostrils.

As I lay there on the cold concrete, the stark reality of my situation burned through the haze of alcohol withdrawal. The filthy jumpsuit beneath my head offered no comfort, only a chilling reminder of how far I had fallen. The tremors in my hand were not just physical; they were symbolic of the internal upheaval that had destroyed my life. The gruesome scene before me, the man devoid of privacy and dignity, was a grotesque mirror reflecting my own decline.

I had all but stopped searching for answers about what happened in my childhood. I'd concluded it was better to bury it and live for the brief moments of euphoria while I gutted out the rest of life's routine than to try to sort out what happened. Yet my life was swirling down the drain while my therapist's assessment lay dormant for over two years; and Holly's apology was but a distant memory.

The irony of it all was crushing. Once, I had a life many would envy: a family, a home, a career. Now, I was witness to my own demise, my existence reduced to this grim spectacle. Every attempt to quit, every fleeting moment of sobriety, had been demolished by the unrelenting grip of my addiction. The stark truth was undeniable: I was on the edge, teetering between life and either an alcohol-induced death or a self-inflicted one.

The cold seeped into my bones, a relentless reminder that if I didn't change my path, I would soon find myself in a darker, colder place from which there would be no return. The echo of my friend's words years prior, "ninety meetings in ninety days," resonated like a lifeline thrown across my bow. It was a clear call to action, a possible path to safety, if only I could muster the courage to take that first step. This was the final crossroads: I could either let the alcohol consume what little was left of me or fight for my life with every fiber of my being. The choice was as clear as the cold concrete floor beneath me.

CHAPTER TWENTY-SIX

Sobering

At noon the next day I drove toward the church, barely noticing the quaint neighborhood I had visited countless times a few blocks from the Powerhouse Pub in Old Town Folsom. The December sun was too bright for comfort. Too glaring, exposing everything, including things I didn't want, out in the open.

My chest was tight and there was a sharp stinging in the pit of my stomach like I had swallowed a paring knife. The alcohol had drained from my system hours prior leaving nothing but a raw, exposed feeling. Like the rock mounds that appeared in Folsom Lake as the water level dropped in the late fall, I felt like a lump of earth or clay that needed to be formed into something. Like an artist's work that hadn't yet taken on any form.

Yet it was unclear what my true form was as I had little to go on. Odd, creepy, sexually inappropriate behavior from my dad. Holly's apology for . . . something. And my therapist's assertion that I had probably been abused as a child. I knew I needed to dig deeper to find out what had happened. I had explored the possibility that I was gay, giving it a full, fair shot and concluding it was not the issue. I also knew unequivocally that continuing to numb out with alcohol would eventually lead to oblivion.

I parked along the street in a row of forty or so cars parked in front of a no-parking sign. As I approached the door I saw groups of people outside socializing. A few of them puffed cigarettes. I quickly skirted two groups and headed inside to find a chair. I kept my head down, not wanting to make eye contact.

"Are there any newcomers?" I heard the secretary say after the opening formalities. This was the part I dreaded. I had always hated the moniker. It seemed to me the word "alcoholic" conjured an image of an old, unshaven, stinky man lying in the gutter, clutching a brown paper bag, having wet himself. But I was desperate and I wasn't going to mince words.

"I'm Phil, I'm an alcoholic," I said.

Something in my ears popped. The tension in my body drained and the tight, pressurized air in my chest exhaled.

Toward the end of the meeting the secretary asked those who were willing to sponsor to raise their hands. I tried to quickly memorize the half dozen or so who'd volunteered. As I crossed the floor, suddenly packed with happy, gregarious alcoholics standing and chatting with each other, I searched for the person attached to the hand I'd seen. I didn't recall exactly who it was, but I vaguely remembered someone tall, big, with facial hair. As I walked toward the edge of the room, I saw a tall, imposing, solid man sporting a goatee.

"Hi . . . were you one of the people who raised their hand to be a sponsor?" I asked.

"Yes," he said, in a measured tone. "My name's Kevin."

"Hi Kevin, I'm Phil." Then in what felt like a gut-wrenching, Herculean moment, I mustered the courage: "Would you be willing to sponsor me?"

"Sure," he said matter-of-factly.

He motioned for me to walk with him over toward a table in the corner of the room and picked up a blue, hardcover book with Alcoholics Anonymous written in big letters on the cover.

"Here, this is for you," he said in a tone both parental and compassionate. "So, when was your last drink?"

"Yesterday," I replied, attempting to suppress my inner embarrassment.

He opened the book and wrote down today's date inside the cover.

"Twelve-fifteen, two-thousand-sixteen: That's your sobriety date."

After a few minutes of conversation, Kevin paused for a minute, looking directly into my eyes. "There is this phrase in the program we call being spiritually fit," he said, his eyes widening as if to emphasize the point.

Something in that comment resonated deeply with my upbringing in Christian Science. While much of the metaphysical work we did had been bizarre dogma, some of it was focused on bettering one's self, evaluating one's thought processes, and keeping one's mind pure of resentment, hatred, and jealousy. I had been very functional once I got into my teens. Not necessarily happy, but functional nevertheless. Based on Kevin's comment, I began to think I could achieve that state again. It lingered in my psyche like a carrot dangling from a stick and drew me toward the program.

"So how did you end up here?" I asked, hoping to shift the focus away from myself.

"Well . . . I was in pretty bad shape. I was a stay-at-home dad, taking care of our two young boys. I spent a lot of time coaching their football teams in the afternoons. But I was drinking all day. I had a Big Gulp cup filled with vodka and Gatorade in the console of my pickup."

"Wow . . . did the people around you know?"

"Some did. A lot of them just looked the other way. At

one point I was at a football game coaching the team. I was fumbling around, trying to act as if I was in control. One of the moms came up behind me and put her hand on my shoulder . . ."

Kevin reached over and put his hand on my shoulder to illustrate.

"'It's OK, Kevin, we know you're drunk.'"

"Oh . . . man," I said, feeling the shame permeate me. "That sounds really awful. So . . . humiliating."

"That's the way it was. My wife had to put up with it for years. When she finally realized what was going on, she forced me to go to rehab. It'll be five years this fall."

* * *

Two months passed. I began working on the Fourth Step. As I attended daily meetings and worked the steps with Kevin, the first thing I noticed was a feeling of no longer being alone. The second thing was that many of those who shared in meetings had similar stories to me.

Not all were rock-bottom drunks who had been living on the street. I even ran across a story in the back of the Big Book that articulated my experience better than I could have myself. I went from feeling messed up and alone to being a part of a group of people who had all been through similar struggles. I identified with many of them.

Some talked about extreme dysfunction in their families of origin, of alcoholism and substance abuse by their parents and older siblings. Some talked about being abused and traumatized as children. It was the first time I had heard people talk openly about the most shameful parts of their lives. I was struck by their honesty and vulnerability.

I began to form a language to explore the difficult times in my own childhood, despite not knowing many details. My mind cracked open just a little bit, allowing me to glimpse what might have happened. I knew about the five-year gray period in my own life, when I couldn't pay attention at school and daydreamed the entire time. I knew about Pam and Holly getting into drugs and alcohol. I knew about my father's odd sexual experimentation and the creepiness I felt about him. It was as though there was some definition forming out of the mist that comprised my younger years.

I continued to listen and attend meetings around the area, slowly expanding my search radius. Cameron Park, Loomis, Roseville, Placerville. Some of the stories were about over-the-top drunkenness: the drunk-a-log.

One talked about having killed someone while driving drunk; and winding up in prison for five years, then getting sober and having a life again.

Every now and then I heard a story that felt eerily similar to mine and this kept me coming. One woman in the Folsom fellowship, the same one in which I had attended my first meeting, told her story.

"I was a wine drinker," she confessed. "I had a glass of wine every evening after work. It slowly transitioned, over the course of a decade, to two glasses a night. I didn't think I was out of control. And I figured, because I drank wine and knew a lot about the winemaking process and many of the different labels, I was sophisticated, and not a drunk."

The story sounded very familiar to me. A glass or two of wine. What could be wrong with that? And it was wine, after all. Drunks don't drink fine wines.

"Then as I got older," she continued, "I found myself increasing ever so slightly to two or three glasses a night. It took years for the progression. Eventually, after another ten years I was drinking close to a bottle most nights . . . sometimes more."

It was a slow burn. A cooking of the frog. Nothing abrupt, just an evolution to slightly more than before. It was as if she was telling my story. The closeness to my own experience was startling—as if she was inside my head. After getting sober, she began to realize and address something that had happened to her as a child. That she had been sexually abused.

I wondered what my own sobriety would reveal to me about my childhood.

CHAPTER TWENTY-SEVEN

Silicon Valley

I continued to struggle finding a job in technology. Sacramento, while having a small, embryonic startup scene, was proving more and more limiting. There just weren't enough technology companies to choose from in this town—at least not ones that hadn't already heard of me.

I had gotten good at interviewing over the years. I suppose if you're forced to do something enough times, you'll eventually master it. But what had held me back as of late was the location question. Whenever the geography question came up, I hemmed and hawed.

"Where do you live?"

I would inadvertently say something coy like: "Well, I have a home in El Dorado Hills, but I have family in the Bay Area and can stay there any time." Hiring managers and HR reps would see through it. They would assume I was trying to finagle a remote position. And the nine-one-six area code of my mobile phone just reinforced their suspicions.

"Why don't you go stay in the Bay Area?" Kevin said

one day over the phone. "Your mom lives there, right?"

It was an obvious move, yet I had resisted it. Maybe it was a sense of duty to my kids. Maybe it was just the feeling of comfort that came from doing the familiar. Maybe I had an aversion to living under my mom's roof again. But Kevin was there to guide me in a positive direction. He had become an ally, willing to give me honest feedback and provide practical advice that was meant to help me have a better life. Kevin had my back, and I knew it.

I packed up two weeks' worth of supplies, my computer, and my dog and headed to the Bay Area to stay with my mother. On the way there I got a call from a headhunter I had been working with.

"Ethan really liked you," she said. "Fareed wants you to interview with a few more people at Agari."

This was great news. And now I could, in good conscience, say I lived in the Bay Area—even if it was only on weekdays.

My goals in visiting the Bay Area were twofold: First, get integrated into the recovery rooms on the peninsula. I knew that recovery was my number-one commitment and any wavering in that would be the end of me. Second, land a job. Once that had been accomplished, I could pursue the task of finding a permanent place to live.

After another round of interviews, I got a call with a job offer: a small, vibrant startup in downtown San Mateo focused on email security. The office was a stone's throw from 3rd Avenue, my former windsurf haunt. Twenty years earlier I would have killed for a job in San Mateo.

Don't mess it up!

* * *

I continued my weekly commute, traveling Sunday evenings to my mother's house and returning to El Dorado Hills on Fridays. Over the next few months, my job flourished, and a newfound stability settled into my life. Amidst this routine, I found solace in attending AA meetings four times a week.

Meanwhile, Brandon celebrated his seventeenth birthday and took up residence with my ex-wife in El Dorado Hills. The weariness of the weekly journey to El Dorado Hills began to weigh on me, prompting a decision to sell the house and permanently relocate to the Bay Area. Within sixty days, the transaction was finalized, and I opted to stay temporarily at my childhood home with my mother. This choice offered both convenience and a nostalgic nod to my younger years, although I couldn't deny the flood of memories it stirred inside me.

One particular Tuesday evening, as my mother and I sat at the kitchen table, she made a move to get up from the table, asking:

"So, Phil, should I not drink in front of you?"

It made me feel like a child—as if my lack of self-control caused her to make life modifications she didn't want to make.

"You should do whatever you're used to," I responded in a blithe, somewhat defensive tone. "Don't modify your behavior on my behalf."

She pulled a bottle of Chardonnay out of the refrigerator and poured herself a glass, then sat back down.

"Congratulations on selling the house," she said.

"Thanks. Yeah, it feels good to be back in Silicon Valley again," I said with a sigh of relief. "And back in the workforce," I added, punctuating the tumultuous career I'd had endured up to that point.

"How are you feeling these days? Are you still thinking about your childhood?"

"Yeah. I keep thinking back about Dad and some of the things you mentioned about him. Can you tell me more about him?"

"Well, Phil, you know he wasn't like other dads. He wasn't the happy, upright, steadfast husband that you'd see in the movies. He had a lot of . . . mental issues." She paused for a moment, collecting herself. "He was a difficult person. And he didn't make me feel secure as his wife, either." She paused again, this time looking down at the floor, her eyes looking tired, worn, and at the same time a little misty as she collected herself. "It wasn't just the . . . incident . . . between him and his sister. He had some pretty weird ideas about sexuality."

"What . . . do you mean?" I coaxed, feeling at the same time curious and reluctant to delve in deeper. "What kind of weird ideas?"

"Well, there was the time just after we were married," she began. "I went back to my parents to stay for a week so he could finish his thesis. But when I got back, he said he hadn't gotten much done because he got distracted by a naked woman."

"What? A naked woman, what do you mean . . . was he fooling around?" I responded, my voice full of surprise.

"Well, practically!" she exclaimed. She went on to describe how the window of their apartment apparently looked across the courtyard into another dwelling. The woman in said dwelling would parade around naked, changing in and out of her clothes without closing the drapes. Apparently, she was quite pretty. And he would watch her as she dressed and undressed and sometimes went about her daily activities unclothed.

"He told me about how he couldn't stop watching her instead of working on his thesis," she said. "And we had been married for less than a year. How do you think that made me feel?"

He told you? His own wife? Why would he do that?

Perhaps he had to relieve his sense of guilt. To come clean to clear his conscience. But in the process of telling her, he created an even deeper rift. Whatever the case, he clearly crossed a boundary, twice. Once with his voyeurism, and a second time by telling his own wife about how he had succumbed to lust and watched this woman parade around her apartment for hours at a time, naked.

And it clearly bothered my mother. I could hear the jealousy in her voice, even decades later. She continued her narrative, pivoting slightly into her romantic relationship with my father. She described his advances as being unwanted and forced. They had clearly had sex—at least five times, anyway. (You can't have a family of five without that.) But there was apparently a fungal issue at one point and they both needed to be treated to resolve it. My father refused medical treatment because of his deep abiding faith in Christian Science. And she had to suffer through.

When my mother recounted this, it gave the impression my father's sexual advances were unwanted, even overbearing. Like he'd forced himself on her. As if he couldn't stay off of her. It felt almost dirty, as if he were a perpetrator.

It reminded me of my own discomfort with him. The way he touched me. Controlling. Invasive. When he put his hand on my shoulder to get me to stop twitching. It didn't feel like a coach or a friend or even a concerned father. It felt dominating, like he was crossing a boundary that I didn't want him to cross. The touch was unwanted. Uncomfortable.

And then there was the kissing. A grown man kissing his son. Granted, it was on the cheek rather than on the lips. But there was the stubble. It was rough and unwanted. It wasn't the same as kissing my mom or hugging her. That all felt good and right. Kissing him felt forced, intrusive. Like it was something he wanted and I didn't.

But I had no choice, his lips protruding outward against my cheek. Then he'd turn as if to insist on me kissing him back. I didn't really feel I had a say in the matter. But he seemed to want it, even need it. Like he would be devastated if I didn't reciprocate. Perhaps this was why I had been so repulsed on that date with the gay man years prior. The way it felt forced, almost penetrative.

After my father died, I felt nervous enough about his motives and his behavior that I went through a series of therapy sessions. In the process I recalled my sister and me in the bathtub together, my father bathing both of us while Cindy and I were naked. My father was on his knees, leaning over the edge of the tub toward us, almost as though he was leering at our bare bodies.

And the way he looked at my girlfriends. I dated Hayley in junior high. She was pretty and spunky, and a good Christian Scientist also. Yet she had this jumpsuit she would wear that was very short and revealing, especially for a junior high-aged girl. It wasn't a dress but more like hot pants with stirrups. It showed off her legs all the way to her upper thigh. My father would look at her and his eyes would widen as he would say: "Hayley, you look really cute today."

It made me feel embarrassed for him because he was exhibiting lust—as a grown man and my father—toward my girlfriend who was thirty-five years younger. It was almost like he couldn't control himself to the point that he felt he had to say something. As if the feelings were so intense and bottled up inside him that he felt compelled to express them.

Then I started dating Inga my senior year. She was even more beautiful: fair, smooth skin, a slim figure at five feet, five inches, short, blond hair, and a shy, demure personality. She told me that when my father looked at her, he would say things like, "Wow, you look really pretty today, Inga. I like that outfit on you."

Inga said to me at one point: "I kind of think your dad has the hots for me." My father's comments toward Inga felt even more invasive than those toward Hayley, Inga being my first true love. His apparent lust for her made me feel as though I needed to protect her from him.

Things were swirling in my mind. I tried to take inventory of it all. First was Holly's apology for something fairly monumental that had happened when I was young; something of which I had no recollection. Next, there was my dad's creepiness and sexual inappropriateness. Finally, I had my therapist's assertion that I had been abused as a child.

Did my dad do something bad to me or the other kids that I just couldn't remember?

* * *

That evening, I had another of those dreams—the heavy, thick, gravitas-laden ones. It was set on a bus deep in the desert of North Africa.

I had gone to East Africa in 1984 during college on an abroad ten-week Kenya program studying conservation and African history. It was a spectacular trip and I had always maintained a close emotional connection to Africa after that.

It was a beautiful trip: the bright colors, the pungent smells, the balmy feel of the breeze on the Serengeti plains, the sounds of animals in the bush. Hearing greetings in Swahili. Dancing with a group of locals at the base camp on Mount Kenya. Swimming in the river just upstream from hippos and crocs, being careful to make lots of noise before entering the water. Seeing one thousand elephants moving through the bush in the Amboseli Game Reserve near the Tanzanian border.

Though the trip itself was idyllic, we had spent a few weeks prior reading up on the problems underlying this incredible country. There was rampant poaching on the animal population and deep corruption within the Kenyan government.

Just like the missing patriarch in my dream about the rotten home just after Holly died, this dream was devoid of any moral compass or benevolent leader. In fact, it went beyond the lack of positive leadership. The alpha male in this dream was corrupt and evil to the core. And he exhibited sexual domination that caused a disturbance in my soul that resonated for weeks.

I was on a bus in Africa with three groups of people: American tourists, African female dancers with colorful dresses, and menacing Somali pirates. My group resided in one corner at the rear of the bus.

One of the pirates came through the aisle and forced each female dancer to bend-over and expose their behind and he would hit them as hard as he could with an open hand causing each woman to scream in pain.

He continued to the next woman who willingly went face down on the seat lifting her leg high above her head exposing her groin for the man to strike. And this continued as he moved closer and closer to my seat.

As he approached, the three groups merged together. It seemed to me everyone must be afraid but covered it up with bravado, while others conformed, acting within the boundaries of the pirates' rules so as not to attract attention.

One of the pirates came over to me with something that looked like a syringe with a very long needle sticking out of it.

He stuck it on my neck and began to press the actuator at the end of the contraption. I instinctively pushed his hand away. He looked sternly at me and said "Dooon't poosh" and he proceeded to pierce my neck with the device.

The sharp needle penetrated an inch into my neck. I felt terrified. Out of control. Forced to do something against my will.

He loitered. About thirty seconds later he prepared to do the procedure again. I had no choice but to comply.

The needle went deep into my neck. It took a few seconds for me to feel the sensation near my throat but when I did, I winced with pain and my face flushed. He saw my reaction and was satisfied.

As he walked away, I began trying to pull the long needle out of my neck. Pinching the end of it with my fingers, I pulled as hard as I could. A six-inch needle slowly emerged from my neck.

I was very afraid that he would single me out again. I tried to stay invisible. I moved toward the edges of the vehicle, searching right and left for a friendly face or a compassionate expression. But none of them appeared to share my fear. They seemed to go about their business, living their lives and taking these minor setbacks in stride. I cowered in the corner as feelings of helplessness and isolation consumed me.

I woke up feeling disoriented and a little bewildered. The dream had felt so vivid and impactful—like some of the recent ones since Holly's death. But in this one I had been on the receiving end of the abuse from a corrupt, powerful authority figure.

Yet there was something else disorienting about my awakening. I looked around and didn't recognize the bed I was in or the paint color on the walls. I racked my brain thinking about the night before. There was dinner. A bottle of wine. My mother . . .

I got up and walked out of the bedroom into the hallway. Things started to come into focus. To my right stood the doorway leading into the hall bath. The same one I had used for twenty years as a child growing up at 12865 La Barranca.

The previous evening's memory began to condense in my brain. Dinner with my mother. Discussions about old times at home. Had I drank?

I didn't feel a headache. Some anxiety was there as usual, but not the electric feeling in my esophagus. I walked into the kitchen and looked in the fridge. There was a bottle of Chardonnay with about half left.

This was never something I would have done—leaving wine in the bottom of the bottle. That behavior was completely foreign. I saw the leftover bottle of non-alcoholic Kombucha next to it. And I remembered.

My mother had consumed two glasses of wine while I drank the Kombucha. I exhaled a slow, long sigh of relief.

CHAPTER TWENTY-EIGHT

The Bad Joke

After hearing my mom's story about my father and having that very disturbing dream, I started thinking more about other signs of odd behavior. As usual, Jared was my "go-to." In the ambient glow of Vesta in Redwood City, the laughter mingled with the clink of glasses as he and I settled into our usual rhythm. We'd picked a spot that felt like an old friend, comfortable and informal, mirroring the ease of our three-decades-long friendship.

"So, how's the new gig shaping up?" Jared inquired, his eyes lighting up with genuine interest, a subtle reminder of the countless times we'd discussed the ups and downs of my career.

"It's good, man, really good. Feels like I'm finally getting my feet back under me," I replied, the relief evident in my voice. The job was more than a paycheck; it was a stepping stone back to stability, a chance to rewrite my narrative.

Jared nodded, sipping his Heineken Zero. "That's great to hear. Dude, they're lucky to have you."

"Thanks, man," I affirmed, shaking his hand, allowing

a moment of comfortable silence before steering the conversation to a topic that had been weighing on my mind. "You know, now that I'm, shall we say, of clearer mind, I've been thinking a lot about my own dad recently."

Jared leaned in, his expression a mix of curiosity and readiness, the kind honed over years of shared confidences and dissected family histories.

"He was . . . pretty inappropriate at times," I continued, probing the fabric of my childhood memories, each thread a mixture of discomfort and revelation.

Jared chuckled, a soft, circumspect laugh. "Yeah, you've recounted quite a few stories that . . . well let's just say they don't paint him in the best light."

"Did I ever tell you about that weird joke he told me at the dinner table," I ventured, unsure of how Jared would react as I followed the uncomfortable thread.

"You mean the one that would make a comedian speechless?" He laughed. "Do tell, and be sure not to leave out the details. I could use a little bawdy humor here."

I laughed, despite the awkward memory, appreciating Jared's ability to inject humor into even the most cringeworthy recollections.

"It was like my dad had no filter, no sense of boundaries," I began, recounting the joke my father had told me at the dinner table after the rest of the family had left for the evening. It was about a man who lusts after a pretty woman who lives in the apartment across the train tracks. He dreams of his manhood growing longer and longer. Out the window, down the wall, across the tracks, up the wall of her building, into her window. "His penis *grows and grows*," I said, mocking my dad's creepy tone in a low, soft, almost sensual tone.

"Oh, dude, that is disturbing. . . . I can feel it myself and he's not even here—wow! But please continue!" Jared said, chuckling again, always comfortable with our propensity to delve deeply into inappropriate subjects.

I laughed outright before setting up the punchline. "Then the train whistle blows and the man wakes up in a cold sweat."

"Ohhh, boom! That is . . ." Jared caught himself just short of a full celebration. "Well, now that I think about it, I can't decide if it's funny or just downright sleazy. How old were you, again?

"About nine years old."

"Wow! That's pretty young. I can see why that would be unsettling, even thinking about it now as an adult." Jared empathized, an act in which he demonstrated his consummate understanding of others' feelings.

"Yeah, I mean it was just a joke, right? Some visual comedy," I mused, trying to downplay the discomfort. "But then again, not knowing your own son well enough to tell a joke that makes him uncomfortable . . ."

"At best," Jared interjected with a knowing look, "it was highly inappropriate of him."

"Agreed." Then pivoting slightly, yet threading the narrative I'd been unraveling: "Speaking of inappropriate, did I ever tell you about him putting his hand on my shoulder when I twitched?"

"Oh dude, I can already feel the discomfort across the table from here," Jared said, his tone shifting towards a more earnest concern. "Was this a regular thing?"

"I remember sitting on the sofa watching cartoons," I said, immersing myself in the memory. "TV always got me worked up. I would shrug my right shoulder and stick my elbow out. As I got swept up in the cartoons the twitch would really ramp up."

"And your love of the screen still knows no bounds," Jared quipped, catching me sneaking a peak at the TV behind him.

"Shit! Caught me," I replied with a lighthearted

chuckle, easing the moment. "But yeah, suddenly, I'd feel his hand on my shoulder, and he'd whisper, 'Phil, you don't have to do that.'"

"Sheesh." Jared sympathized, shaking his head. "That might be the exact right thing he should do . . . to *reinforce* the twitch!" he exclaimed, dramatizing the last words with a flourish.

He paused, seemingly struck by a thought, his expression signaling a moment of clarity. "It's weird, though," Jared mused, his gaze introspective as he swirled his beer. "It's like, by confronting these memories, you're also . . . what's the word? Unshackling?"

"Unshackling," I echoed, the term striking a chord within me. "Yeah, by facing these past memories, maybe I'm ready to put them behind me and start anew."

Jared lifted his glass, eyes sparkling with camaraderie. "To new chapters, then. And to the unsuspecting ladies awaiting your charm."

Our laughter blended with the surrounding din, a shared release. Discussing these deep-seated issues openly, especially with someone who understood the gravity, yet could lighten the mood, was profoundly liberating.

As we wrapped up our meal, the discussion subtly pivoted towards the future, particularly towards my foray back into the dating scene. Jared, ever the wingman, was brimming with encouragement.

"Speaking of ladies, you've got your life pretty dialed in, man. Do you think, maybe, it's time to put yourself out there?" he asked, his grin contagious.

"Hmmm . . ."

Driving home later, I mulled over our conversation. Jared was right. My job was stable, I was reconciling my past, and for the first time in a long while, I felt ready. Ready to meet someone new, to explore possibilities, to experience the thrill of a first date again. The thought was exhilarating, a testament to the distance I'd traveled from the tumultuous shadow of my father's influence, through the darkness of alcoholism, and to the promising horizon ahead.

CHAPTER TWENTY-NINE

Kathy

As the conversation with Jared resonated through my mind, I began to think, perhaps if I had a woman in my life, I would be complete, no longer searching for something. I decided to take the plunge.

I resurrected my Match.com profile that had been dormant for five years. I took a new picture, touted my new career in cybersecurity, and reposted the bio. Now, in the year 2018, Match was no longer the hot site for dating, but it had worked for me in the past. And it was fairly straightforward with the least propensity for duping and catfishing.

After a few false alarms, I ran across a profile that caught my interest. Her name was Kathy. She had photos of herself in running clothes, and many outdoor pictures. There was one of her in a sleeveless cocktail gown, showing her fit arms and lean form. There was even one with her parents. Pictures with family were rare in most dating profiles that I had seen. She talked about liking tennis and being enamored with Roger Federer.

At some point we moved from Match.com to texting.

We set a time to talk by phone, Tuesday evening at 6:30. On the phone she was somewhat circumspect—even to the point of seeming disinterested.

"I teach at Woodside Elementary School," she said. "I've been teaching physical education there for twenty-five years."

"Wow, you really stay with a job," I observed. "I really think teaching is a noble profession," I added, only vaguely aware that I had used this same line years earlier with Aly.

"Well my goal, aside from helping them learn lifelong fitness, is to help them learn to be good human beings."

The comment sank in. It was a profound statement. She clearly cared about her job and about making an impact on the kids. And she had longevity. I wasn't used to people on dating sites in their fifties showing a huge amount of stability.

"That's pretty amazing," I said after a few moments passed. Then without thinking too much about it, I added "Where exactly is Woodside?"

"Wait . . . you don't know where Woodside is?" she asked incredulously. "I thought you grew up in Los Altos Hills." I could hear the tone in her voice shift toward doubt, and then into suspicion. "Isn't that, like, eight miles away?"

I could envision the wheels turning in her head. I was some guy on the other end of the line she had only just met from Match.com. And catfishing was common in the online dating scene.

"Well I just recall riding through it on a road bike, but I don't think I ever drove there. I mean it's a really small town. I don't think I had any reason to go there." I became suddenly aware I was overexplaining and stopped myself.

"Oh," she said. Then she was silent.

She wasn't interested.

The flat tone, the lack of emotion, the absence of excitement in her voice. I couldn't just keep wooing her, thinking she was hating it and just waiting until she could finally get off the phone.

"I don't know how to say this but . . . it sounds a little like you are bored with me," I finally said impulsively, with a slight chuckle. I was a little surprised by my own abruptness.

"No, it's not that I'm bored," she told me. "I just don't like talking on the phone. . . . It makes me uncomfortable."

I was quickly bolstered by a glimmer of hope. My heart lifted. It was time to ask her out. I began thinking through my schedule for the next week. My buddy had planned a birthday dinner for Sunday evening. Saturday was booked.

"So, what about having lunch on Monday, Memorial Day?" I asked.

"Yeah, my weekends are usually a combination of relaxation and work," she continued on a previous thread, ". . . pulling together lesson plans."

I waited while she finished her thought.

"And I'll usually get a run in or two."

Had she not heard me? Was she just being coy? I thought she had expressed interest, but maybe she changed her mind in the last two minutes.

After what seemed like an eternity, Kathy said in a fairly casual way, "As far as Monday, yes, I think that will work."

She'd kept me hanging for almost a full minute. I let out what must have been a huge, audible sigh.

* * *

The Shoreline Boathouse held a certain bucolic, happy place in my heart. It was beautiful, it was outdoors, and I had always felt a connection with the venue. I had windsurfed and inline skated there for years. It was sunny, breezy, and sat adjacent to a good-sized saltwater lake.

I arrived ten minutes early. After a few minutes she texted that she had just parked in the overflow parking lot near Michaels. I headed across the pedestrian bridge to meet her. As I looked across the slight grade toward the parking lot I saw her walking toward me, about thirty yards away. She had brown curly hair, and her hands extended outward like a cheerleader as if to say, *Heyyyy...here I am!*

In stark contrast to her phone-call demeanor, her body language was open, lighthearted, playful. Almost like a smiley-face emoji. Perhaps it was something that came from working with young kids for twenty-five years?

I was immediately drawn to her. A warm sensation grew in my chest, the feeling of a budding romance combined with attraction combined with a sense of feeling safe. All this was wrapped up into one welcome feeling of elation.

Lunch was busy and crowded. Tables were hard to come by. I secured one along the side of the restaurant facing the lake. I set my phone on the table to stake our claim as we went inside to get our food.

"Did you really hold the table using your phone?" she said. "You really are from Los Altos Hills." I couldn't help but chuckle at her silver-spoon reference.

Despite the hectic atmosphere, we managed to engage in conversation, joking about society and how odd people can be. She was funny—much more so than I had thought from our initial phone call.

I don't recall if it was my idea or hers but, instead of walking on the Shoreline paths, we decided to drive to the Stanford Dish for a hike. She suggested we take one car for ease of parking. Her shift from being very reserved, even suspicious, to trusting a stranger enough to drive in his car, surprised me a little.

Heading up the first hill, I started huffing and puffing, as was my usual beginning of a workout. The hill was steep, and we were going at a good clip.

She seemed unfazed, her athleticism instilling a somewhat intimidating sensation in me. We walked and talked for the better part of an hour, noticing the views, watching birds, and getting to know each other.

On the way home I asked her to pick out some music on my phone to listen to. Later she would tell me about her surprise that I had been transparent and trusting enough to let her look at my phone.

"I like country music," she said.

Dammit! Country.

I was suddenly afraid. I'd never liked country music. Doubt crept in. This would never work. I mustered up what resolve I could and gave it my best shot with an open mind. She chose a song and cued it up.

"If it's meant to be, it'll be, it'll be, baby if it's meant to be." The chorus by Bebe Rexha and Florida Georgia Line came across the car stereo. *Nice,* I thought. Country wasn't my genre, but, somehow, I began to feel a connection with her nonetheless.

After we listened to a few more country tunes, I put on a few of my own selections: Dave Matthews, Hootie and the Blowfish, Train, Goo Goo Dolls.

"OK . . . it's not terrible," she said after listening to a few songs.

"Is that how you're going to describe this date on Facebook," I said with a chuckle. "Not terrible?"

She laughed, a deep, hearty tenor laugh.

I found her open, trusting, approachable. Yet every now and then she would shift to seem circumspect, almost suspicious. As we joked and chatted on the way back, I made another move. Not wanting the day to end, I asked, "So do you want to get a cup of coffee at Starbucks?"

Instantly, she responded, "I think I'm good."

Danger, Will Robinson.

What was going on? Why was I constantly misreading her? My confidence was flagging, and I felt a twinge of foolishness.

Back at the Shoreline parking lot, I found an open spot next to hers and parked the car.

"I'll walk you to your car," I quipped.

She laughed. I felt a little bit of redemption and my confidence inched up just a notch.

I walked her one space over to where her car was. I put my hands on her waist and leaned in, not fully sure what would happen.

She leaned in toward me. I felt her soft lips against mine and suddenly we were in a passionate kiss that felt both infinitely long and way too short.

My life was shifting. Things were changing, moving. I felt a strong connection for the first time in many years. Anxiety about the trauma in my childhood and the possibility that I had been abused still lingered, but it became temporarily stayed as the excitement of dating took precedence and my career began to rebuild.

CHAPTER THIRTY

Email Insecurity

Things began to feel more comfortable being a sober man in the Bay Area. My AA fellows shared that their lives had changed for the better after they stopped drinking. They were employable again. Relationships improved. People shared stories about their loved ones and colleagues, complimenting how great they looked with the new changes.

Occasionally, however, people would recount anomalous experiences. Ones that ran counter to the mainstream. One woman who had gotten sober said that her husband decided to also get sober a year later, mostly at her behest. To his credit, he did. He joined AA and stopped drinking.

But something strange happened. "Our relationship actually got worse when he quit," she said.

I began to hear some stories about the deeper malady. The "ism" as some people called it. There was the "alcohol." But then there was the "ism."

Some stories recounted how the problem hadn't been solved by quitting. That, in fact, drinking had been their solution. Was this a cute play on words? Or was there something deeper going on?

They talked about how alcohol had made them feel better, had removed the feeling of self-loathing, and had helped them interact socially and not be afraid. Removing that protection the alcohol provided, for some people, was like thrusting them in the middle of a gladiator pit with no armor.

One member recounted a discussion with his sponsor. "I want to feel better."

"Oh . . . you'll feel better," the sponsor warned. "You'll feel joy better, you'll feel pain better, you'll feel depression better."

It was a cautionary tale. And one that scared the living daylight out of me. I thought I was doing the right thing. Drinking had caused me immense problems. Quitting drinking was surely the answer. Yet some of my fellows were recounting unexpected outcomes after quitting.

Things were going well at Agari. I was steeped in technology, working toward a more secure cyberspace, and protecting the complex world of email, including corporate inbound email, and protecting employees, corporations, and individuals from cybersecurity attacks. The FBI was quoting statistics in the billions of dollars for losses from cybercrime.

I was assigned a huge project. It was a white paper articulating Agari's core technology and how it was head and shoulders above our competitors. It had to be smart. It had to be clear. It had to be right. Most of all, it had to be convincing.

I immersed myself in the task with a passion and commitment I hadn't had since the Cisco days. My primary contact was Markus, a smart, highly educated European man who would suffer no fools. He spoke with a slight northern-European accent (Danish or Swedish, I think) and had an elitist air about him.

Markus was the right-hand man of the founder, Pat. I had heard stories about Markus getting indignant with certain coworkers and excommunicating them from his projects. It seemed that if he didn't like one's style or resonate with their business acumen things might not go well. Our English field marketing lead had been cut off from working with him. She still worked in our England office, but she was forbidden from contacting him. Our PR person told me some stories too. Don't anger him or you'll pay the price.

Rather than jump straight into the task, I decided to pause for a moment and get to know Markus. We went for coffee at Philz in San Mateo. He seemed to appreciate the gesture. We built a good working relationship with clean and frequent communication. We were moving ahead, making good progress, and working fastidiously together on the project. By six weeks we had a solid draft.

Pat tore it apart. He redlined the Executive Summary. He made four bullet points about problems with the structure, the grammar, and the clarity of the paper. But he did this on the physical print-out of the Executive Summary rather than on the digital copy—a nod to his old-school heritage. He made no comments whatsoever on the rest of the twenty-page piece.

It was a failure of epic proportions. I prepared to gather my belongings, but Pat didn't seem greatly concerned. His demeanor was counseling and educating, like a teacher or a coach: "Go back and work through it, not just the Executive Summary but the whole paper."

So we went back to the drawing board. Markus and I worked for another three weeks, getting it right and elucidating the technology, yet being sure not to give too much away and tip off our competitors.

The project was a challenging one with immense visibility throughout the organization. In addition to the founder, Pat, our VP of engineering had a strong interest in it, as well as my boss's boss, our VP of marketing, Ethan.

The farther along I got, the deeper I became immersed in our core technology. I knew Pat was a technologist and the paper wouldn't ever be sufficient if our technology wasn't well articulated.

My research eventually drove me into a series of conversations with an engineering director in our organization, a very clever, bearded man with a sharp wit and a solid grasp of the technology who had a team of developers working for him. He looked like Ernest Hemingway, if Hemingway led a team of developers.

I asked Hemingway to weigh in on a particular technical issue and received an answer back that felt reliable.

I circled back with Markus and told him what I had learned. But he said, "No, Phil, you're wrong."

Who to believe? I decided the only way to get to the bottom of it would be to get the two of them together. I crafted an email to the two of them, laying out the issue and asking for clarification. Markus said the same thing to Hemingway that he said to me.

Hemingway responded: "Well . . . no, Markus, I don't think that's quite right," and explained his view of the technology. He copied some others in engineering also.

There was no rebuttal from Markus, just radio silence for about four hours. I decided to pause and pivot to a different project, temporarily, as I awaited resolution on the issue: an infographic on email cybersecurity. Then I walked to get some lunch in downtown San Mateo.

After a lunch break I got back to my desk. The phone rang. It was Ethan, our VP of marketing.

"I'm pulling you off the white paper," he said.

What?

"Don't worry about it. It's not a big deal. We're assigning it up the chain to the VP of engineering."

Something didn't feel right. Despite Ethan's casual

words, and blithe demeanor, this felt pretty significant.

I called my boss, Fareed. "What's going on?"

"Markus didn't want you on the project anymore."

"Markus? Do I even have an opportunity to defend myself? I mean—"

"Just stay clear of him," Fareed said. "It will probably blow over."

Thirty days later, a new coworker showed up and sat next to me. He was young, smart, and articulate, if not a little brash.

Fareed split the two products amongst us. Brash was handed the fast-growing Enterprise product. I was relegated to the legacy Service Provider product, the one that was on the decline. Despite this, I jumped in hard.

Months passed. We moved to a new facility in Foster City, and a new chief marketing officer named Armin was hired between the CEO and Ethan. A month later I got a calendar invitation to a meeting in our main conference room on the top floor of the tallest building in Foster City.

The room was large with a twenty-foot table and twelve chairs around it. A ninety-inch television monitor was mounted to the front wall. Windows surrounded the room on three sides. The main window—the one along the long outside of the room—looked out over the Foster City shoreline. Kiteboarders were already out on the water, powered by the mounting afternoon winds. I was moving closer to the water, just five minutes from Third Avenue. I could get used to this. I had to pinch myself to believe that it was real.

Ethan and our HR manager came into the room and sat down across the table from me. "Well Phil," Ethan said, "I know you've been working here a while and you've done good work. And Armin asked you to do that project so you've had a lot of things going on in parallel. . . . How did that turn out anyway?"

"Well, Armin asked me to do it but I was answering to

a couple of different bosses at the time. Frankly I kind of think Mike and Armin had different visions for how the project was supposed to—"

"That's nice . . ." Ethan said. "Well anyway, Phil, hopefully this won't come as a surprise . . ."

* * *

I began to reevaluate my time at Agari. And Ethan himself. I respected him. Well, no . . . that's not exactly right. I admired him. He was big, strong, confident. He had a self-assured demeanor and imposing build that compelled me to obey him. His power and heft were vaguely reminiscent of my father.

As I gathered my things, I tried to put a finger on the feelings that were pulsing through me. Ethan didn't know me . . . not really. Nor did he, apparently, care about my success. He was exerting his authority and ending my job.

Something about it was familiar. The power. The blithe demeanor. A quick, almost incidental decision that would negatively affect my life for a long time to come. It was reminiscent of that first decade of my life when I felt completely out of control and at the mercy of an evil authority figure.

I had been in this situation before. It was, however, my first firing in sobriety. This was new and unexpected. I was sober and thinking clearly. I had a higher power called The Universe. My judgment was sound, or so I surmised. I wasn't coming into work with a hangover nor getting drunk at team-building events. I wasn't clouding my judgment with a constant stream of alcohol. I felt I had achieved stability in my life.

This was uncharted territory.

CHAPTER THIRTY-ONE

Big Man

"Jared, I don't know how to say this . . . but it happened again."

Jared and I found ourselves nestled amidst the hustle and bustle of Philz Coffee in Palo Alto on a Wednesday afternoon. The Alma location was particularly inviting with the aroma of freshly brewed coffee intermingling with the chatter of customers. Despite the horde of people, we managed to secure a table snug against the wall, offering us a semblance of privacy amid the commotion. The murmur of voices blended into a comforting white noise. Safety in a crowd.

"But this time," I sighed, frustration evident in my voice, "I was sober and clearheaded. I was thinking straight. I thought I had a grip on my triggers and was making the right choices."

"So . . . what happened?" Jared asked, leaning in with genuine concern etched across his face.

I took a moment, recalling the twists and turns of my final months at Agari. "Well, when Armin stepped in as CMO, I made it my mission to establish a connection with him. He was the new top dog, positioned right between Ethan and the CEO—"

"Ethan was your boss, right?" Jared interjected, his eyebrows raising in surprise.

"Yeah," I confirmed with a nod. "And once Armin took the reins, it felt like a shift in power. I thought it would be safest if I aligned with him."

"Interesting," Jared pondered, sipping his coffee as he processed the information.

"Armin asked me to switch over to work on a slew of projects for him as the new CMO," I explained, a hint of uncertainty creeping into my voice. "It felt like a great opportunity, but here's the thing: Ethan still wanted me to handle my previous tasks. Essentially, I was juggling two roles at once. I didn't feel right about it, you know?"

"Well, yeah, Phil, but that happens in business," he replied, his tone pragmatic yet empathetic. "Sometimes you have to juggle a couple of things for a while."

"Yeah, I suppose," I conceded with a sigh. "I ended up crossing Ethan . . . really got on his bad side. It's like I reached a breaking point with him. It seemed like he was overstepping his bounds. He didn't hold the same power anymore with Armin coming in above him. But he still acted as though he was top dog. Ethan is a big, commanding guy, you know? Tall, with his swagger and booming voice. When his influence in the organization waned, I felt pressured to adapt, to align myself more closely with Armin."

As Jared mulled over the situation, a look of certainty flickered across his face. "Well . . . this is interesting," he remarked, his tone shifting closer to resolve. "You've had triggers around women before. But this time it's a guy. A large, imposing authority figure. Is that reminiscent of anyone?"

"Well, if I'm being honest, Ethan reminds me of my dad," I confessed, a heavy sigh escaping me. "Unrealistic expectations, always demanding more. And yet, wielding power in a way that feels abusive."

"Tell me more about this power dynamic," Jared asked, ever diligent in following a lead.

"Well, when I was working for Armin, Ethan seemed completely oblivious," I explained, frustration evident in my voice. "He essentially gave me the green light to follow Armin's directives, but then he still expected me to maintain the same workload for him without missing a beat. It was like trying to juggle two full-time jobs at once. I felt stretched thin, and it seemed like he didn't even want me to succeed."

"Yeah, but again, that's business," Jared replied, his tone matter-of-fact. "Everyone's just looking out for themselves."

I paused, my gaze drifting past Jared to fixate on the wall behind him as I wrestled with my thoughts. His words struck a chord, resonating with a truth I was reluctant to acknowledge. It left me feeling unsettled, like I was somehow out of sync with the rest of the world.

"He seemed . . . sinister," I finally muttered softly, the confidence waning in my voice.

"Sinister?" Jared echoed, his tone incredulous, yet at the same time compassionate.

"Yeah, I know that's a strong way to put it but . . . it seemed like he was, kind of. . . ." Jared stared at me with an expectant look on his face. I struggled to articulate my thoughts. "Almost having his way with me. Satisfying his own desires while I was being belittled, even violated." I felt my face flush with embarrassment after this last comment, wondering if this meant I was going crazy or psychotic.

"Do you think that's about your father?" Jared ventured, his voice gentle yet probing.

I paused and let out a long, slow breath. There were feelings swirling through me about the job loss and about my family in the sixties. And they were beginning to blur together.

"Well, yeah I do," I finally admitted after a long pause. "And when my dad lost his power in our family, I realigned with Holly. It's like Holly became the leader of our family and, when that happened, I wanted nothing to do with my dad. In simple terms, it's like Ethan is my father and Armin is my older brother."

"Ooooh, that is fascinating. So as you saw the power dynamic shift in your family you switched your allegiance to Holly and rejected your dad as the bad guy," Jared said, his eyes lighting up with intrigue.

"Basically, that's it," I confirmed.

"So . . . was he the bad guy?" Jared prodded with heightened curiosity.

"Seems like it. But then everyone in the family says nothing happened and that there was no abuse," I replied, a hint of frustration creeping into my voice.

"Well . . . families can be very, very complicated," Jared offered, his tone sympathetic.

"Thank you doctor," I said wryly, a faint smile coming to my face.

"Seriously, Phil, you're talking to someone who grew up in a very complicated family. My father ruled the household with fear . . . and even some level of emotional abuse. And my mother was an enabler of all of it. So I know the kinds of dysfunction that can happen in families. And I also know that the actors around the abuse often go out of their way to cover up what's going on."

"Why would they do that?" I asked, perplexed by his assertion.

"Well, that's a big question. I mean I don't claim to have all the answers. . . . I think it may have something to do with saving face or trying to keep the family intact. Maybe not wanting to rock the boat."

"Well, when the boat's full of holes and taking on water, it's a little late for that."

* * *

On the way home from the coffee shop, my head still reeling from the conversation about Ethan and my father, my cell phone rang. It was my mother, her voice laden with urgency.

"Phil, could you take a look at the retaining wall? It's starting to get a lot of water above the wall. One of the tenants noticed it. I'm worried the wall might fall over and flood the barn."

"Sure," I said. "I'll drop by tomorrow morning."

CHAPTER THIRTY-TWO

Dad's Unfinished Ark

The next morning, I dropped by 12865 La Barranca to survey the property. For years, my dad had worked on a retaining wall just above the barn, which had since been converted to a two-dwelling apartment. My mother and I had built the main wall behind the structure. At least that's the way I remember it. She and I rented a gas-powered auger and drilled postholes twenty-four inches into the soil. We set redwood posts in concrete, and then added two-by-twelve planks to hold back the dirt.

We were quick and efficient. The whole project took us three days.

But there was another section around the front corner of the barn where the newer stairway had been constructed to go up to the second story. My father had dug it out, then put an earth anchor way back and down in the soil so that the wall wouldn't slip or lean. A regular retaining wall wasn't good enough for him. This had to be indestructible.

The problem was the design was very complicated and required special materials—huge, long steel rods that were threaded at both ends and half an inch in diameter. Then each of those pieces needed an anchor on the end (imagine a poma ski lift but with the seat portion set into the dirt behind the wall to act as an earth anchor). And on the wall end it was also threaded and needed a large washer and nut. These materials were specialized and hard to find. And he kept having to go back to the hardware store to get the correct pieces. Every time he would get close to having everything in place, the rains would hit and the dirt would slump, so he'd have to dig out the dirt and reset the anchor again. This cycle continued over and over for what seemed like an eternity.

"Why won't you just finish that silly retaining wall?" I recall my mom saying to my dad. There was often more than a hint of cynicism in her voice.

"Shan, don't rush me," he'd say. "This has to be done the right way." In his mind, cutting corners was a sin. He'd seen it with so many builders and contractors and it was a constant thorn in his side. He wasn't going to leave that legacy for his future self or his progeny. This was a moral decision.

My mom would scoff. Then she'd laugh outright and put on a decidedly snarky tone. "You're never going to finish it—you can't finish anything!" This wasn't lighthearted fifties Yiddish dialogue that seems harsh but is really endearing. It had a distinctly mean tone that bordered on contempt.

And, without consciously meaning to, I played into her game. At one point I got frustrated seeing the constant futile cycle of his work being undone by the elements and went up the hill to the barn on a mission. I placed the anchors roughly where it looked like they belonged, then shoveled dirt on top of them. Over time, went my reasoning, the wall would hold the dirt in place long enough for it to compact down and that, in turn, would hold the anchors in place. Then we could tighten things up nice and snug once everything had settled.

The next day my dad dug the dirt back out and started

over. He said in an angry tone, "Don't meddle with my projects."

In the end, I don't think he ever finished it. I don't recall if he died first and one of us came in to fix it or if my mother brought in a contractor to finish the job while he was still alive. In either case he never saw his concept translated into reality. He just got too old and tired to finish the job and basically gave up.

As I stared at this botched, yet overbuilt, project, memories of his relationship with my mother and my siblings came flooding back. It seemed like not only could he not finish projects, but he also had lost the admiration and respect of his wife and family. Each failed project and ensuing humiliation chiseled away at his manhood in the same way that diabetes eventually chiseled away at his foot. Over time, he became depressed, sedentary, and isolated.

It seemed to me that at some point my father became inadequate as a man. Men take care of their homes. They build things. They don't allow their properties to be flooded. They are admired by their wives.

It seemed to me that my father wasn't able to do any of those things. Especially to be admired by his wife. He had alienated her so much that they ended up living in separate ends of the house for the last twenty-five years of their marriage. By that point my mother had shut down all of his romantic advances.

In some sense he was no longer a man, given his wife wanted nothing to do with him sexually. I began to wonder what other side effects might have developed from this now-loveless marriage. Was it possible he redirected his sexual frustration somewhere else in the family? Maybe Holly's apology in the therapy session was actually a reference to something my father had done and Holly was blaming himself for not protecting me.

As I looked over this corner section of the retaining wall, I saw some water puddling above it. A small clump of branches were keeping the water from flowing down around the corner onto the lower section and into the drain.

I removed the branches and the water flowed out where it was supposed to. An easy fix.

CHAPTER THIRTY-THREE

Tides of Truth

Clearing the obstruction from the retaining wall was straightforward. It felt good to see the water flowing freely again as it was supposed to. My thoughts shifted from the resolved issue of the retaining wall to my impending date with Kathy.

We'd made plans for a Saturday walk on the beach. She loved the ocean and felt a sense of connection with the coastal environment. After a forty-five-minute drive over the coastal range, we arrived at Pescadero State Beach and walked about half a mile to the end of the beach for some privacy.

She turned to face me, her expression somber. "There's something I need to tell you," she began, her voice wavering slightly. "It's not . . . easy. I'm afraid of what you'll think of me when I tell you."

She took a deep breath. "I've struggled to find a healthy relationship in my life," she confessed. "I've faced a lot of loneliness and haven't yet had the committed relationship I've always wanted." Her words were honest and heartfelt, revealing the depth of her longing and resilience. There was a hint of vulnerability in her eyes, a quiet acknowledgment of feeling a little unworthy for not having found that relationship before now.

I told her what I knew about myself. About my family and being raised in a cult religion. About my father and all the inappropriate, odd sexual behavior he exhibited over the years. About suspecting he had abused me as a child, though I couldn't fully remember it. How the trauma expressed itself in my life through heavy drinking and taking prescription drugs.

About getting sober in 2016.

After the walk, Kathy and I went to dinner and talked some more. She was circumspect, though. Despite the restaurant being relatively intimate, she seemed uncomfortable talking in public with people around who might hear us.

Back at the school parking lot I told her I needed to stop at the grocery store on the way to my place.

"What for?" she asked.

"Just something . . . I need."

She looked at me suspiciously.

"Dude, I'm unprepared. . . . I need to buy condoms!" I finally blurted out.

She burst into laughter. Thirty minutes later we met back at my place. We unfolded the pullout bed in the living room at my rented pool house in Atherton so we could watch a movie and chill. One of her favorite movies was *Love Actually* so we put the DVD on. We made out for a while. Life was good and we'd leveled with each other. We'd been honest and vulnerable, and the stage was set to consummate the relationship.

But I was nervous. It'd been a while, I told myself. But that wasn't really it. I'd always struggled with sex toward the beginning of a relationship. And this time I was sober. It was harder than I remembered. I had a bottle of blue diamond-shaped pills. But something inside me wanted to do this clean, unaided.

I fumbled. The moment came. Failure to launch. The same feelings of inadequacy from years earlier came flooding back to me. I went into the bathroom and took a Viagra, kicking myself for not having done that in the first place. In my mind, I felt connected to Kathy. There was nothing that could screw that up. This was meant to be, I had told myself. Nothing could interfere with that. But there was something deeply painful and traumatic that was rooted deeper than I could comprehend. And it wasn't going to let go.

This wasn't the way it was supposed to begin. I wanted to be a hero: strong, masculine, and confident. Instead, I felt like a weak, self-doubting little boy, dependent on erectile dysfunction pills to engage in the natural act of sex. After years of therapy and sobriety I was still at the mercy of my own psychological dysfunction. The injustice welled up inside me. Why did it have to be this way? Why did this have to follow me around for the rest of my life?

The remainder of the evening was a blur. We had sex. I only know this from talking to Kathy later. For the rest of the evening things felt pretty flat. I didn't feel the excitement. In fact, I didn't really feel anything. Despite being there physically, my connection with Kathy was cut off. I'd still managed to be kind and engaging, perhaps even charming, so I'm told. I was a little like Adam Sandler in the movie *Click* who fast-forwards parts of his life he doesn't want to, or can't, deal with.

I knew what happened. But I'll never know just what the moment felt like. This seemed to me a terrible injustice. It was a tormenting paradox: to be with someone I loved and respected, yet unable to shed the weight of the past, and unable to truly appreciate the moment. And it was so demoralizing, all thanks to my father's actions.

I had to find a resolution, and quickly.

CHAPTER THIRTY-FOUR

My Meeting with Andre

While the last job had ended abruptly—and let's face it, they all had—this time I was prepared. I had seen the writing on the walls and looked around, interviewing extensively. By the time I was fired from Agari, I had a new job already lined up. A vibrant startup in the pentesting space called Synack, which was faster-growing than Agari, better capitalized, and a darling in the cybersecurity space, located in San Mateo.

Amidst these career transitions, Kathy and I made a significant move ourselves. We bought a house in Emerald Hills and settled into it seamlessly. It was a milestone—a tangible sign of stability in the midst of my professional upheavals. Kathy, in stark contrast to my constant career changes, had been anchored in her job for thirty years. Fortunately, there was no employment gap for either of us so that we could set out on this new chapter with a sense of security.

Yet another perk was that my new company was big on social justice. I had big questions looming in my mind about my childhood. Synack was involved with the post-trauma military and socioeconomically underprivileged communities which gave me an opportunity to explore my own trauma.

I had been looking forward to the Diversity, Equity, and Inclusion speaker meeting for days. Dr. Laura *somebody* was speaking, and Andre was the host. Andre had established a persona in the organization for raising awareness about trauma and creating forums for employees to discuss the topic in a safe space. In a brief messaging exchange just before the meeting he shared with me that he had been through traumatic incidents while in the military. I felt a sort of connection and thought he and I might share some common experiences.

Once I got into the virtual meeting, I heard the speaker talking about trauma treatment and something called the *stellate ganglion block*. I quickly looked it up and found that it's a technique that calms the nervous system when one is in fight-or-flight response, and helps people who are having severe symptoms of PTSD achieve a calmer state.

I scanned through the forty-five attendees to see if high-level personnel in my organization were there. Jim Hyman was the senior attendee. He wasn't in my organization but was a powerful executive in our company and his presence gave me pause. If he relayed negative things back to my own chain of command, it wouldn't go well. It was enough to keep me quiet . . . at least for the time being.

After about twenty minutes, however, I felt a burning need to ask the speaker about childhood memories. I had recently heard Tim Ferriss's podcast episode: "My Healing Journey after Childhood Abuse," and it resonated deeply within me. All the triggers I'd had, the assessment from my therapist, Holly's apology, and my father's inappropriate behavior all added up to one thing: I had been sexually abused. But somehow it had been erased from my memory.

I had to get to the bottom of it and retrieve those memories. Because if I didn't, then all of that trauma-driven psychic clutter would sit down in my subconscious and continue to control my life. Yet I also wondered if the discovery of childhood memories would be worth it, given the risk of retraumatization through the recollection of vivid memories.

This woman seemed empathetic and kind enough that I was comfortable asking the question. So I wrote the question in the chat window and prepared to send it to Andre as the host:

I believe I may have repressed memories from childhood. Do you think it is necessary and important to resurrect the memories through any means possible in order to process; knowing there is a risk of being further traumatized when they come back?

After typing the message, I paused before pressing the RETURN key, as I mentally assessed the risks. What would people think? Will it get back to my boss?

Eventually the speaker began to wind down her comments. I heard her say "I'm going to open it up for questions now."

Andre spoke up and said that he had been through significant trauma from fighting overseas, and having guns and bombs go off near him, and seeing many of his buddies get injured or die. I began to feel at that moment like this forum was a safe space. If Andre could be vulnerable here, couldn't I?

I brought my right index finger, which had been poised a half inch above the RETURN key, down, sending a direct message to Andre.

Moments later I heard him announce:

"We have a question from Phil March who asks . . ." Then he read my full question out loud, verbatim.

Shit . . . that was way more overt than I expected. At the very least I had thought he would couch it as anonymous. *Oh God, this is a disaster*

I scanned the gallery, looking for Jim to see what his expression was. Was he shocked? Was he suspicious? Was he disappointed? Scanning . . . scanning.

After scanning the full list of names in the participants list, it became clear: Jim had left the meeting.

Thank God!

Then the speaker commenced to answer the question in a manner that gave me some pause.

"Memories typically come back when we are strong enough and feel safe enough to face them."

It seemed like a sound assertion. I had seen an example of this before. Something way, way back in the newspaper, from twenty-five years earlier. There was a story about a woman in the *Mercury News* who didn't remember that her father had abused her. It went well beyond that. Her childhood friend had died when she was very young. It wasn't until she was in her late thirties and her own daughter looked at her with a certain expression on her face, that she recalled what her father had done. He had not only abused her, but he had murdered her childhood friend.

I had known about these things intellectually but hadn't really considered the concept in relation to my own experience. Emboldened by the speaker's response, I asked a follow-up question:

> *Tim Ferris talks in his podcast about having resurrected memories through medicinal means during a retreat and how he was re-traumatized . . .*

Andre responded in the chat: "I am familiar with that episode and that modality of therapy."

Toward the end of the meeting, I sent Andre a direct message and asked if he'd be willing to catch up one-on-one over the next few days.

Within twenty-four hours we were on Andre's private zoom account having a conversation that started deep from the outset. He explained his journey, first with sexual trauma as a teenager, which had largely been repressed, then with post-war PTSD after tours in Iraq.

I told him about my own struggles in a dysfunctional family and my long bout with substance abuse, about being in recovery for the last four to five years, and coming to the conclusion I'd been sexually abused by my father. I mentioned my desire to try to finally get to the bottom of it after all of these years. At that point, Andre went into a detailed account of the medicinal-plant-based retreat he had attended the previous summer.

"It changed my life," he said.

He explained how he had been able to become a better partner, a better colleague, and a better steward to those who needed his help in their mental health recovery.

By that weekend Andre and I were exchanging emails about how the medicinal modality might be engaged safely and in a secure manner. I was receptive, for sure. Yet the illegal nature of the substances that were commonly used—psilocybin, ayahuasca, MDMA—gave me pause.

"I want to introduce you to my partner, Amelia," Andre said. At first the word "partner" made me think of a business partner. But he explained that he and Amelia were a couple. They were in a romantic long-term relationship, but one with a fairly unusual complexion.

"She works with a lot of people who have experienced post-trauma," he continued, explaining that she had been in the military and helped work with women who had been sexually traumatized.

After the call ended, I immediately got on LinkedIn and looked her up: Amelia Jane Harper. I was captured by her online persona of pretty woman with a devilish smile, yet someone who was clearly out of the box. Her hair was buzzed on the left side of her head, yet was long and flowing on the top and right side. She sported a wide-brimmed black hat and blouse. There was something decidedly mystical, even Wiccan about her looks. A juxtaposition of opposites. Masculine plus feminine. Beautiful yet daunting. Affable but at the same time mystical.

Despite the many questions hovering in my mind, I knew I had to do something. Bad things had clearly happened to me as a child. And whether I knew consciously about them, or if they remained hidden in my subliminal brain, they were there either way. And they were going to destroy me. I would spend the rest of my days losing jobs, falling in and out of love, and being forever on the outside looking in.

I decided it was worth the risk.

CHAPTER THIRTY-FIVE

Amelia

"I'm a life coach," Amelia stated. "I'm studying for my masters in psychology with a thesis in 'Instigating Social Change Through Plant-Based Medicine.'"

I was on a private video call with Andre's life partner, Amelia, getting acquainted. She was just as attractive as she had been in her LinkedIn profile. Her long flowing sandy-blond hair was combed over the other side of her head, covering up her closely cropped buzz cut. I realized she had the ability to go two different ways with her appearance. She could let her hair flow down one side and show her buzz cut on the other, or she could comb it over creating a dramatic, sweeping flow and all but cover up the shaved side. This gave her the ability to appeal to different demographics, depending on the situation. And for this occasion she had chosen the conservative route, apparently on my behalf.

She had refined, baby-face features with near-perfect fair skin. Her eyes were discerning, as if they could pierce through my protective boundary layer, even over a video conference call.

"What motivated you to get into this field?" I inquired.

"I've dealt with mental illness around me since I was young," she said. She described having a brother who was "simple" (her words), a mother who struggled with depression, another brother who struggled with addiction and then went to AA and later became a doctor, and a sister who struggled with Borderline Personality Disorder.

"Then, once I got into the military," she continued, "I found myself spending a fair amount of my time coaching women who had been through sexual assault. My captain asked me to create a program to help a number of women who had gone through sexual trauma."

She forwarded me a link to the article, and our conversation lasted for over an hour. Soon enough, it felt as though we were old friends.

She described the weekend-of-recovery process: ninety minutes of prep work over video conferencing, three days together, meditation and breathwork, and plant-based medicine. She used mostly psilocybin which is derived from magic mushrooms. Then she suggested microdosing for the next ninety days.

For the second video conference I requested that Kathy join us. She had already become my confidant and soul mate. Her levelheaded thinking had become invaluable to me in these kinds of decisions. And she had always had a caring, compassionate approach to our discussions around my childhood trauma. I also cared about how this kind of a process would affect her. I wanted to make sure she was on the same page and agreed with the plan.

We met again on Amelia's private video conference line. Perhaps sensing there could be some jealousy on the part of Kathy, Amelia started out the call with a preemptive, bold approach, saying, "It's so visible and powerful . . . and so tangible, the love the two of you have for each other."

We discussed the medicinal weekend of recovery

concept. We talked about plant-based medicinal products, including psilocybin. We talked about legalities, civil disobedience, and about her commitment to recovery using these, and other techniques.

After the call, Kathy became fairly introspective.

"What if you end up having a psychotic breakdown while you're there?" she asked. "You don't really know anything about this woman or about taking psilocybin. It seems pretty risky."

"Well . . . she isn't just someone we found off the street," I said, feeling a little defensive, yet trying my best to stay calm and stick to the facts. "I know Andre, and he's a decent guy. He seems legit. And he's with her." I explained how Amelia had references and articles written about her. And she must embody a level of discipline to have made it through the military. I sensed myself pushing at some point.

"What if you get arrested for possession of an illegal substance?" Kathy said.

I took a deep breath.

"Look, I know there are risks associated with this," I began. "But I also know there are risks with the do-nothing approach." I went on to describe the effects of my own family's dysfunction. And the likely abuse by my father that had ruled my life for decades. I knew I couldn't go through the rest of my life feeling like I was damaged inside, but I'd never really processed what happened. I don't know if it was because I coerced her or because she truly believed in the process. Or maybe she cared about me enough to not want to see me in pain. Whatever the reason, Kathy approached me a couple of days later.

"I want you to know I support you and I want you to be able to explore what you need to," she said, her words delivered in a careful, measured tone. "And I give you my blessing to do this weekend with Amelia."

It was a gift of immense trust, not to mention kindness

and compassion. She was willing to have me spend a weekend in a rented home with a woman neither of us had met in person. She saw my pain and wanted me to feel better. This, despite the fact that the activity clashed with every ounce of carefulness and rule-following in her character.

I reserved an Airbnb in Half Moon Bay and blocked out the weekend in my calendar.

CHAPTER THIRTY-SIX

You Had Me at Open

"She said Prozac is numbing me out," I said with a hint of resentment.

"Seriously? Seems a bit over the top," Jared responded.

Six weeks after Kathy and I had agreed I should move forward with the unconventional weekend, Jared and I sat at a table outside the Sandwich Spot in Redwood City. Every few minutes a train would come into the Sequoia Station and blare its horn multiple times. The blasts were spread out just enough that our conversation was interrupted every few minutes.

"Well yeah . . . I mean she didn't exactly tell me to stop. But she implied I might not have the full recovery experience if I'm on an SSRI. Like it might impair my progress."

"So what did you do? I mean, the whole thing is this weekend, right?" Jared asked with heightened curiosity.

"I decided to get off meds," I responded resolutely

"Really, you stopped all your meds?" Jared exclaimed

"Well, it's not like I'm on a thousand things. Just Prozac and—"

A train whistle blared, vibrating me to the core. I gathered myself.

"The only two things I'm taking are Prozac and—"

Hooooot!

Another train whistle. I waited. Then, after I was sure it was over, I resumed:

"Prozac and—"

Hooooot!

A third whistle.

"Dammit!"

I paused for a full thirty seconds, waiting for another horn. Then, not wanting to endure another interruption, I said, "Prozac and Effexor." The words tumbled out of my mouth, loudly followed by a hint of embarrassment at sharing my personal information with other diners on the patio.

"So you just stopped taking both of them?" Jared continued, leaning in, his voice almost a whisper.

"Well, no, I mapped it out," I replied in my characteristically analytical tone. "I halved one of the meds for two weeks, then quartered it for another two weeks. Then did the same thing with the other med. The whole process took six weeks."

"You did that by yourself?" Jared asked, his tone a mixture of surprise and concern.

"Mostly. I did talk to my doctor to formulate the plan," I clarified.

"Wow," Jared said, taken aback by my boldness, even brashness, in making big life changes swiftly. "So, how did it go?"

"It was rough!" I responded in a tone conveying both

hardship and relief. "I mean, the Prozac was easy: after a few weeks I stopped it and was basically OK. But cutting back the Effexor was really tough."

"R-e-a-l-l-y?" Jared drawled, his tone combining astonishment and care.

"Yeah . . . the worst part was—get this—just before I cut back the Effexor, I had a conversation with a friend in one of the AA fellowships. She had mentioned going off meds in her group share. She told me she had decided to do a recovery weekend with Ayahuasca. She went off Venlafaxine just before the weekend. But then she started—"

Hooooot!

I paused for a moment. "She started drinking again and—"

Hooooot!

"Mother f—!" Another pause. "She went off the rails. She relapsed so badly she—"

Hooooot!

I paused to make sure the noisy disturbance was completely over. As I saw the train leave the station, crossing Broadway to the north I continued.

"She relapsed so badly she lost her therapy license."

"OH . . . MY . . . GOD . . . you're kidding?" Jared exclaimed, flabbergasted.

"I kid you not. She is still trying to get her life back in order and it's been over a year."

"Holy shit!"

"Yeah. That stuff is pretty potent. It's not like Prozac or Zoloft," I continued, shifting back into my analytical persona. "It affects norepinephrine in addition to serotonin, the fight-or-flight chemical."

"So Phil, I know this is your life," Jared began in a very measured tone, choosing his words carefully. "But are you sure this weekend is the right thing for you to do?"

"I . . . don't know," I replied, my tone laced with uncertainty and a hint of defeat. I thought about the years, even decades, I'd struggled with these demons. About exploring my own sexual orientation. The years of therapy that had led to a dead end. About my decision to stop drinking under the assumption that alcohol was my problem. About my therapist's assertion. About my father.

"This stuff about my dad," I continued, searching for the right words. "It won't resolve on its own. And I can't go through ten more years of just . . . not knowing."

"I get it," Jared responded gently. "I've seen you struggle through all of this and I know how rough it's been for you."

I stared out across the boulevard. Sunlight filtered through the trees along Broadway Ave. Sparse, white puffy clouds dotted the deep blue Northern California sky.

"In other news," I said, relieved to change the subject, "I had the weirdest conversation with Amelia's partner yesterday."

"Oh yeah? How do you mean?"

"Well, you remember I'm spending the weekend with her, right?"

"Oh, believe me, I remember. I seem to recall you saying she was gorgeous."

"Uh . . . well yeah, there's that. Anyway, Andre, her partner, reached out to me and wanted to talk. I wasn't really sure why. But then when I got on the call with him, he volunteered that they have an unusual relationship."

"What kind of unusual relationship," Jared said cautiously, yet moving in so as to attend more closely.

"I'm still trying to figure him out," I said, wrestling with the uncertainty. "Like is he trying to ice me? Is he washing his hands? Is he signaling a green light? Is this some sort of passive-aggressive way of saying he's checked out . . . like he's indifferent? Or is it some other ploy—"

"Phil, what are you talking about?" Jared implored, a blend of amusement and impatience in his voice.

"Well, here I am, planning to spend the weekend with his romantic partner," I continued, "and he tells me that he has an open, nonmonogamous relationship with her!" The words hung in the air conspicuously like the white clouds that drifted across the expanse of the blue sky.

Jared's eyes grew wide. Then his initial shock transformed slowly into a mischievous grin, the kind that signaled he was about to flip the script with his trademark humor. There was a beat of silence as he leaned in, his expression loaded with anticipation, ready to deliver the perfect comedic line.

"Phil," he began, his voice dripping with exaggerated sincerity, channeling his inner movie star, "you had me at 'open'!"

Hooooot!

CHAPTER THIRTY-SEVEN

The Shroom Whisperer

I drove into the older suburban neighborhood in Half Moon Bay at 5:45 on Friday evening. The weather was overcast—as is typical for Half Moon Bay. There were picket fences with trees in the yards and lots of ocean-going crafts in the driveways: small sailboats, stand-up paddleboards, and kayaks. It was within walking distance from the bluffs overlooking the Pacific Ocean.

I parked in the driveway next to the basketball hoop. I opened the key lock box and unlocked the door. Inside, the house was relatively nicely decorated. Nothing lavish but . . . decent. It would do.

Amelia arrived about fifteen minutes later. She was pretty and outgoing and very fit and petite at five feet, two inches. Her smile was devilish and mesmerizing, yet she had a kind, approachable demeanor. We hugged each other like old friends. After a quick tour of the inside we planned where we'd do the various activities.

She made a vegetarian dinner from the organic groceries she'd brought for the weekend. Over dinner, we immediately began talking about deep, emotional subjects: about my chaotic childhood, abuse and my father, and about her struggles in the military as a lower-ranking, attractive female. We were both vulnerable. The barriers were coming down.

"So," Amelia began, speaking with just a little more import than before, "have you ever gotten really mad at him?" The subject change caught me off guard.

"Well, yeah, kind of . . . I don't know. How do you mean?"

"I mean, have you ever just said, 'Fuck you, you're a fucking asshole for doing this'?"

Her stark, unfiltered language rattled me. I collected my thoughts and tried to think back over the last few years. He had died years ago and I had never talked to him about it.

"But . . . he's dead," I said, after a pause.

"Yes, but you can still confront him. You can still have a conversation."

"Well, I . . . I thought I had gotten angry back when I first suspected it," I said. "I know I've gotten very sad. I've gotten resentful . . . even been very afraid. But I don't know if I've really gotten angry. Now that I think about it," I contemplated, "I've really gotten angry at other people. Even other *things*. Like, for example, I get really, really frustrated at work when my computer glitches. Or when my mouse malfunctions and registers a single click instead of double. Or a website doesn't do what I expect it to do."

"Of course," she said.

"Of course?" I asked, genuinely perplexed. "Why do you say that?"

"Well . . . it's a lot easier to get angry at an inanimate object."

"Why is that?"

"It's safe," she said.

I thought for a minute. "Well, maybe I need to learn how to just express anger about him instead of objects." It seemed an obvious conclusion. Yet, as the phrase goes, be careful what you wish for; sometimes the truth can be more overwhelming than expected.

As Amelia and I sat at the kitchen bar next to each other, talking about these vulnerable thoughts, I sensed another feeling come over me: part confusion, part arousal. It had to do with my conversation with Andre before the weekend and the nature of their relationship.

"I think if we're going to work together the rest of the weekend, I have to clear the air. And part of it is that Andre called me just before the weekend and told me about you guys being in an unusual relationship. I don't want to have confusing feelings and have them lingering like an elephant in the room."

"Yeah, we have an open relationship," she said in a tone that was more matter-of-fact than I expected.

"Does that mean either of you can just go out and have sex with another person?" I asked in an incredulous tone.

"No, it's not like that," she said. "We stress open communication. We have had others in our relationship."

Others?

"We had a girlfriend for a while," she offered. "But it only happens if we both agree to it."

"So are you bisexual? Or—"

"I would call myself omnisexual," she said conclusively. "And Andre . . . he would consider himself pansexual."

"Oh, gotcha."

Despite my feigned confidence, I had no idea what she was talking about. However, after discussing these sensitive topics openly with Amelia, I started to feel a little more grounded, less triggered, less on autopilot, and more intentional.

"Tonight, before you go to bed," she pivoted toward the end of the evening, "I want you to record a video on your phone saying what it is you want to get out of this. Just speak about why you're here, how you're feeling, and what you want to get out of this process. We'll use this later on to see your progress and decide if you've met your goals."

A few minutes later, I made a recording:

OK, this is my "pre" video. I am . . . scared shitless.

What is my intention for this? It is to find myself. To see myself as I was as a child. To get to the bottom of it. To be able to resolve these things and to not have the reactions happen automatically—these triggers—without me having anything to say about it.

I've definitely cut myself off from who I am. I think Amelia nailed it. I've cut myself off from my six-year-old self but also from that side of me that is vulnerable and I'm afraid is weak and/or might get me in trouble. I think there's a war going on with this twitching that I've had since I was a kid.

And this "boundaries" thing—I don't have emotional boundaries so when someone near me experiences something, I can't have my own sovereignty, Amelia calls it. When I think about my own kids . . . I definitely caused them not to be secure. I didn't have emotional boundaries; I couldn't let them have their own emotions without me experiencing them even worse than they did.

And I think that makes kids unsettled and insecure. Like they're drifting . . . and they can't rely on the people around them. I think I fell into their every emotion and stress and strain, and I only made it worse.

I touched the screen to end the recording and contemplated what I had just said. I was struck with an immense amount of sadness for what my kids had been through, for the pain I had caused them. I knew in my heart of hearts I didn't want to continue living my life this way.

Act III:
Promised Land

CHAPTER THIRTY-EIGHT

Ancient Migration

The next morning, I awoke with an emotion that sat somewhere between anticipation and terror. It was the day of reckoning, and I had no idea what was going to happen.

Memories could be unlocked and revelations could lead toward resolution; or they could traumatize me beyond anything I have ever experienced. Or there could be nothing . . . just more of the same repression. There were no guarantees and I had no idea—across the spectrum of possible outcomes—what was going to happen.

I got up and showered, brushed my teeth, dressed, and walked into the kitchen. Amelia was making coffee and preparing food. She looked awake and alive and glowing!

She wore a white jumpsuit, the style of which I couldn't quite place. It was somewhere between a white yoga outfit and hospital scrubs, yet there was a hint of maternity about it. I want to say she referred to it as a "birthing suit." She was there to bring the new me into the world. It felt slightly unsettling, but I put my reactions aside and decided to roll with it.

After some coffee and breakfast—leftovers from dinner combined with bagels and cream cheese—we talked about the day.

"We'll take the psilocybin, then do yoga," she said, laying out the itinerary. "Then we'll engage in the core portion of the ceremony with music and incense."

After some cleanup and dishes, Amelia pulled out a box containing the mushrooms. She set the open box in front of me, along with a small bowl, and asked me to select three or four mushrooms for the ceremony. I was a little perplexed. In my ever-so-scientific mindset I wanted more clarity.

"What's the criteria I should use to select them?" I asked.

"Just whatever moves you," she said, unhelpfully. "This is your ceremony. So you get to choose which pieces to use. You can use the shape, the size, more stems, more tops, whatever you think makes sense and whatever you connect with."

I chose a few pieces—a mix of all of the above, a fair representation, a sampling of stems, tops, big and small. I was being careful that I didn't overuse certain parts of the mushrooms that might have a higher concentration of the substance. A good statistical sample, being the scientifically minded, analytical person I am. I put them into the bowl and handed it to her.

She placed them on a cutting board and minced them up. Then she put them back in the bowl and folded in honey, mashing up the whole mixture with a mortar and pestle.

"Are you taking them also?" I asked.

"Yes," she said. Then, probably sensing my nervousness, she added, "So that I'm on the same page with you. But I'll be taking a smaller amount."

After some ceremonious words she directed me to eat the concoction which I did, obediently. It tasted like an odd, chewy combination of bitter and sweet.

She did the same.

The deed was done. There was no turning back.

We moved into the family room with a large picture window that looked out into the front yard landscaping. We began with some yoga moves, stretching, downward dog, cat, cow, melting heart. I was nervous that, amidst the yoga activities, my mind would suddenly launch into a hallucinogenic state with no warning.

"How long does it typically take for the mushrooms to kick in?" I asked her.

"Usually about thirty to forty-five minutes."

I felt terrified not knowing what to expect when they finally did kick in. Yet, steadfastly, I continued the yoga and we finished and moved into the living room.

First, she directed me to sit next to the mattress we used as a makeshift bed. She said in a somewhat parental tone that if, at any point, things got scary or overwhelming, I should bring my attention back to my breath. She told me to close my eyes. Then she started the music.

And that's when the magic began . . .

* * *

Suddenly, a transient image catches my eye. At first, I'm not sure if it's a random figment or an anticipated aspect of the process. However, as the beat of the music persists, more images begin to emerge. They are very colorful, even psychedelic, and start to move and bounce in unison with the music.

In between songs, when the music stops, there is nothing. It all goes blank. But as the music resumes, the images appear again. They dance around and morph and roll, as if psychedelic serpents or worms. I wonder how the music is controlling my mind like this.

The images are a little scary. Some of them start to feel overwhelming.

I focus back on my breath, and it brings my awareness back to my body. Things settle down.

As the music builds, I see incredibly colorful, vivid images. Moving. Twisting. They look like multicolored, ringed worms or snakes.

Amelia directs me to lie down on the makeshift bed. I feel somewhere between a massage patron and a sick hospital patient. I close my eyes. She puts a cover over my eyes to help block out the daylight.

I smell incense burning. Sage and palo santo. The music continues. The show resumes.

The wormlike creatures are emanating up from the ground like the fireworks from the sixties called "snakes." When I was young, we used them out on the brick patio behind the house. They were the same ones I had dreamt about over the years, but instead of ash, animals emanated out of the pavement. They had turned out to be recollections of roadkill along the street that Holly would stop and inspect as we explored the neighborhood.

As the music continues, I hear the chanting of what sounds like Native Americans singing. I begin to feel a growing sense of unity swelling in me. It's as though I'm part of something immense—something much greater than myself. It's like we're moving across the desert in a large group migrating to some new place with more opportunity. It is something from tens or even hundreds of thousands of years ago. A hereditary memory?

The impact of the chanting, the pounding music, gives the familiar feeling of migrating through the desert as part of a nomad community, getting to the next destination, to greener pastures, anvil-shaped thunderheads looming huge in the distance. Moving between hills, tableaux. Traveling together as a community. A wise, benevolent alpha male leads all of it.

I feel part of something. I'm not alone. The singer has a deep voice and there are multiple people chanting, one echoing the other as if animals, calling one to another.

* * *

After a few minutes the visuals started to subside. Amelia stopped the music and directed me to sit up and remove the eye covering. It was like waking up to a harsh reality after being in the most exquisite dream.

The lights seemed alarming, but her voice was soothing and calm. It pulled me gently out of the mesmerizing dream I'd just been through.

"What time is it?" I asked her.

"One o'clock," she said.

It had been three hours.

As I collected myself after the intense experience, trying to understand exactly what I'd been through, Amelia suggested we have some lunch, then take another small dose and take a walk on the bluffs. Moments later as we walked along the cliffs above the beach, the sun peeked through the fog. The flowers were vivid and beautiful. Despite having just been through a monumental, mind-altering experience, everything felt calm and peaceful, even serene, as we walked through the foliage, just within sight of the ocean.

During the ceremony, I'd heard animals calling to each other. Benevolent males steering the community, moving us to a destination of opportunity. It felt right and safe and very very far from evil. Like I was settling into some part of the universe that was good and sound and exactly as it was meant to be.

I continued trying to process it all as the brightly colored flowers played on my mind like a pleasant cocktail. There was something under the surface that felt huge like an iceberg with most of the mass hidden from view.

It seemed I had tapped into something very important. As if I had come within close proximity to some massive beast, a mammoth presence.

I knew it was big, powerful, and meaningful. But I just

couldn't make out its true form.

The next morning Amelia suggested we work on something a little different. "I want to do an exercise that deals with emotional sovereignty."

"OK ..."

"I've noticed you have a tendency to be strongly affected by other people's emotions," she continued in her benevolent, coaching tone. "You take on other people's feelings. This exercise will help you with that."

Despite her encouraging, compassionate demeanor, the feeling of being a lab rat, of being observed, even scrutinized, began to build up again in the form of a growing level of defensiveness. Then, I recalled our Friday night discussion and my pre-video. The things I had said about creating an unsafe emotional environment for my kids. About taking on their emotional state instead of letting them experience their own feelings, independent of me.

Something clicked.

We sat down on the living room floor, cross-legged, facing each other. She told me to close my eyes and listen to her.

Then, suddenly, she launched into a persona that was completely different than I had ever seen in her. It was as if she was an actress, displaying her craft. And this particular character was very angry.

"I CAN'T BELIEVE YOU DID THAT," said Angry Amelia. "Do you realize how that made me feel? Do you have any decency at all? That was an awful, terrible thing to do...."

My chest felt crushed with immense pressure, like a four-hundred-pound gorilla was sitting on it. Then, as if a hypnotist had just snapped their fingers, she came out of character.

"OK, Phil," she said in a soft, kind voice. "How did that make you feel?"

Oh my God, I'm sharing a house with a schizophrenic. Who is this person?

"Well, that felt absolutely fucking awful," I blurted out in an unregulated, almost angry tone. "You seemed so mad at me. I felt guilty . . . like I was a terrible person for . . . whatever it was that I did."

"Good. Now we're going to try it a little differently," she continued as if this was all just part of the process. "Now I want you to imagine that from your heart center there is an energy field. It's green. It grows out around you and protects you." She briefly explained the Ayurvedic heart center, the fourth—or Anahata—Chakra.

Then we repeated the exercise. Angry Amelia returned. Her voice exhibited the same angst, the same pointed, accusatory language. But something changed for me.

I was aware of her anger. Yet I didn't feel the same reaction. I felt protected, safe, even. It was as though I was strong, autonomous, unfazed. This, despite the fact that she was emotionally venting. I was aware of her disturbance, yet it wasn't governing me.

We repeated the same exercise with Sad Amelia and Embarrassed Amelia. Each time, she went in and out of character seamlessly, as though I was sitting face-to-face with a polished Hollywood actress.

In each instance, she exhibited the same intensity of emotion. I sat the same distance from her. It was the same Amelia, yet when I maintained the vision of the green aura emanating from my heart, protecting me, I was able to witness her emotional state without taking it on or succumbing to it.

It was exhilarating, experiencing a different reaction. A way of moving I'd never engaged in before.

At the end of the weekend, before saying goodbye, Amelia told me to record another video to document my thoughts about the weekend vis à vis what I had set out to do at the beginning:

Man! What an amazing experience that was! The visuals were so intricate and interesting. There was intense meaning. Like symbols trying to tell me something profound.

At one point, the music was flowing and the drumbeat was driving. And the aroma of the incense was intoxicating. I felt as though I was part of a moving caravan, going to some mecca land where we belonged. There was a male voice calling out in a foreign language and another echoing from a different location. The feeling of being part of this group, this caravan in the high desert somewhere. Thunderheads off in the distance. It was safe and profound.

Now . . . does it tell me about what happened with my father? There's no vivid memory, per se. But rather it's more like it doesn't matter because I feel there is something so much more profound and greater than me. And I'm safe as part of it. It was like being with a mentor, a brother, a father.

A few days after our weekend together a small, unmarked package arrived in the mail. In it was a small jar of dark brown glass with a small wooden spoon. This was my microdosing regimen. A diluted mixture of spiced honey and minced mushrooms. Amelia instructed me to start it immediately and do it for ninety days.

I was on cloud nine. Although memories hadn't flooded back, there were fewer questions in my mind, and I was supremely more confident in who I was. I better understood what I had been through. I had turned the corner.

CHAPTER THIRTY-NINE

Growing Sideways

"Oh . . . My . . . God!" Kathy exclaimed. "What happened?"

Three days after I began microdosing, Kathy came home from her job teaching at Woodside Elementary to find me crouched down on the back lawn.

"I'm . . . dethatching the lawn," I said.

I had researched the concept of dethatching grass on YouTube earlier that day and decided that thatch was the problem. All the undergrowth had to be removed to make the lawn healthy again. It was choking off the other grass, starving it of light, oxygen, and nutrients. To grow lush and green it only had to be dethatched. It needed to have those sideways vines removed so only the vertical grass remained. I embarked on a mission: raking and combing and trimming . . . for hours. I continued the work between meetings and on my lunch break, and then again after work.

"Dethatching?" she said, noticeably shaken. "It doesn't look like you dethatched it. It . . . it looks like you dug it up and threw it away."

Kathy's exclamation snapped me back to the present. I stood up and looked over the area. It didn't look like a lawn anymore. Rather, I stood amid a twenty-by-twenty-foot plot of land that was mostly barren. Where there had been green grass there were only a few tufts of turf here and there, and a lot of dirt.

As I surveyed the damage, a feeling of embarrassment crept in. The view reminded me of the Richard Dreyfuss scene from *Close Encounters* in which he shovels large amounts of dirt into his house through the kitchen window and builds a monument to the flat-topped mountain.

As embarrassment slowly shifted to shame, I began to try to understand what was going on. I had started microdosing three days earlier. Was that the culprit? Was I experiencing hallucinations? Was I becoming psychotic?

Or was the drug just causing me to think differently about things? And that meant approaching a gardening problem in an aggressive, somewhat unorthodox way?

Or was the answer more complicated? Perhaps the lack of psych medications that I had been taking before was the culprit. And this was causing me to descend into a highly obsessive state. I had never been diagnosed with OCD. Yet I knew that anxiety could sometimes exhibit itself as obsessive behavior.

Or . . . was this some element of post-trauma finally beginning to bubble up from my subconscious? But instead of an actual memory, it had transformed subconsciously into a vendetta against the lawn?

I thought more about the microdosing regimen. I didn't feel euphoric. I wasn't having any hallucinations.

I contacted Amelia to understand the strength of the microdosing mixture. Then I did some research on the web to compare it to that of the "full" dose. I was taking about one-eighth of the "typical" dose. I ran across a quote in healingmaps.com about microdosing: "This dosage isn't enough to create a high, but only minimal, acute drug effects that can help long term."

I didn't feel drugged. There were no hallucinations. No breaking from reality. Yet my behavior had changed. And I was acting differently around the house and toward Kathy.

Questions flooded my mind: *Should I quit micro dosing? Should I restart my previous medications? Was I a monster?*

I had—while trying to do something for our home that would enhance and beautify it—actually damaged it. I was moving backward, undoing what I had previously accomplished. I had set out to beautify but had destroyed instead.

It seemed as though something foreign was taking control of me. A massive creature the size of an elephant had roused inside me, gotten angry, and demolished the lawn. And I was worried it might react again at any moment and do something worse.

CHAPTER FORTY

The Suffering of Job

Two days later I found myself pounding my fists on sofa cushions.

It started with me trying to meditate on a Wednesday morning after a terrible night's sleep. It was week two of micro dosing and I felt like hell. The small amount of psilocybin in my system had drained the emotional cushion around me, leaving my emotions exposed and raw.

I had gone outside to do my meditation routine along with a teaspoon full of the shroom and spiced honey mixture. In what should have been a very simple, routine move, I picked up the small patio end table to set it next to my chair. As I grabbed it, my fingers touched the underneath of the table. I felt a very sticky substance. I didn't know what it was, but it felt gross and invasive.

It was on my hands, and I knew it was still on the bottom of the table. It had to be removed. I tried to wipe it with a paper towel. But the paper just ripped and stuck to the underneath of the table.

"Use Lysol wipes. They work really well," Kathy

offered.

I grabbed them from under the bathroom sink but the plastic tub was almost empty, and the remaining ones were in a soupy clump at the bottom of the container. I pulled off the lid, all the while getting incrementally more agitated. I tilted the tub, and they came out in a wad of wet, sloppy wipes in my hand. Worse, the saturated wipes wouldn't dissolve the sticky substance on my fingers.

Already pushing the clock trying to get ready for an analyst briefing at 9:00—it was already 8:25—I started to feel the hair on the back of my neck stand up and my chest tighten. I rushed to the laundry room to get some Simple Green and a rag to wipe down the table.

The irritation began building into anger. I sprayed the Simple Green onto the rag and began wiping furiously to get it clean enough to touch. I tried to sit down again and meditate. But the sun was too bright. I could feel the anger compounding. It was welling up like an ocean wave, peaking, getting ready . . . To . . . break.

I ran to the office and closed all the windows and drew the shades. I started screaming and pounding on the cushions as hard as I could, yelling:

"Fuck this shit, fuck this shit, it's so . . . fucking gross, so fucking sticky, fuck this shit . . . this sticky, fucking—"

As I said this, the relevance of the word "sticky" emerged into my conscious brain. It propelled me into a different realm, one infused with a connection, albeit distant and perplexing, to sexual trauma. I didn't know exactly who or where. But I knew when. As with the dreams, I could always place the timing by the emotional tenor of it. There was terror, lack of control, huge forces revolving around me, and the feeling of powerlessness, as if I were being dragged down a rapidly flowing river. The combination of these sensations took me back to a now-familiar decade: the sixties. My screaming and pounding stopped. The rage passed.

The creature calmed.

CHAPTER FORTY-ONE

Reposado

"So, tell me how the weekend went," Jared said, his voice infused with excitement, the anticipation evident in his high-pitched tone. We were seated at the bar in Reposado, Palo Alto, the following Thursday, just after work. The evening crowd hadn't yet arrived, affording us the seclusion of a mostly empty restaurant in a public setting—one where we were unlikely to encounter anyone we knew. It felt like a sanctuary where all topics were fair game.

"It . . . Was . . . crazy," I began. "I had the most profound experience I've probably ever had."

"Tell me everything," he said, honing his attention toward me.

"Well, once we started the psilocybin, I started having all these visions: weird serpents and snakes rolling . . . " I continued, my tone laced with wonder.

"That's . . . kinda creepy!" Jared remarked, his concern subtly interwoven with curiosity.

"Yeah but after a while things transitioned beyond that.

I got to a place of feeling connected with all of mankind," I marveled. "But not modern day . . . it felt like hundreds of thousands of years ago. A simpler time. A simpler social structure . . . a simpler human kind. Without all the strife and politics and all of that."

"Wow . . . so you're cured?" Jared said, chuckling.

I stared back at him with a forlorn expression. Something inside me didn't want to reveal the next piece of information. I wanted to be OK and cured—just as he had joked. Yet I knew better. Things were happening deep inside my brain—disturbing things that were starting to worry me.

"Something . . . changed in the last few days. Some kind of rage kicked in," I offered, in a tone that mirrored our lighthearted discourse yet acknowledged the seriousness of the situation.

"Really?" Jared said. "Wow . . . that sounds rough. Man, there have been a lot of twists and turns in this journey, haven't there?"

"Tell me about it," I said, puffing out the words. "I had this really awful experience during my morning meditation the other day. I picked up a small table to move it out of the way and…well, it had this sticky, gross texture on the bottom of it."

"Ewww . . . that is gross," Jared said empathetically.

"Yeah, but it gets worse," I continued. "It gave me this disgusting feeling like I was," my eyes wandered the wall behind Jared as I searched for the appropriate words, "like I was being subjected to . . . a man's bodily fluids."

"Oh my God," Jared cried, the volume of his voice echoing our longstanding friendship. "So, do you think," he continued, returning his voice back to a confidential whisper, "this is a memory about the abuse?"

"Maybe," I conceded. "I can't say for sure, but it was the most disgusting feeling. And at the same time, pure hopelessness. Life had no meaning. Just a big void."

"Dude . . . I'm sorry."

"Thanks, man. I keep thinking I'm getting toward the finish line," I lamented, "but it seems like every time I get close there is another layer of the onion. All I know is I can't keep this up. It's demoralizing and exhausting."

"Hey," Jared interjected, his voice carrying a tone of hopefulness combined with gravitas. "Here's an idea: Have you ever tried EMDR?"

"EM—what?"

"A friend of mine did this thing called EMDR to deal with a lot of subliminal stuff that had to do with her childhood. She said it really helped her to understand what happened."

"Hmmm, I'll check into it."

That evening, perhaps as my subconscious brain grappled with the prospect of going through some form of deep, disruptive therapy, I had another thick, monumental dream from the sixties.

I sat in a huge elongated room, seats all facing the same direction, like a theater, but a very long, narrow one. The white noise numbed my ears as I pressed my face to the window.

My body felt traumatized, as if I had been shaken to my very core. A penetrative, unwanted feeling lingered in my lower abdomen. I had no idea of my whereabouts prior to that moment.

I stared through the window viewing a piece of land below with piers jutting out radially from the curved shoreline below me. I heard the captain say in a military-style voice:

"Approaching Runway One-Niner . . ."

I woke up with a feeling of nervous tension—of having survived something traumatic. The dream lingered in my consciousness like a faint fog. It seemed as though I had weathered a storm and the aftermath left me feeling raw and exposed.

The image of the land below, with its curving shoreline and protruding piers, seemed strangely familiar, as if it was a place I had once known. The captain's voice, authoritative and clear, reverberated in my mind with a weight that I couldn't shake off.

The transition from the surreal theater-like setting to the stark reality of my bedroom was disorienting. I blinked, attempting to clear my head. As I glanced around the familiar walls of my room, the feeling of unease persisted. This unexpected journey through my own subconscious had left me shaken and unsettled.

CHAPTER FORTY-TWO

Joy

In the late 1980s Dr. Francine Shapiro, while walking through a park, stumbled upon the principles of what would evolve into EMDR. Her discovery was serendipitous, a byproduct of her own wandering thoughts and physical observations. At once, she noticed her eye movements were somehow soothing her psychological turmoil. This accidental insight laid the groundwork for a groundbreaking therapeutic technique.

The evolution from a simple discovery to a structured therapeutic approach was no small feat. Shapiro didn't just stumble upon a novel idea; she mined it, refined it, and presented it to the world with the sort of conviction that comes from knowing you're onto something transformative, yet wholly aware of the arduous journey ahead.

But like any new discovery, the legitimacy and effectiveness of EMDR encountered scrutiny. Shapiro, propelled by her initial findings, ventured into a realm of psychological exploration against a backdrop of skepticism. As EMDR gained traction, its narrative was punctuated with debates, endorsements, and critiques. The therapy was a disruptor, challenging the status quo of trauma treatment. Critics were quick to cast doubt, questioning whether this new approach was anything more than a placebo. Yet, as the method withstood scientific scrutiny, it secured a legitimate place in the therapeutic community, offering hope to those caught in the persistent grip of trauma.

The story of EMDR is not just about the therapy itself but about the broader dialogue it initiated in the psychological community and the lives it touched. It's a testament to human ingenuity and the relentless pursuit of solutions that can sometimes emerge from the most unexpected circumstances. Dr. Shapiro's journey with EMDR mirrors a story common to innovation: a blend of serendipity, insight, and a touch of defiance that coalesced into a practice that would reshape the field of psychology.

In the grand scheme of things, EMDR's history isn't just a chronicle of a therapeutic technique; it's a saga about challenging the status quo, about the intersection of chance and science, and the enduring quest to alleviate human suffering.

EMDR's promise lured me like the sun's gravitational field. It offered me hope in the face of overwhelming discouragement. Here was a therapy that dared to dive into the depths of my psyche, to confront the demons that lurked in the shadows, where traditional approaches dared not go. It wasn't just another treatment option; it was a lifeline.

So, nearly forty years after EMDR's inception, with most of the bugs ironed out and its efficacy well-established, I stepped into my new therapist's office. With a deep-seated desire to understand and confront the source of my mental anguish, and knowing full well that conventional therapy was powerless to help, I committed myself wholeheartedly to this form of therapy, hoping to alleviate the pain that had plagued me for so long.

* * *

"Something changed," she said. "Your expression, body language, something shifted. What were you thinking about?"

It was my first session with Joy, in a small, well-decorated office in Mountain View. She was a slim, feisty woman in her late forties with curly brown hair, lean features, and a gleam in her eye. Her demeanor was quick and energetic. She was one of those rare people who is all-in, one hundred percent present, and attends to your every word. She had instructed me to put on headphones and switched on a CD of nature sounds. As the sounds of trickling water oscillated slowly back and forth from one ear to the other, I fell into a dreamlike state. Accompanying that was a feeling of being outside my body. As I looked down upon myself, I saw a vision of me as a young toddler.

"I don't really understand it," I explained, "but I had a vision . . . it's awkward and embarrassing to explain."

"Take your time. Don't judge. Remember, this is a safe space."

I paused for what must have been minutes, trying to both sort out what I saw, and at the same time not present myself as delusional. It seemed too far-fetched, too outlandish to recount, and yet incredibly vivid. More tangible than reality itself.

"I am . . . well . . . I . . . see myself as . . . a cherub baby." I tried with all my might not to judge what I was seeing, to just let the vision form and articulate it. "I'm in a sexy pose. I have my right arm up and my hand behind my head . . . like I'm imitating Marilyn Monroe."

I explained how the vision didn't feel like any other memories I had ever had. I could tell from the vibration of it that it was me from many decades ago. The vision was reminiscent of the cherub statues in Italian and French architecture. I was a small baby naked with one arm up behind my head.

"Don't try to make sense of it," Joy said, sensing the

high degree of self-judgment in my anxious state. "Just sit with it. Let it come in its own time."

At the end of the session, she said, "I'm going to break protocol. If you're feeling up to it, when you're at home, you can try tapping on your knees while sitting in a chair."

At home, as I let the image resonate inside me, it reminded me of a family picture from decades ago. I rummaged through the chest at the foot of my bed and ran across a photo of the four of us: Holly, Pam, Cindy, and me. The three of them were dressed formally, but I was in a skimpy jumpsuit, looking like a baby sailor, fleshy, angelic, fair-skinned, and pudgy. I was donning a baby-faced smile. In the picture I was a few years old and Peter was not born yet. Was this what my mind was pointing to: me as a toddler with my older siblings?

A few days later, I found some free time once my meetings had finished for the day. I sat on my couch and closed my eyes and began to tap. Left knee, right knee, left, right, left, right . . .

The tightness in my chest started to subside as the tension of the workday slowly melted away. I drifted further and further into a scene that was darker, shadowy.

My head seemed to lift up away from my body. I began to feel as if I was floating. I sensed an electric feeling in my stomach. Then an image gradually came into focus, as if pinch-zooming a picture to reveal a clue from a crime scene, something that you had been searching for. An answer that was suddenly revealed.

A canopy of trees as seen from above snapped into focus. Their clumpy, billowy dark green foliage was unmistakable. I saw myself looking down upon a canopy of oak trees from a height of two hundred feet.

I knew that something important had happened in or around this image. However, this was baffling because I couldn't recall as a child ever being suspended above a grove of oak trees. We weren't a jet-setter family and didn't stay in tall skyscrapers when I was young.

And what about the cherub baby image? I couldn't see how this would relate to any real scene or experience. Yet there I was as a cherub baby in an erotic pose. It was as if I had undergone some sort of child pornography photo shoot but had no recollection of it whatsoever.

These images were very impactful, even monumental. I knew that something important, possibly even traumatic, had happened in or around them. Yet, incongruously, it was unclear whether they were good or bad. I didn't know if I wanted to pursue them or run as fast as I could away from them.

* * *

"OK, so things are starting to move," she said. "I think this is progress." I was back in Joy's office, recounting my recent experiences. After a pause, she added: "Do the images remind you of anything?"

"The trees, that image looks a lot like when I was on a business trip in New York in a hotel near Central Park. I could look down and see the oak trees from a hundred feet up. But as a child I never went there. It was only as an adult."

"Have you tried looking around?" she said.

"What do you mean?" I asked. "I'm not there now. . . . How can I look around?"

"Your mind knows a lot more than you consciously know. You can look around. You can move forward in time, even backward in time," she said.

Forward and backward in time? This was something new. I had never thought that I could search an image or a partial memory for more information. I just assumed what I saw was all there was.

Neither of these visions made sense to me, but they were compelling images. Not because of the content but rather the feeling that accompanied them. It was the experience of remembering something significant that you had forgotten about. Something monumental that had a big impact on your life. Maybe it was traumatic in some way. It was the feeling associated with the memory—the taste that accompanied it—that told me it was important. The sudden rush of adrenaline.

I couldn't think of any time in my childhood that I had been in a high-rise building looking down on trees. I hadn't been in a tall building until well after adulthood. And, as far as I knew, I hadn't flown in an aircraft either.

CHAPTER FORTY-THREE

The Trees

"Do you remember me flying in a plane as a child?" I asked my mother. After my second session with Joy and the very vivid image of the trees, I needed to understand its origin. I had called her over my lunch hour to find out more about where I had traveled as a young child, and whether we had stayed in any high-rise hotels.

"Well . . . let me think about that," my mother said, pausing for a good ten seconds. "Well, we did fly to Tulsa on our way to Table Rock Lake for the family reunion."

"When was that?" I asked with a growing sense of curiosity.

"Hmmm . . . let me think. You were about six and Peter was a very young toddler. So it would have been . . . probably the summer of 1966." She went on to describe how we had flown to Tulsa, then taken the whole family, including her parents—a total of nine people in two cars— to Arkansas for a family reunion.

As she recounted the details, a nervous energy tingled through me, memories stirring like leaves in a gust of wind. I recalled the reunion, vaguely. But had forgotten about the aircraft. As a child, I had developed an affinity for flying on airplanes and a strong desire to sit in a window seat. I loved looking at the landscape and roads and cars below. It pulled me out of myself and gave me a sense of awe. It was logical that I would have looked intently out the window as we landed and took off and would have noticed the trees.

But what was my brain trying to tell me about this trip? As I thought more about the reunion I remembered some other things. The boat slips on the shore. Swimming in the pool. Getting reprimanded for it. Peter, my younger brother, being just a baby. But what did that have to do with trauma? And if it even did, why couldn't I recall anything bad happening?

I got in the car, heading home from San Mateo. The sun was just setting over the coastal mountains as I drove toward Crystal Springs Reservoir on Route 92. As my brain adjusted to the twilight, a memory condensed in my mind.

The inside of the room looked like a bus, but the long tubular shape lurched and shifted sideways far too much to be a bus. The wheels couldn't possibly move like that . . . the motion was all wrong.

I looked out the window and saw that we were hundreds of feet above the trees. And they were moving rapidly below us. I pressed my face hard against the cool plexiglass trying to see the trees, the grass, animals, maybe insects . . . closer, closer. Then an abrupt BUMP as the wheels hit the tarmac.

That night I had another dream. It had such a vivid reality to it and a feeling of importance that told me it came from the same era as the others.

I was in a big pond with rocks and footbridges and gazebos. I had to get to the cove where the young child was still sleeping. (Was it my son? My younger brother? A younger version of myself?)

In my hand was the handlebar of some sort of contraption: like a Razor scooter that rode on water. Not a Jet Ski but a waterski with propulsion.

I hit the throttle and scooted across the water, quickly approaching three boulders that blocked the cove. I gassed it again and careened off the first boulder onto the second. I bounced off that sharper, more upright boulder and headed for the third: the final test. In one spectacular motocross move I ricocheted off the third boulder and into the cove, pulling up to the shanty that stood on the beach.

I went into the room to find the young boy sleeping in a high bunk bed, safe from the poisonous insects and spiders that inhabited the lower portions of the shack.

"Are you OK?" I asked.

"Yeah . . . just resting." I felt a huge sense of relief come over me.

I sped back to the main lake, to the gazebo and footbridge and let off the throttle. Just then I heard the captain's voice from a jetliner far above over the radio:

"Now approaching Runway One-Niner."

I was instantly transported into the aircraft above and looked down on a familiar coastline with piers and waterways fanning out from the edge of a highly populated city.

I woke up with the realization that this was another significant dream and clearly relevant to whatever it was my brain was trying to work out. But it had a lot of mixed themes and was complicated, to say the least.

The airline reference mixed with water was confusing. When had I ever heard that kind of lingo? And what about the piers and waterways? And why were water sports mixed with flying aircraft and visuals of piers?

I sat down and spent a few minutes sketching out the coastline I'd seen in the dream. From the texture of it, I guessed it was around 1966. It seemed correlated with the other dreams around that time as if coming from the same sedimentary layer. I also knew from the conversation with my mother that I had flown on an aircraft in 1966, at age six.

Triangulation. Like identifying the scene of a crime.

Viewing the sketch, I backed away to gain some perspective. Something about that image resonated in my mind as if I'd seen it before. Maps and satellite pictures I'd been exposed to as an adult told me it might be related to San Francisco. Pulling up a series of aerial images from the web, I came across the section of coastline along the wharf.

It was a dead hit.

The piers fanning out radially as the coastline curved from Fisherman's Wharf and the Ferry Building to what is now Chase Center matched exactly the drawing I had just made. Somehow, I had seen this image from hundreds of feet up.

But what about the nautical lingo and the phonetic alphabet occurrence? I couldn't grasp how, as a child, I might have heard that language.

I thought back about flying in aircraft as a young teenager visiting family on the East Coast. In those days you could put headphones on and listen to a choice of different stations. One of them was the raw audio of the cockpit crew talking to the tower. They didn't have televisions in the seats at that time, so audio was the next best thing. Maybe I had heard the phrase "Now approaching Runway One-Niner" in the headphones on that flight. But why was this significant enough for me to remember it fifty years later? And was it even real or some made-up fantasy?

I continued my web search, looking up "Runway One-Niner" in relation to SFO. Another direct hit. It turns out that runways are named according to their orientation relative to due north. For example, runway "nine" means ninety degrees from due north (they drop the zero).

I recalled windsurfing for years out at Third Avenue off the coast of Foster City. Aircraft were constantly cued up to land as they flew low over the San Mateo bridge, heading westward toward San Bruno and the San Francisco Airport runway. But this didn't line up with the image in my dream. The typical landing pattern at SFO brings you over the portion of the bay near Foster City, not the wharf. I wouldn't have seen that image.

In my obsessive state I had to know the truth. If the facts didn't line up, then perhaps this whole thing was fantasy on my part. And if it was fantasy, then perhaps the other dreams and flash-frozen memories I was experiencing were unreliable as well. Perhaps I had made them all up and I was just a neurotic person, disturbed for no particular reason.

On the contrary, if the facts did line up, then maybe there was something real to my disturbance. And if there was something real, I had to get to the bottom of it. Otherwise, I'd be denying my own experience. And in doing so I would be that lost soul, forever plagued by ignorance, unable to accept what had happened to him.

As I continued my research, I found that there was another runway at San Francisco International Airport. It's not the main one and it's shorter. It's used in less common weather conditions and for lighter aircraft that don't need as much run-up. And it's oriented toward the south-southwest. Aircraft landing in a southerly wind will typically land on this south-facing runway: Runway 19. And it is verbally articulated as "runway one-niner." (In radio vernacular "nine" is distinguished from the similar-sounding "five" by adding the extra syllable.)

Viewing the whole configuration in Google Maps, I saw that the approach toward Runway 19 took the aircraft just south of the Fisherman's Wharf region of San Francisco, which would have been viewable from a window on the right side of the plane. The image of piers, the aircraft, the water, and the audio all lined up to the moment when we approached SFO on our way home from the reunion.

But why was my subconscious brain so fixated on that particular flight back from Tulsa? Did something happen on the flight? Or did something happen before or afterward?

It seemed important, somehow, to know what my brain was trying to tell me. This compact little experience had clearly had a major impact on my life. I had immersed myself in windsurfing as an adult. Skimming across the water at thirty miles an hour had become my new drug. It seemed to hit something central within my subliminal mind and satiate my nervous system.

Windsurfing—particularly as I got good at it and graduated to smaller, faster gear—was like flying over water. The mylar sails were like wings. The short, sleek boards like Jet Skis. And once engaged in windsurfing, I was compelled to call the SFO weather line each afternoon, exposing myself daily to the same language I'd heard from the airline captain fifty years earlier. Two disparate modes of transportation—aircraft and watercraft—using the same weather information and the same language.

I began to consider if gravitating to windsurfing as an adult was a way for my brain to re-create this image from 1966. The activity, the language, the visuals. The sound of the rushing wind across the aircraft. The view of the white caps on the bay as we came in for our approach. The feeling of being shaken by recent experiences. The way that chaos in my life was being mirrored by the motion of the aircraft on our approach.

I wonder sometimes if the events in our lives are less random than we think. If the human brain subliminally orchestrates our experience to bring us into proximity with the vaguely familiar, but for reasons that are unclear, at least to our conscious brains. Wind, water, tumultuous motion, mixed with the sounds of authority figures. All of this had been wrapped up into a bizarre dream that seemed, like a screenplay written in code, to come from the summer of 1966.

CHAPTER FORTY-FOUR

Blood of the Lamb

Back in Joy's office, eager to get to the bottom of these dreams and other mental clues, I recounted the images that I had seen following the first few EMDR sessions. There were two of them and a faint third. The trees, the cherub baby, and one other. This third image was less ambiguous, less benign than the first two.

While sitting on my own sofa a day earlier, in a dreamlike state, tapping rhythmically on my right and then left knee as I transitioned my breath to a slower, calmer state, my consciousness had been assaulted by a gruesome, violent scene. I had seen in my mind's eye, a vision of a bedsheet soaked with an immense amount of dark-red blood.

I recounted this latest image to Joy. If she had any feelings of shock or repulsion, she didn't show them. The two of us sat in silence for a period of time as the image lingered like an elephant in the room.

As I sat with the unsettling aftermath of the images, the idea of delving deep into my subconscious again felt daunting. However, amidst the discomfort, there was also a sense of urgency, a recognition that confronting these demons head-on was necessary for my healing journey.

"Would you like to try some more EMDR now?" she asked softly, as if any blunt or overly candid words might destroy me. I knew it was a step I needed to take, despite my trepidation.

Joy led me into a mindful state. This time, instead of headphones or her oscillating hand, Joy opted for a tactile approach: a set of paddles that vibrated with the electrical signal supplied to them. Something that might resonate with a different part of my consciousness, perhaps? After some preparation and deep breathing, I began to sense myself sliding into a calmer, less-inhibited state. The paddles began to vibrate: left, right, left, right . . .

Suddenly the paddles transformed themselves into something much less innocuous. Warm, firm, slippery. There was no mistaking the sensation of holding in my hand something of someone else. Something so personal and erotic that it didn't belong in the office, much less in my hands.

I threw the paddles on the floor. "Aaaaaaah . . . YUCK! That was . . . disgusting!"

"Tell me what happened," Joy said in a voice that bridled surprise with a layer of confidence and mentorship.

"It was," I began, trying to collect myself, "it was a man's . . . organ in my hand."

"You can say the word, penis," Joy said matter-of-factly.

"Fine . . . it's a man's penis. I could feel the heat of it, the texture. And it was slippery. Like it was covered with . . . semen." The graphic indecency went against every ounce of modesty that resided in my being up to that point, instilling a raw, exposed feeling in me.

Joy looked at me with measured curiosity and little to no surprise. "How old are you in this scenario?"

"Well, pretty young . . . maybe nine years old" I responded.

"Is there anything else associated with the feeling? Any smells or other feelings."

"There's . . . a cool breeze on my face. The smell of water and dirt," I continued, pondering, digging deep into my other senses. There was something vaguely reminiscent about the sensory input I was receiving. As I plunged into the experience, a faint memory came into mind.

"It reminds me of a creek I used to go to as a child," I continued after a long pause. "A place behind the Friedmans' house where the water flows out of the huge concrete pipe into the creek below the 280 freeway. We called it *The Pipe*.

"Who's there with you?" Joy inquired in a tone moderating curiosity with a layer of reassurance.

"It's the Friedmans," I began carefully, not wanting to exit the trancelike state I was in. "Chase, Rachael, Anne. Chase was the same age as my older brother but I don't remember interacting with Holly much. They are all laughing and almost...mocking me."

Joy paused, contemplating, planning her next move. Then her look shifted to one of confident resolve. "Tell me more about Holly."

"Holly? Well, he and my older sister were pretty big partiers in their early teens," I began. "A lot of alcohol and pot. I don't really remember it, but he told me about it later. Then in the late eighties and nineties, he seemed to turn things around." I recounted to Joy the sense I had during those later years, that he was a changed man. He'd become centered and thoughtful, as if he had evolved into a whole human being. It seemed we'd developed a relationship that was positive. "I've always felt we had a really close relationship. Like we were soul mates," I said proudly.

"Anything else?" Joy asked in a tone moderating

eagerness with infinite patience.

"Well things shifted when he met his new girlfriend. And it seemed like things changed back. It was during the last couple years before he died. He seemed like he got back into the drinking and drugs . . . as if . . ."

"As if he were engaging in risky behavior again?" she offered, her question carrying an air of finality to it.

"Yes," I said, pausing briefly to collect my thoughts. "It made me really sad to see that. More than sad . . . almost . . . afraid. But I don't really know what it has to do with these memories. I mean I don't recall anything bad between him and me when I was young."

As my mind grappled with these thoughts and questions about my past, that night ushered in another profound dream that resonated deep within me.

I rode on the back of a motorcycle, speeding along a path constructed of fresh soil that had been worked and shaped into a dirt road.

We circled in a clockwise direction up the grade toward the east, then to the south. As milliseconds passed, I began to recognize the location: the cloverleaf onramp from Page Mill onto Highway 280 northbound. But it was constructed of dirt.

I was on the back of the vehicle, holding onto . . . someone.

We rolled over rocks and gravel, jumping over branches and careening up embankments as I held onto some unknown form in front of me. From my perspective the motorcycle seemed huge, like it was built for a giant. In my mind's eye we were twelve feet off the ground.

There was an urgency to get to our destination, which I didn't fully understand. Finally, we rode up to the level of the "living." There were houses and fences and landscaping. We had to make it back by dinner.

After the final ascent, we meandered through the neighborhoods from this shack to that mansion. We had risen to the "human" stage where the zombies were no longer.

I clung to his torso — I had no choice or I would fall off. And the faster he rode, the stronger I gripped. It was as if I were forced to show intimacy by squeezing him as we rode; but really it was self-preservation.

The next morning, as my head cleared, the previous night's dream percolated into my consciousness in a way that was both daunting and baffling. I recognized the location of the cloverleaf. But it should have been paved, not dirt. After all, it was the entrance to a heavily traveled freeway.

I got onto my computer and looked up the history of the 280 freeway. After a few minutes of digging, I learned it was built between 1964 and 1966. In those years, the cloverleaf was, indeed, unpaved earth. Somehow, I knew I had been there. On the back of a motorcycle. I now had multiple data points that triangulated to a time: 1966.

I decided to shift my research to the old neighborhood, to the Friedmans across the street and the Weltys next door. I got on Ancestry.com and looked for various kids— who would now be adults—who were there during the sixties. My eyes became tired. My metabolism slowed. A feeling of grogginess seeped through my body.

* * *

"Dude, I don't know what it is," I explained in a perplexed voice, "but every time I try to do research about my childhood I . . . can't seem to do it."

"What happens?" Jared asked with anticipation, always eager to uncover the hidden psychological mystery. We sat across from each other in a booth at Wahlburgers in Palo Alto, having lunch on a Thursday. A few groups were scattered across the dimly lit restaurant, the three TVs above the bar shining brightly above the ambient light.

"I've tried three or four times to do the research. Sometimes I drift off to sleep, and other times I find myself unable to focus, as if my mind is avoiding the task altogether. It's almost like there's an invisible barrier, like a cow sidestepping a cattle guard."

"Hmmm, that's . . . interesting," Jared remarked, his tone taking on the compassionate demeanor of a therapist and friend.

"And when I do get around to it, the process becomes very . . . confusing. Things that I can usually do, like web research, are suddenly incredibly difficult. It's as if I don't even know how to work a computer any more. Like my head's in a fog." I contemplated for a moment. "My thoughts even drift back to my third sister, Sally, the one we haven't seen in years."

"Wow! Sounds like it might be a mental block," Jared observed, his empathetic tone ever present. "Like maybe your subconscious doesn't want to let you go there."

I regarded him with skepticism, unwilling to acknowledge that my subconscious might be getting in the way of my own self-discovery.

"What are you trying to figure out?" Jared continued. "Maybe I can help. I'm not working these days, so I've got time. I'd love to help my buddy out," he added, in a phrase so characteristic of our longstanding friendship. Jared had just been laid off from his recent job at a small startup where he had acted as interim CEO for over half a year, but he had retained his VP salary while the board tested him out.

"Well, somehow it looks like I interacted with Holly more than I thought. I just had a dream where I'm riding on the back of a motorcycle. But it wasn't my dad—he never rode a motorcycle. The only one in our family that did was Holly."

"When was this?" Jared asked with a sharply inquisitive tone, like a detective following a hot lead.

"Around 1964 to 1966," I said.

"And he was . . . how much older?"

"Eight years," I offered. "So he would have been fourteen."

I gave Jared a short list of names I had gathered from my vague recollections around the time, friends and neighbors from the sixties. I didn't know if it would lead to anything, but feeling at a loss in my own research, I hoped he might uncover something.

CHAPTER FORTY-FIVE

Budweiser Bob

"Did you invent the weed wacker?" the disheveled, unshaven man across the table said to me.

"Why do you ask?" I responded in a tone combining deep fascination with a layer of skepticism.

I sat at Alice's Restaurant on Skyline Boulevard across the table from Bob Friedman, my childhood friend. Jared had located Bob during his research into the old neighborhood, along with his older brother and sister, Chase and Rachael.

"I remember when we were kids, you'd take a long thin branch and swing it close to the ground and chop down blades of grass with it. I honestly wondered if you were the one who invented it. I remember you being the smartest guy in the neighborhood."

"Oh ... well, thanks for the comment," I said nervously. "I remember you being really into gardening," I continued, eager to change the subject.

"I was . . . in fact I told my dad when I was in high school I wanted to be a farmer. He just laughed at me and said that was ridiculous."

Bob ordered his third Budweiser. The food hadn't yet arrived.

"So what happened to your family?" I asked. "I lost track in the seventies. It seems like things kind of disintegrated."

Bob told the story of his sister Anne, who died of cancer years ago, and his younger sister, who no longer speaks to him. Of Rachael, the eldest sister who struggled with health and relationship issues over the years.

"What about Chase?" I asked. "What was he up to back in those days?" I knew Chase and Holly were about the same age. Something in the recesses of my mind told me the two of them had hung out together, though I couldn't remember anything specific.

"Chase was a rebel. He and my dad didn't get along. They fought constantly."

I had known there was some trauma in their household, mostly because the siblings had all struggled so much afterwards. But I had never known exactly what. That combined with my own alleged abuse and post-trauma symptoms got me thinking that maybe his family had been hit by the same thing. And perhaps he had seen something.

After getting up my nerve, I looked at him until he looked back into my eyes: "Bob, did you ever see any sexual abuse in the neighborhood?" The question emerged from my lips in a more terse and abrupt manner than I intended. And perhaps too early in the conversation.

Bob's brows went up and his eyes got big. His face went pale. "Oh . . . oh no, I never saw anything like that . . . no. Huh-uh." It was as though I had said something grossly inappropriate. Yet I sensed there was more under the surface. His words were saying "no," but there was some sort of evasion, some sort of denial going on. Maybe he couldn't get at it. Maybe he didn't want to recollect it. I knew I needed to dig deeper. But tonight wasn't the night.

After dinner we went back to his residence, the basement of a home owned by his sister, Rachael. There, on his kitchen counter were no less than twenty empty beer cans.

"Dude, if you ever want to go to AA, I'll take you," I said, carefully, not knowing just how he would react.

"Ha-ha-hah! I don't need AA, that's for losers" he said. "I drink twenty-three Budweisers a day and I'm fine with it."

"Twenty-three?" I said, astonished. Then, catching myself so as not to appear judgmental: "That's just one short of a case. Seems like you're leaving one on the table."

His blank look evolved gradually into a wry smile, as it sank in. "Haaaa-ha-ha."

"I'm worried about you though," I said.

"Don't worry about me," he said. "I'll probably die of liver failure but, hey, we're all going to die eventually. I might as well enjoy life in the meantime."

I contemplated his situation for a minute. I knew he was on a downward spiral. He had been for years. I really didn't want to lose him. He was my first—really, my only—childhood friend. It had taken me fifty years to reconnect with him and I hated seeing him abuse his body like that. But I also knew he was a grown man, at age sixty-three, and had his own ideas about how he wanted to live. He had his own history. His own trauma. I wasn't going to change him, not if he didn't want to get sober. It was a fool's errand.

We looked over pictures from the old neighborhood. I felt like memories were being slowly filled in for me. The events of the 1960s on La Barranca Road were becoming more more clear.

Back outside and up the stairs, we walked past the deck and saw Rachael and her daughter smoking weed while

Rachael's eighteen-month-old granddaughter milled around the deck exploring and playing with her doll.

Bob introduced me to his sister. I was struck by how misshapen and obese she was. Her stomach and lower abdomen hung down between her legs as she sat on the bench, forming what looked like another appendage. And her bright red hair took me back to a time many years earlier.

I so much wanted to ask her questions about 1966. What did she know? What could she remember? What would she even be willing to tell? I would have to find a moment, later, to ask her, when the moment felt right.

CHAPTER FORTY-SIX

Holly's Friends

"So I found some more contacts you were trying to locate," said Jared as he approached me outside the Marufuku Ramen shop in downtown Redwood City.

"Dude, you are a true bud!" I sang. "I tried a bunch of times to look into that but . . . well, my brain just wouldn't let me do the work."

"What are friends for?" Jared said in his high-pitched, eager-sidekick tone.

The hostess escorted us to the well-lit bar backed with natural antique wood adorned with fishbowl pendant lights. Sake bottles lined the back of the bar.

"Well, you have no idea how helpful this is. So what did you come up with?" I asked.

"Well, before I tell you what I found, do you mind if I ask you something?"

"Sure, anything," I responded.

"So . . . what do you remember about hanging out with Holly back in the sixties?" Jared asked in a tone that sat somewhere between inquisitive and perplexed.

"Well, a lot of things . . ." I stared off to the right across the low-slung second bar into the kitchen where five or six chefs were working feverishly preparing food. I thought back to those years. About our bond and the many interesting and exciting times we'd had together. I dug deeper and thought about those younger years, contemplating our interactions.

"Well, that's odd," I said, after a long contemplative pause. "I'm trying to recall—I mean I know we spent time together—but I can't remember much." As my mind searched for the plethora of experiences with Holly, nothing except two random memories came into focus.

We had gotten home from somewhere on a weekend—perhaps from church—and each hurriedly eaten a couple of leftover pancakes and walked outside to his car, got in, and headed up La Barranca. I couldn't remember where we were coming from, nor where we were going. Once on Elena Road, a minute or two later, we both had the sensation of choking as the dry pancakes slowly made their way past our esophagi. We glanced at each other as we each put our hands to our throats, trying to help the cakes down.

The other memory was when the plastic model biplane I'd received as a gift broke a wing. It had a string attached to it so that I could twirl it around above my head as if it were actually flying. I recall going into Holly's room. It was dark. He inhabited the space like a mobster, puffing a cigarette. But in this case, the smoke emanated from his soldering iron instead of a cigarette, which would have been forbidden in our Christian Science household. He offered to weld the plastic back together. But in the process, he suggested we put some bat-like scallops on the trailing edge of the wing and the aileron. While ostensibly asked my permission, it was more of an announcement of what he was going to do. I was in no position to argue. After ten minutes passed, while I observed his every move, he completed his work. All that remained was a melted, deformed airplane, a mere mockery of its previous form. The break in the wing was only just barely holding together. The bat-like squiggles on the trailing edge exhibited grotesque bulbs of melted plastic.

I recounted the two seemingly innocuous memories to Jared.

"*W-e-i-r-d dude!*" Jared uttered in a haunting tone. "And those are the only two you remember?"

"Yeah, but that doesn't make any sense," I protested. "It seems like a lot of memories about my younger years are . . . missing."

"Well, you were pretty young," Jared offered.

"It's puzzling," I continued, ignoring Jared's conjecture. "Why does it seem like there are gaps in my recollection that should be filled with a bunch of memories about Holly?"

"Well . . . I can't say for sure," Jared said, pivoting into the mainstream topic of our meeting, "but I think there is some really strange stuff going on with the old neighborhood. I did a lot of research . . . went to the county courthouse; I went to your old high school and looked through yearbooks and old school newspapers."

"Man, I totally owe you," I interjected, not sensing the gravity of where he was going.

"It became a pretty dark journey, if truth be told," he continued, his voice growing softer, laden with solemnity. "It kind of filled me with a feeling of dread. Wasn't at all what I expected. After a while it started to really kind of weigh on me."

"Really? How so?" I asked, my cheeks flushing with embarrassment for not realizing what he'd been through on my behalf.

"Well," he began, "I started researching people in the Gunn yearbooks and some of them just seemed to disappear without a trace."

"That's weird," I said, as I drew nearer to him.

"And the more research I did, the more evil characters showed up."

"Really . . . evil?" I responded, as an ominous feeling began to creep slowly through my body.

"For example," Jared continued, his tone resolute yet cautious so as not to overwhelm me, "this one friend who now lives in Santa Cruz was arrested and lost his therapy license for sleeping with one of his patients." Jared turned his phone toward me to reveal a web page from a Santa Cruz newspaper. The headline sent a chill through my chest:

> *John Spurr of Santa Cruz was accused of inappropriate behavior with a patient from 1990 to 1994, according to Tom O'Connor, the board's executive Officer.*

"Jeez . . . that's creepy," I said. "John was a close friend of Holly's during high school."

"There's more," he said. "Hold on to your hat. This one takes the cake!"

I felt a nervous, jittery, electric feeling in my abdomen.

"Remember that other friend of Holly's, Kerry Mock?" he asked.

"Y-e-e-e-s-s-s . . ." I said cautiously.

"Well, he's in prison in Georgia for sodomizing a young boy. I'm pretty sure it's the same guy."

Holy shit! This can't be happening. Two of Holly's closest high-school friends are sexual deviants.

Jared showed me his phone again, this time displaying a web page from Homefacts.com:

> *Kerry Nelson Mock, Registered Sex Offender.*

A chill ran down my spine as the gravity of the revelation sank in. The realization came crashing down on me: Those unsavory characters had been regular fixtures in our home, possibly lurking in the shadows plotting unspeakable acts as I went about my business. Had I ever been alone with them? The thought sent a shudder through me.

Over the next couple of days my mind roiled with questions and unease. Memories of the family reunion in Arkansas began to materialize, accompanied by a nagging uncertainty about what transpired during those nights. Where did I sleep? Who did I share a room with?

I peered into the recesses of my memory, probing for answers. But instead of clarity, I was met with a void—a massive black wall placed ominously in front of me, hiding secrets I knew I needed to uncover.

CHAPTER FORTY-SEVEN

The Roommate

"Who did I room with?"

Back at 12865 La Barranca, my mother sat next to me at the kitchen table sipping a glass of Chardonnay. I'd had a day of meetings at Synack and was eager to sit down and decompress. But I needed to pursue the events around the family reunion in 1966, and the subject matter was too charged for me to completely relax.

"Well, let's see, Pam and Cindy roomed together. Peter was just a baby so he would have stayed with your father and me." She paused, staring across the table as she collected her thoughts.

"Well . . . I guess it was Holly," she finally concluded.

"Holly . . .?"

Something in my gut tensed up. I didn't remember anything about staying in a room there, with anyone. It was as if we had traveled there and I had swum in the pool, done some boating activities, but never slept anywhere, in any room, with anyone.

"I roomed with Holly?" I repeated, as if trapped in a

repetitive loop I couldn't extract myself from. "Well . . . that's weird. There's a lot that I do remember about the reunion. How could I not remember who I roomed with?"

"Well," she said, "it was a long, long time ago. You were so little . . . maybe five or six."

"But . . . I remember swimming in the pool by myself. I remember Aunt Robena's cookies. I remember her dachshund. . . . I just don't see how I—"

"What is it that you're trying to piece together?" she interjected with a hint of frustration.

"I know I went through some kind of abuse during the sixties. I thought it was Dad originally but you said you never saw anything. What about Holly. . . . Did you ever see anything going on between us?"

She slowly set her glass of wine on the table, still holding the stem, staring across the room. Sun filtered through the overgrown planter bed through the kitchen window as shafts of light illuminated glass crystals hanging from the chandelier, sending rays out in all directions.

"Well, do you think something happened?" she said with her characteristic inflection. Up then down at the end, like a British person articulating a statement pretending to be a question.

"Well, yeah. But I can't remember it. I was hoping you could shed some light. I mean, like you say, I was really young. You were an adult. . . . Didn't you see anything?"

I looked over at my mother who had a contented smile on her face, as she brought the glass full of amber liquid to her lips, sipping slowly, gazing out the window.

I sipped my water, contemplating and trying to sort out what was going on. But I didn't want to put unnecessary pressure on her.

"Hmm . . . do you think something happened?" she said again, using her British inflection.

Thoughts swirled in my mind, a whirlwind of doubts and fears that threatened to overwhelm me. Was I ready to confront the memories lurking in the recesses of my psyche? Was I prepared to face the truth, no matter how painful it might be?

As my mother echoed her question, her voice trailing off, I found myself grappling with a decision. Should I delve deeper into the darkness of my past, to uncover the secrets buried deep inside me? Or was it safer to remain in the comforting embrace of ignorance, shielded from the hard truths of reality?

CHAPTER FORTY-EIGHT

The Tempest

The motivation should have been there. And I had plenty to go on. The neighborhood was beginning to reveal itself, despite my mother's systematic denials. I was convinced the time had come to reach the end of the trail and reveal the secrets of my youth.

But something pulled me away as if shielding me from an onslaught of unwieldy thoughts and memories. The same overwhelming feeling that plagued me in my young career—the tension building up with no release in sight— hit me again, drawing me away from the fear and toward nature. Toward some sort of intensity that would both occupy my conscious brain completely and offer some relief to the anxious task at hand.

In the nineties, I had balanced things out by windsurfing on the bay. Whether it was healthy or dysfunctional had never been clear to me. Yet I needed an activity to nurture my soul, connect me with nature, and at the same time generate adrenaline to purge my being of latent tension.

So instead of diving full force into sleuthing the old

neighborhood and putting together the pieces, I embarked on a different journey—an activity that would make me feel like I was still alive and vital. Whether I was avoiding the newfound revelations or I was actively drawn to something else, one cold day in early April, I launched from the Oyster Point Marina on the back of a Jet Ski in a light drizzle. Even with a 4 mm wetsuit and a neoprene hood I felt chilled to the bone.

I'd found a local pro who owned a kite school at the marina, a solid guy with dark hair who had been involved in the Big Wave circuit. His rugged looks and messy hair just amplified the big wave, risk-taker motif.

The cold—the unwelcomeness and the harshness of it— was amplified tenfold as Big Wave and I motored out of the marina and across the Oyster Point bay. The strong winds sent stinging drops of frigid water across my face as we made our way over to Tigers.

We came to a stop and Big Wave shut off the engine. Two hundred yards away I could see planes taxiing along the south-facing airport runway. Suddenly I realized I was just below the approach zone to the same runway upon which we had landed when returning from Tulsa in 1966. Just as in my dream about the Jet Ski and the aircraft flying overhead, there we floated, directly under the aircraft approach. In my mind's eye I could hear the captain articulating over the radio: "Now approaching Runway One-Niner".

The winds blew offshore, sending me toward the deeper, colder, and more tumultuous water. It was daunting, even with the Jet Ski nearby. Big Wave's casual approach and intermittent attention to me between checking his phone for messages only intensified my feelings of exposure. There were moments in which I drifted so far downwind I could no longer see Big Wave. Just me, the chaotic water, and strong, stinging winds, leaving me ultimately alone to fend for myself.

At that moment I felt I could quit. I could bail out and no one would judge me for it. After all, who would want this for themselves? But there was something I felt deep in my core: if I endured this and didn't give up, I would be rewarded. If I went through this combination of fear and discomfort—dragging through the choppy water, occasionally ingesting mouthfuls of the chilled, brown, salty liquid—I would eventually become competent and self-sufficient. I would rise above. Like the satisfaction that comes from climbing a mountain peak. There was something pulling me through this pain toward a better place. Moving me toward my future happiness.

Despite my anxiety prompted by the extreme conditions, I managed to get up twice and it was exhilarating. Skipping across the water with a ten-meter kite pulling me felt more exciting and faster—even freer— than windsurfing. It was a moment of pure elation. At the end of the lesson, Big Wave told me to eject the kite.

"How do I do that?"

Big Wave looked at me suspiciously. "You don't know where the eject is?"

He pointed to the red cylindrical-shaped plastic piece between my harness and the control bar. "That's your eject. Pull that." Then he paused for a moment, then added: "That's like driving a car and not knowing where the brake pedal is."

I knew that engaging in this sport involved a fair amount of risk. Ironically, though, the biggest danger I experienced during the entire day had been self-imposed.

I decided to take my final lesson at Third Avenue with Big Wave's colleague. I was told to look for Giovanni. I showed up at Baywinds Park—my old windsurf haunt and the site of my near-death mishap in the 1990s. It was much cleaner and more gentrified than I remembered. Neat, professionally laid artificial turf replaced the many pieces of donated used carpet that had sparsely covered the mud in the setup area decades earlier. A building with restrooms and two outdoor showers had been constructed. Two park benches were installed in the rigging area.

The space was mostly empty except for two men sitting on one of the benches. Both had dark hair, and one was stout, Caucasian, about five-foot-ten, while the other was a very short Vietnamese man, about five feet tall, shirtless, sipping a Budweiser.

"Do either of you know where I can find Giovanni?" I asked.

"That me," said the short one who couldn't have weighed more than 135 pounds.

"Really . . . you?" I said. The Italian name combined with Vietnamese accent and features was an unlikely combination. Surely he was joking with me. Just having a laugh or two. But the man next to him just nodded.

"Yeah, my name come from long time ago. My original name Tran but people call me Giovanni. Long story."

"Oh . . . OK," I said.

"So you ready for lesson?" he said cheerfully.

"It doesn't look like it's going to blow today," I said, looking out across the launch past the limp windsock to see glassy water and barely a ripple on the bay.

"It blow today," he insisted. "You wait. Two o'clock it blow."

I chuckled. I wasn't going to argue with him. I had sailed here for thirty years, and I knew the pattern. Nevertheless, I went back to my car and put my wetsuit on mostly to humor him. I didn't want to seem like I was stonewalling or unexcited about the process. Maybe we would do some beach work or some kite ground-handling. Or perhaps we'd wade into the water and explore the rocks around the kite launch.

I got back to the windsurf setup area just before two o'clock. Incongruously, I heard waves lapping against the rock levee. I looked out toward the launch ramp. There in front of me stood the flag flapping vigorously in the breeze and the windsock jutting out horizontally, away from the pole, blown by a stiff, twenty-knot wind. From zero to twenty in fifteen minutes? Maybe this quirky, compact little man did have some magic up his sleeve.

We headed to the kite launch, about a quarter mile upwind. It was high tide, and the lagoon was filled with thigh-deep water.

"It time for safety brief," Giovanni said.

"I've already been through the safety lecture with the other teacher," I protested. It was partially true. I had been through the safety briefing a couple of years earlier when I'd tried it with a friend. And Big Wave had told me a few things about safety the previous week.

"You right hand or left hand?" Giovanni asked.

"I'm right-handed."

"Why you have emergency release on left side?" I looked down at my harness.

"What emergency release . . .?"

Giovanni stared at me. His eyes grew wide. He slowly pointed to the small red tube that surrounded the line attached to the left side of my harness.

I knew where the main eject was. Big Wave had drilled that into me. But I really had no idea what the other cord with the smaller red tube was.

"If you need release the kite completely, you pull this," he said. He pulled the red sheath which was held in place with a bungee line. As he pulled the sheath, a cord appeared inside which was held in place with a long metal pin. Once the sheath was out of the way, the pin disengaged and the whole line separated.

"You need be able release completely. You about hit rocks, you pull this."

Then he fixed his eyes on me and added: "You drive car and not know where brake is?"

I passed it off as an oversight rather than a major safety issue. This, despite seeing stories in the news about kiteboarding students getting dragged across rocks and over fences. It seemed I was less afraid of dying than I was of flat day-to-day living.

That afternoon I managed to get up on the board a few times. I executed a few twenty-second runs, harnessing the wind for brief, yet exhilarating, moments. Over the course of the next couple of weeks I built my competence and began riding consistently. I pieced together a quiver of four kites and a board and spent most afternoons that summer on the bay, carving, jumping, learning tricks.

It was mesmerizing and, at the same time, soulful to be out on the water again, twenty-five years later. Launching off the sharp wave peaks in the open water and screaming across the smooth flat water inside the lagoon.

My kiteboarding sessions became ubiquitous during late afternoons and weekends. Yet no matter how much I tried to immerse myself in the thrill of the sport, thoughts of my conversation with Jared, memories of Holly and his friends, and the unsettling events from my past at the age of six would inevitably resurface. Even as I sought out this sport that allowed me to soar with the wind, I found myself tethered to the memory of 1966, unable to fully escape its grasp. And the irony wasn't lost on me: I sought solace in kiteboarding, only to find myself confronting the very place from my nightmares . . . the waterway leading up to Runway One-Niner.

CHAPTER FORTY-NINE

Into the Woods

As the winds began to die off toward the fall of that year, I found myself with more free time to think about the unfinished business of understanding my past. I decided to reach back out to Bob, my childhood friend. Maybe something we talked about had jogged his memory and he was ready to discuss it. I called his cell phone multiple times with no response. Usually he got back to me within a few hours to a day, even in his chronic state of inebriation. But I heard nothing.

I decided to reach out to the only other person I knew who was connected to him, and to that part of my own history. I exchanged a few texts with his sister Rachael and eventually made an appointment to meet her at her home off Skyline Boulevard on a Saturday afternoon.

I had been there once before, when I met Bob for dinner. I had never actually talked to Rachael—at least not as an adult—and this situation felt different. She lived in the mountains in a remote location about a mile southeast of Alice's Restaurant.

As I drove along La Honda Road past the Woodside

Library, I began to feel a growing sense of fear and doubt in my chest. Who exactly was Rachael? I had known her as a child but who was she as a grown adult? Holly's other friends had turned out to be unsavory characters. What would a face-to-face meeting reveal about her?

I took the right fork at Portola Road and headed up Route 84 with its steep incline. Suddenly I wanted to turn around. To call the whole thing off. I had no idea who this person actually was. She could be a serial killer for all I knew. I'd be in the woods in a remote location with no one else around. Kathy was out of town and had no idea where I was going. I would ask Rachael some very pointed questions. I had no idea how she might react. And it seemed as though she had some kind of power over me with her stocky build, her abrupt, even bossy, demeanor, and her fiery red hair.

I could cancel over text and just say something came up. She would understand. And even if she didn't, I would be in my own space, not hers. I would be safe.

I pulled off the road onto the shoulder and prepared to make a U-turn. Then, as I sat in my car, preparing to head back down the hill, I wondered: is anything in my life safe . . . I mean, really safe, if I'm not facing my past? If I'm ignoring the scared, damaged creature inside me, will I ever feel truly at peace? I sat in the car, thinking. Acid bubbled up as it always did when I felt nervous. I twitched my right elbow and shoulder involuntarily. Then, my other elbow. As my left arm hit the inside of the car door, I was jolted back to the present moment to that location in Woodside halfway to Rachael's house, halfway to answers, to resolution. I couldn't make the fear go away, but I could push ahead, despite the fear. It suddenly became clear to me that this was something I had to do. Fear or no fear. Dangerous or not.

I pulled back onto Route 84 and continued up toward Skyline.

CHAPTER FIFTY

Poor Bud

"So . . . did you know?" Rachael said as I approached her in her front courtyard. Her bright red hair, fair skin, and stocky build looked a little more like Rachael from my childhood. She had lost an immense amount of weight since I had seen her last while visiting Bob. The frontal appendage was gone.

"Know what?" I responded.

"About Bob."

My heart felt heavy like a weight was pushing down on my chest, growing more forceful by the second.

"I . . . I tried to reach him a few weeks ago and he didn't answer," I said. "Is he . . .?"

Rachael handed me a newspaper clipping from the November issue of the *Woodside Almanac*:

Robert "Budweiser Bob" Friedman, 63, a Woodside resident and gardener/landscaper, died on Nov. 12, 2021

"Shit!! I'm sorry."

"Yeah . . . it sucks." She waved me into the door of her home. "Come on in."

Rachael had a way of talking that reminded me of a five-year-old telling a "big fish" story. She would say something impactful and exhale, as if laughing through the end of the sentence to punctuate how immense, even outlandish, it really was. It conveyed a sense of feigned import. As if distancing herself from the grueling topic of conversation, like a five-year-old girl telling how she just saw a horse poop on the side of the street and it was r-h-h-h-e-a-l-l-y b-h-h-h-h-h-i-g.

"Yeah . . . I put it in the *Almanac*," she said. Then, not wanting to deal with the awkward silence, she quickly added: "I heard if I just put a notice in the paper that people could search for it. I didn't want to do a long thing because they wanted th-h-h-h-r-e-e . . . h-h-h-u-n-d-r-e-d . . . b-h-h-h-u-c-k-s. I wasn't going to do that."

Then she added matter-of-factly: "But it was free just to put a line in the paper with his name and the date . . . so I did that."

"Sure, I understand."

"That whole thing was hell. . . . It was pure hell," she said.

"So what happened, exactly?" I asked.

"He just kept getting sicker and sicker. He cut himself in the groin . . . and it turned into gangrene and . . . it was terrible."

"Oh . . . Jeez . . . Wha . . .?" I wanted to ask how he had cut himself in the groin. How could he possibly have gotten a wound there? And on top of that, to let it fester enough to become gangrenous? Then I remembered he was an alcoholic. Self-care was a big issue with that crowd—I would know. I let it pass.

"He never wanted to eat," she continued. "His stomach was killing him. At that point he couldn't walk, he couldn't breathe. So I said 'We're taking you to the hospital.' He said 'No, no I'm not going.'"

"Well, yeah…sounds like Bob," I said. "He wasn't big on being coddled."

"But then later that night," she continued in her hurried fashion, "he called me from downstairs and said, 'I need to go to the hospital.' So I took him down to Sequoia."

"This just sounds incredibly traumatic," I consoled.

"It was s-s-s-s-o-o-o-o-o-o traumatic," she said. "They did tests. Then they said 'We need to do an operation on his groin to clean it out.'"

"Wow . . ."

"Then they came back and said 'We didn't get it all. We need to go in again.' Then . . . after the second operation they said he wasn't coming through anesthesia like he should. His organs weren't working. He was shutting down. He had a ruptured stomach. He had sepsis. They asked if he had been drinking and I said 'Yes.'"

"Oh my God," I said, searching for something comforting or insightful. But my mind was blank with shock.

"The doctors said they could go in and repair his stomach, but if they did that, he might not come through the operation. He was very, very sick. Very thin. They called me the next morning and said 'He's getting worse.' I said I know. He wasn't waking up. He was so frail."

"That's terrible!" I said empathetically.

"They said if they do the next surgery he may die," she said. "And even if he *did* come through, he would have to be on three months of assisted living. He w-h-h-h-ouldn't . . . w-h-h-h-a-n-t . . . t-h-h-h-a-t!"

"No . . . he wouldn't," I agreed. "Back when I talked to him last year, he always said 'We're all going to die of something.'"

"Yeah, Bob and I had talked. We always said…if anything happens p-h-h-h-u-l . . . the . . . p-h-h-h-l-u-g."

"Right," I said.

"Finally, they called and said, 'It won't be long.' So I told the doctors to put him on the ventilator and keep him going until we get there. When we got there I talked to him. We played all his favorite music. I held his hand. Five minutes after we got there, he passed."

"Jeez . . . I'm really sorry you had to go through that," I said.

"Yeah . . . he lived with me for forty years . . . since 1984. It's as close as a husband and wife. My brother . . . we did everything together. I'm still mourning. I still hear him downstairs," she said. "I can still smell his cigarette smoke."

He was gone. My hopes of getting him into recovery, taking him to meetings, sponsoring him, helping him turn his life around—those were all gone. He could never realize his dreams. Could never be something. And all the memories he had were gone with him. He could never bear witness to the terrible things that had happened to me.

I decided to sit down again with my mother and see if I could learn anything more about Holly.

CHAPTER FIFTY-ONE

"Decent" Exposure

Mary Baker Eddy founded Christian Science in the late 19th century. Her book, published in 1875, called *Science and Health with Key to the Scriptures,* became the central text for the religion that would grow to include 270,000 members at its peak. Eddy described the religion as "a return to primitive Christianity and its lost element of healing."

But as to its legitimacy, you be the judge. Eddy, who grew up in New England and had chronic ill health most of her life, began searching for solutions, medical or otherwise, that would offcr relief. She had also become recently impoverished after the death of her husband and breadwinner and had lost custody of her son to foster care at age four.

At that point, Eddy not only needed something to believe in and help her through her suffering (and maybe even heal her), she also needed something that would generate a lot of cash. She began poring through writings from the metaphysical movement that had gained substantial traction in the late 1860s.

In 1866 Eddy fell on the ice in Lynn, Massachusetts and incurred injuries. A few days later, in front of a number of her students (she had cobbled together a small group of followers at that point), she was handed a Bible, and, shortly after reading a passage about one of Jesus's miracles, she rose up out of bed claiming she had been healed.

Most public accounts of Eddy and her character don't reveal nearly as much as that of a close family friend. One of her staunch followers wrote a book that unwittingly revealed a significant amount of misconduct and showed her to be a fairly manipulative and unscrupulous character.

In Bliss Knapp's *The Destiny of the Mother Church*, he goes about the process of trying to venerate her as the founder and leader of the movement. He describes how he and his family had spent their life supporting her, both physically and financially. Knapp's family were very wealthy and big contributors to the church and even housed many of Eddy's church-related meetings and special activities.

Yet while Knapp sets out to extol Eddy's virtues, he writes in great detail about a number of odd and irregular activities that the typical observer would recognize as quite manipulative. In the book he doesn't, himself, seem to realize the obvious conclusion of many of Eddy's actions. Yet as he happily and naively writes the account about his fearless leader, he actually shows her to be a master of trickery and mental manipulation.

For example, in his recounting of her story, people appear and disappear at various times as if orchestrated by Mrs. Eddy. And in two instances, he closely connects her to the sudden disappearance of large amounts of cash belonging to the church.

Knapp felt strongly about his book and the importance of telling Eddy's story. So much so that he requested in his will that the Mother Church publish it. In that request he willed a large sum of money, one hundred million dollars, in payment if the church agreed to publish it.

Decades later, in a moment of incredible irony, the now-impoverished church decided to publish his book as authorized church literature. They got the money and a short while later stopped publishing the book. After publication ceased, it became virtually impossible to find it. I secured a used copy in 2005 and read it cover to cover.

But despite a plethora of shenanigans, parlor tricks, and even fraud—not to mention the shameless borrowing of ideas from other movements like Transcendental Meditation and the works of Phineas Parkhurst Quimby—the religion grew and peaked around 1936 to over a quarter of a million followers, just in time for my mother to become fully indoctrinated at age six.

* * *

"He didn't really show his privates," my mom scoffed. "He had an engine part in his hand so that's probably what the older man saw."

"Wait," I interjected. "So what happened, exactly?"

I was back at 12865 La Barranca. My mom sat next to me at the kitchen table, drinking a glass of Chardonnay on a Friday evening. She recounted the bizarre episode in 1966 when my brother had been arrested in downtown Los Altos.

"Well, I had taken him downtown to Los Altos because he wanted to buy a part for his car," she continued. "I thought I would drop him off and do some shopping in the meantime. He was on the corner waiting for me to pick him up and an old man, I mean he was really old, saw him and tried to say Holly had exposed himself." She let out the last phrase with an exasperated huff of air. "And then he called the police!"

"The police? What? Did he get arrested?"

"No, when I got there the police were questioning him. They finally decided to hand him over to me and I took him home."

"And you don't think he did?" I asked with a hint of incredulity.

"Pshaw . . . no. The man was senile. He had no idea what he saw. Holly had a part for his car he had bought at the auto shop and that's what he was holding. I think this man—he was pretty old—I think he just couldn't see very well."

I was skeptical. My mother had been quick to deny the whole incident as a misunderstanding. And invalidate the man's observation in the process. Yet the event was large enough and impactful enough for her to recount it decades later. Did she herself even believe that it was a case of mistaken identity? Or was she trying to tell herself a narrative that would ease her heart and mind about the nature of her eldest son?

A few minutes went by. We talked about the yard and about my mom's walk around the neighborhood with the dog.

Then my mind went in a different direction. I had a vague recollection from years prior about my mother recounting when Holly came home from camp at age twelve. It was a Christian Science camp for teens called Verdant Vales up in the North Bay. My mother had mentioned something had shifted in the family around that time.

"So . . . you mentioned before you thought maybe something happened at camp?" I asked the question as delicately as I could.

"Well...yes. When Holly came back from Verdant Vales . . . well he just seemed different," she said.

"In what way?" I asked.

"Well, he was more depressed . . . and he seemed detached. And he started to be . . . Well . . . oppositional." She thought for a minute and added: "And also there was this new business of peeing on the front edge of our property facing the street. Sometimes cars drove past while he was doing it." She laughed nervously through the final sentence. A hint of embarrassment combined with bravado.

An eerie feeling came over me. My mother was recounting another behavior from my brother that seemed bizarre and possibly even antisocial. Yet she passed it off as insignificant.

"So . . . you think something happened?"

"Well . . . yes, I had a feeling that something happened at camp. Maybe something with a counselor or with one of the other boys," she said. She was loose now, after a glass and a half of Chardonnay. More lucid and forthcoming than usual.

"Wow . . . that must have been rough for you," I said.

"It . . . was . . . AWFUL!" she chimed. "We were Christian Scientists so we didn't use therapists or psychiatrists. All we had was Christian Science practitioners."

As I sat there in the kitchen watching my mom sip Chardonnay—something that would have been absolutely forbidden as practicing Christian Scientists—I imagined her there in 1966 with five kids, no doctors, and no psychiatric support, facing the prospect that her eldest son might have been damaged, using the only tool she had available: prayer.

My mother's account of Holly's behavior was startling. It felt invasive, like someone had taken over my brother even just during the recounting of his story. Like the events were being retold with him cast as a villain instead of who he was—my friendly, lovable brother.

"By the way," my mom said, shattering my dreamlike state, "the barn flooded again. Could you take a look at the retaining wall and see what's going on? The downstairs tenant said there is water pooling up and she's afraid it will flood her kitchen."

"Sure, I'll take a look in the morning."

CHAPTER FIFTY-TWO

The French Drain

When I arrived back at 12865 La Barranca the next morning, Saturday, I feared that the retaining wall had failed, that there might be mud slumped against the uphill side of the barn—the same barn I had helped build, around which my mother and I had built a retaining wall forty years earlier. The same wall my father had struggled to complete in the late nineties with his earth anchors and massive hardware.

I was relieved to see the wall was still intact. There was a slight lean in it near the middle section, but it still held the earth back from the structure. As I looked down, it became very clear what the problem was: surface water was building up between the wall and the barn due to the heavy rains we recently had.

I seemed to remember my dad burying some sort of drainage system underground next to the foundation, but it had been some forty years ago, and I didn't trust my memory. My dad was meticulous about everything he did. He was an engineer at Lockheed for thirty-five years, working on satellites and other space-bound craft. When he designed something, he made it to last. That is, if he ever finished the project.

I got out a shovel and pick and began digging. I couldn't imagine there hadn't been some drainage placed here. That would be highly out of character for him. In the faint recesses of my mind I seemed to remember something about a French drain.

After three or four shovels full of mud I hit something solid. It wasn't rock, I could tell that. It had the feel of something softer, tackier—plastic or a tar-like substance. I was working amongst two inches of standing water on top of a few inches of mud that had washed into the area. As I continued to dig around the object, the water began to drop, and I heard a faint gurgling sound.

I used to think when my father built these very rugged retaining walls, foundations, drains, and set posts, he tended to over-engineer things—a habit that spilled over from his engineering work at Lockheed. This perfectionist mentality, so it seemed, kept him from completing projects.

But as I uncovered his old work down under the mud, I began to think differently. I saw he had buried thick, large-diameter ABS drainpipe one foot down and it was perforated throughout its lower half. There was gravel above that with a layer of tar paper covering the gravel. The pipe was intact, and the gravel was still relatively pure, not clogged with mud.

As I located the various tributary pipes he had placed to drain water from behind the barn and underneath the deck, I discovered a whole network of arteries, carefully glued together. There were many surface drains connected to underground pipes. I followed it around the back of the barn and saw that it had been meticulously laid along the foundation, perfectly graded for water flow, around the south corner where it eventually terminated with a clean-out plug just under the surface of the dirt at the uphill end of the line.

I took out a hose and ran it into the clean-out. I was sure the pipe had clogged after forty years. But when I turned on the water, I realized it was unobstructed. Essentially two hundred feet of networked pipe my father had buried thirty-five to forty years ago was still working perfectly.

After a quick trip to the hardware store, I spliced three surface drains into his original drainage pipe, tested them, and the drainage problem was solved.

It used to really bother me when my dad would spend so long on things, how he seemed to overbuild things all the time. But when I uncovered the work he had done—and as my own childhood history with him began to emerge in my consciousness—I began to recall helping lay some of the pipe, gravel, and tar paper when I was about twelve years old, working shoulder to shoulder with him for hours.

I continued my work, tying drains into the lattice that he and I had built years ago, appreciating each glued joint and noticing how straight and solid the pipe was. I marveled at how it still hadn't clogged with mud forty years later.

My dad had passed away years before. But on that afternoon I felt I was receiving an ancient message: an artifact he had buried to act as a communication device, telling me something about him.

About us.

As I reflected on my recent discovery of my father's meticulously constructed drainage system, memories of our shared experiences flooded my mind. One recollection in particular surfaced from a half a century earlier with vivid clarity.

* * *

It was 1969. I was nine years old, sitting at the table after dinner. My father was on my right with his hands clasped behind his head, wearing a satisfied smile.

"Don't both of you have something else you need to

do," my mom barked from inside the kitchen in a tone that was impatient, bordering on mean.

"We'll just be a little longer . . ." he said, in a placating, yet confident tone.

He turned to me and continued his story. "Scientists used to think we were at the center of the universe. It's a common mistake by humans, thinking we're at the center."

He explained to me how the outer portions of the cosmos were receding away from us, and this prompted scientists to assume we were at the center of everything. But over time, they realized that the whole universe was expanding—that everything was moving away from everything else. This only created the illusion that we were at the center. Galaxies were moving away from each other and the further away a galaxy was from us, the faster it was moving. We didn't have to be at the center of the universe for this to make logical sense.

"The redshift shows us that."

"The red what?" I asked.

My dad explained how, when an object that's emitting a sound is moving relative to the listener, the waves get piled up on each other (or more spread out, depending on its direction). If a train is coming toward you, the sound is higher as it's approaching, but then as it passes you, the pitch drops.

Then, my dad being not only a consummate storyteller but also having a huge propensity for slapstick comedy, imitated the sound of a train as it passed by, using his best falsetto voice which lowered toward the end:

"Whhhaaaaaaaoooooouuuuuwww!"

We both laughed like it was the best thing ever.

"But this is true for light as well as for sound," he continued. "But instead of hearing the change, you see it. The light rays pile up or spread out and the color shifts from blue—like the train coming toward us—to red as the train moves away from us."

I stayed at the table, sometimes for hours, despite being aware that it irked my mom. These conversations were chock-full of scientific progress, innovation, and soul. They felt zen and safe to me. Nothing could be bad or sad when the secrets of the universe were being revealed. And through these conversations, I developed a love for cosmology and science in general, something that would later give me an immense sense of purpose, as I pursued a degree in physics and a career in technology.

But it went beyond that. Over the years, as I became an adult and eventually began to ponder the true nature of my childhood, I would view these sessions a little differently. It wasn't just that science interested me or that I could get lost in the imaginary world of thought experiments (Gedanken experiments, as Einstein described them). Nor was it that I was gifted in science, physics, and math—a characteristic that none of my siblings shared.

My habit of sitting at the dinner table with my dad, talking for countless hours—long after the dishes were cleared and everyone else had left the table—began to take on a different meaning. As I thought about myself as a child, I couldn't help but wonder why my father would spend that kind of time and energy teaching me fascinating laws about the universe if his goal was to objectify and defile me?

I began to ponder if, perhaps, my father was intent on occupying my energies, so that I wasn't engaged in less wholesome, even nefarious activities.

CHAPTER FIFTY-THREE

Cheeseweed

"I've uncovered another memory—this one feels pretty vivid."

I was back in Joy's office recounting an image that had come to mind during a recent meditative state. The previous evening, as I sat in front of the gas fireplace, another memory had soaked into my consciousness. In it, I was crouching in the green, tall leafy weeds in the backyard of our home at 12865 La Barranca.

"This one is a little confusing. It's crisp in my mind but it doesn't seem directly related to anything else."

"OK," Joy said in an encouraging tone. "It sounds like things are continuing to move. Tell me about it."

"Well, it's me, out in the backyard, crouching down in the tall, lush grass and cheeseweed—those plants with round scalloped leaves that branch out like a sphere and sometimes get huge. It's late winter or early spring, damp and lush. I'm very young . . . maybe seven or eight."

"Is there anything else that comes with that image?" she said.

"Like what?"

"Well, can you look around?" she responded.

Oh yeah . . . look around.

I remembered her comment from months earlier. In my mind's eye, I looked around me: tall, lush green weeds and grass, tall enough to obscure me completely as I crouched like a tiger, intent on not being seen. I looked to my left and saw the walnut tree on the slope heading toward the neighbor's house up on the hill. Then I looked ninety degrees to the right to see the back of our house and the sliding glass door that led into the family room, the curtains drawn.

"All I see is the back of the house," I said.

"Try going backward in time," she said.

What? Backward in time?

What a strange suggestion this seemed—a completely foreign idea. In real life, traveling backward in time was impossible. But maybe in the recesses of my mind there was more content to draw from.

I began to rewind the mental video.

"Well, if I go backwards, I'm moving around to the right side of the house . . . I don't really see anything."

"Keep going. Try to stay in the scene. . . . Don't try to judge or edit what you're seeing," she responded in a firm yet gentle tone.

"I'm moving through the side yard, past Holly's window . . ." I said cautiously.

I let the scene surround me on all sides.

"There's a door . . . the one that goes into the side of the garage . . ."

I approached the door. It was open.

"I'm going through the door into the garage."

"Good. Keep going . . ." Joy coached.

"I'm walking through the garage . . . it's dark. I'm worried I might trip over something."

"Take your time," she said. "Don't rush."

"Walking past the front of the car. . . . OK, I'm at the steps that go from the garage into the laundry room," I continued. At the top of the steps, I faced the interior of the laundry room with its blinding bright light. At that moment, a daunting feeling came over me, the familiar vise clamping my chest.

"I'm afraid," I confessed, sensing my own vulnerability.

"It's OK . . . I'm here with you," she guided. "There's nothing to be afraid of. You're in a safe place."

I tried to regroup. To see the steps again. They began to materialize out of the darkness. A shaft of light came down the steps. The door from the house into the garage was open and light emanated from the laundry room.

"I'm going up the steps . . . into the laundry room," I continued.

The dryer and washer were on my left. Just beyond that, I saw a Formica counter covered with bottles of detergent, spot remover, rags. I continued walking slowly.

"OK, I'm leaving the laundry room. Just ahead of me is the family room door. To my right is the hallway to the kitchen. I'm turning left . . ."

As I slowly rotated left, I saw a bedroom door two feet away.

"It's his bedroom. I'm . . . going into Holly's room . . ."

I slowly took one step forward. Then another. I saw the door crack open just ahead of me. I craned my neck to try to see what was inside. I pushed the door open slowly . . . Slowly . . . As the door opened wider I peered in. Then—

The vision disappeared.

Bewildered and surprised, I began to open my eyes. The stark brightness of the dimly lit space hit me. As my eyes adjusted, I looked around. Chair, window, desk, sofa. I was back in Joy's office.

CHAPTER FIFTY-FOUR

Rubber Vomit

"He put *what* on his drum set?" I asked.

"Rubber vomit."

I wanted to find out more about Holly. There were many clues pointing toward my older brother being involved in some unsavory activities, though I wasn't sure exactly what. I reached out to my third sister, Sally, to see if she recalled any negative or inappropriate encounters with him. She began to recount a story that I didn't expect.

"So . . . why did he put that on his drum?" I asked curiously.

"He wanted to lure me into his room," she said in a matter-of-fact tone.

She was talking about Holly and the room in the far north end of the house, next to the laundry room. The same room I had envisioned myself walking toward while in Joy's office the previous week. Sally's tone was steady and sure. She was lucid and focused, even uncharacteristically calm. It was as if she had suddenly transformed from her chaotic, ever-frantic self into the adult that she could be.

"What happened when you went into his room?"

"He closed the door," she said. "Then he told me to get up onto the bed—you know that small twin built-in bed that was wedged between the wall and the bookcase?" Her voice continued in its steady tone revealing no emotion.

"Yeah, I remember the built-in."

"Then he turned off the light," she continued.

A daunting feeling gripped my chest. My throat pinched a little, impeding my ability to breathe. I tried to collect myself. I had to hear her story, to stay in the moment.

"Were you afraid?" I asked her.

"Yeah, well kind of," she responded, "but also I was trying to just figure out what he wanted."

"How old were you?" I asked incredulously.

"About eight."

I calculated that would have made me about six years old. Yet another independent data point leading to the same time frame, and now the same person.

"Then he told me to take my clothes off." As she spoke, I felt my chest tighten and my shoulders tense up. I twitched my right elbow involuntarily.

"This sounds absolutely terrible," I said after shaking off my momentary paralysis. I was both eager to know the rest of the story and, at the same time, unwilling to hear it based on the awful feeling of trepidation for what might come next. Part of me wanted to go somewhere and hide.

"So . . . what happened?" I forced myself to say.

"Well he was rubbing me with something long and hard. . . . I thought it was one of his fingers or his thumb, but I didn't know exactly what it was."

I couldn't discern which was more alarming, the content of the story she was recounting to me, or the fact that her voice continued in its steady, unwavering, unemotional tone. She didn't seem horrified or even afraid. Yet to me this felt very, very bad. I sensed a triggering in my own soul as she recounted the story. Where would it end? Was it going to transpire as expected, her innocence lost?

"Where was he rubbing you?"

"In my groin," she said, again in a very unfazed tone.

It was almost too much for me to bear. I wanted to jump in and ask where it was going, to cut the suspense. Yet I didn't want to hear what was coming next. I knew the story was important and that I needed to hear it. But I also didn't want to be taken to the place she was going.

"Did he . . ." I began, trying to muster some sort of response while the words froze in my throat.

"He told me to lay there," she continued, "and not to move, while did whatever he was doing."

"Weren't you . . . afraid?" I asked, shocked by the dark, sinister nature of her story, which sharply contrasted with her calm demeanor.

"Well, I didn't know what it was. I remember asking him at one point if it was his finger or . . ."

"Jeez . . . this sounds . . . awful," I said, trying to imagine what must have been going through her heart while this very imposing fourteen-year-old boy did these things to her. It seemed to me the next part of the story would be unbearable, sending me off the deep end. I didn't know how to ask what happened next. I wasn't sure I could even cope with what happened next.

"Then, I got scared, and got up and ran out of the room," she confessed, breaking the silence with the final revelation.

Instinctively I exhaled a sigh of relief, followed by a flood of self-doubt and feelings of inadequacy.

"Wait . . . you just ran out? He didn't try to stop you?"

"I was nervous, and something didn't feel right," she said. "So I got up and ran out. He didn't stop me. Maybe he was just afraid I would say something."

It seemed like an almost incongruous transition. Going from a victim under his control to suddenly fleeing the scene. How had she been able to do that? This seemed to me to constitute a monumental act, something incredibly strong and resolute. Somehow, Sally was able to tap into, and trust, her flight reflex.

What makes some victims run and others stay? We're all human. We have similar instincts for survival, feeding, and reproduction, to protect ourselves from danger. Yet the same circumstances that one person might walk away from might cause another to freeze, leading to the destruction of their childhood, their soul.

What Sally had just recounted was the first tangible account of sexual abuse in the family, and by a person I was beginning to suspect of abusing me. After all these years and countless conversations—ones that had revealed nothing about my family's true nature—Sally had revealed a narrative that was chilling and incriminating. Yet I had never heard anything about this before. Had I just not listened? Or had she been too embarrassed to recount the story up to now, even to anyone else in the family?

Things were swirling around, moving inward toward the eye of the hurricane. First, still images adjacent to our 1966 family reunion. Then Holly's deviant friends. Following that, my vision of being in or near his room. Then dreams about riding on the back of his motorcycle.

And finally, Holly and my sister, right there, under the same roof.

CHAPTER FIFTY-FIVE

Alpha and Omega

The next day, as I sat at my desk trying to engage in my various marketing activities, my sister's recounting about being sexually abused continued to reverberate through my soul. I didn't know quite what to do with it and how much it had to do with me. But I had to keep exploring. As the workday began to wind down, I decided to drive to the old neighborhood and go for a run. Part of me wanted to explore my old haunt, yet another part of me just wanted to get outside and release some stress.

I wasn't in the mood to visit my mother on this particular day, so I parked about a mile away from 12865 La Barranca and headed up Elena Road under the 280 freeway overpass. At the hairpin turn, I forked off to the right, up the dirt path through the thick vegetation. Then eventually I turned left on Taaffe Road to connect with the Packard Trail (the same name as the powerhouse Silicon Valley company, Hewlett-Packard).

Just as I approached the trailhead, I saw off to the right ahead of me, a lone shack standing on the top of the hill. Something in my lizard brain resonated with that shack, telling me two things. First, *danger! It's off-limits.* Second, *I think I'll go there.*

I walked up the hill to the shack and peered in. In the back of my mind, I had a vague recollection that Holly had lived here for a period of time after he had been kicked out of our home on La Barranca Road. This shack lay about half a mile from our home as the crow flies. It was a bit circuitous to get to by road from 12865 La Barranca. But I recalled there was a path that ran between our street and Elena. A shortcut.

As I looked into the shack the layout resonated with something far, far back in my brain. In my mind's eye I saw the room from fifty years earlier matching, like an old tattered, worn-out glove matches the form of a hand, the image in my consciousness. The orientation of the wall where the bed used to be, and the bathroom door just to its right. And the tiny kitchen around the corner from that.

As I slowly turned from the view of the room and looked out over the landscape, I saw the grassy hill drop off down a steep embankment, out of sight to the south. Then, as the terrain rebounded about a quarter mile beyond, I saw a hill rise up in the distance about two hundred feet below my current elevation, densely populated with oak trees, creating a canopy.

That same image I'd had during my EMDR sessions: the canopy of oak trees.

Was this a different vivid image of oak trees? Did the image come from this shack instead of Tulsa Airport? And if so, did that mean that my very vivid memory was unreliable, as it had transferred from one instance to another many years later?

Which was the true source of the image? It had to be one or the other.

But why?

What if, instead of the image coming from just one of those sources, it was somehow both? What would that mean? Holly had lived there starting around age eighteen, at the end of 1970. Any memories I had about this shack had to happen after that time. So perhaps 1971, when I was eleven. I had flown into Tulsa Airport in 1966 on the way to the family reunion. This constituted a five-year period between these two pivotal moments. The sense of foreboding—of having endured trauma for five years— vibrated through my very core. These years marked the beginning and the end of my suffering, the Alpha and the Omega.

CHAPTER FIFTY-SIX

Bookends

"It seems like parts of my memory have been completely erased." I sat across from Jared at Pizza My Heart in Palo Alto. The noon rush filtered in as we sat in a booth on the south side of the restaurant, eagerly soaking up the sun streaming through the window.

"I-n-t-e-r-e-s-t-i-n-g," Jared said, very slowly, as if carefully observing a big clue. "So . . . what's an example, what's a memory, that seems inconsistent?"

"Well, for example, I have memories of Bob in those days, but not Chase or Holly. I have memories of riding my bike, but not Holly's motorcycle. Yet I just ran across a picture of me sitting on the back of Holly's motorcycle when I'm, like, nine years old. I would have remembered that."

"Jeez . . . that's bizarre. It's like your mind shut some things out but it didn't erase all of it. Like . . . there's a leftover residue."

"Totally. It's kind of like . . ." I paused, trying to put together the metaphor, "as if I went to the grocery store and something traumatic happened . . . and my mind just wiped out the whole memory. But then later at home, I see bags of groceries on the counter, wondering where they came from. I mean it's obvious—everyone knows where groceries come from. Yet my subconscious . . . it tried to erase the bad memories, but didn't do a thorough job."

"Tha-a-a-a-t-s . . . s-o-o-o . . . w-e-i-r-d!" Jared exclaimed with genuine surprise.

"It's like my subconscious was acting like a child," I continued my narrative, "trying to fix something in a clumsy way. Covering up muddy footprints with a pile of toys. Even the most unobservant parent could figure it out. The story looks like Swiss cheese. Some memories are there. Others are gone. For example, I had memories of school but not home."

"Nice try, subconscious! You can do better than that," he said, chuckling like a skeptical parent unraveling a child's fib.

"And sometimes I don't have any memory of an event that I actually know happened. I have memories of the before and after. Kind of like . . . bookends." I paused for a moment, searching. "And then . . . there is that weird thing that happened with the swim team."

"I remember you mentioning being a really good swimmer as a kid," Jared said, embracing the tonal shift.

"It's true," I said. "I was a gifted swimmer in the six-and-under category. I won a lot of swim meets. I've got a bunch of blue ribbons sitting in a box somewhere. I could race a full lap without taking a breath as a six-year-old."

"So . . . what happened?" Jared asked as his curiosity heightened.

"Well, in the summer of . . . let's see . . . 1967, I graduated to the next age category: seven-to-eight year olds. But something happened."

Jared leaned in. His eyes grew big, his brows raised in anticipation. "What happened?"

"Well . . . my aerobic capability plummeted," I

responded. "I could barely complete a lap without gasping for air. Some of the time I had to dog-paddle part of the lap."

"What? That's . . . baffling! What do you think was going on there?" he asked, his tone urgent.

"Something changed around seven years old. I was cutting through the water like a knife at age six. But by age seven I was slogging across the pool, gasping for air. I couldn't breathe. I ended up dropping out of swimming."

Jared's expression shifted. His eyebrows, once raised in shock, softened and lowered. The edges of his mouth dipped slightly, quivering with genuine concern.

"Oh man," he said softly. "I'm really sorry to hear that. That sounds absolutely horrible. Even soul crushing. It's like the best part of your childhood—it was just taken from you."

There was a long silence as I stared at the wall over Jared's right shoulder. My chest felt empty as if part of my heart had been singed around the edges and now empty gaps filled the space that it once occupied. Jared wanted to help, to somehow take away my pain, or at least share it. I knew he could feel what I felt. It was his superpower.

"I've been thinking about me as a sexualized toddler," I began after gathering my thoughts. "The bloody sheets. The daunting images before and after the reunion. Holly's behavior around that time. The fact that I roomed with him at the reunion, yet I have no memory of interacting with him. My five years of grayscale images as I spent long hours in the elementary-school classroom dissociating. Being a great swimmer, then barely being able to swim a lap. And . . . the trees. I saw them on the way to the reunion in 1966 and then again at the shack in 1971. Those were incredibly vivid. The stuff in between—the stuff that went on for five years—that was the part that was hard to figure out."

Jared's expression shifted again. His large inquisitive

eyes transitioned to something softer. His brows lowered, the lines on his forehead disappearing, as a faint smile formed on his lips.

"You remembered."

CHAPTER FIFTY-SEVEN

The River Jordan

Over the next few minutes, I recounted the scene that had only recently come into focus to Jared as he stared wide-eyed at me. A composite of still images, memories, flashbacks, supplemented with research. I triangulated yet went beyond the margins, filling in the middle of the trauma itself.

It was the summer of 1966, just after my sixth birthday. We were at the family reunion at Table Rock Lake, Arkansas.

I walked slowly down into the pool, one step at a time. Right . . . left . . . right . . . sinking lower into the water with each step. My right shoulder twitched in a shrug-like motion combined with an elbow protrusion. Once on the third step—chest deep in the water—I pushed off and glided with only my head above the surface.

At 3'6" I was not tall enough to stand up in the pool, even in the shallow end. I glided slowly into the deep end as I'd done many times at the neighborhood pool. But this time I looked detached, numb. My face was blank — empty, as if in a trance.

As I swam, the water flowed across my body, smoothly and gently, cleaning and soothing. Purifying. I had no idea what had led up to this point. It was as if I had been suddenly transported here to this pool at this exact moment, coming from nowhere and going to nowhere. All I knew was that at least at this moment, in this environment, I was in a safe —

"OH MY GOD, WHAT ARE YOU DOING? GET OUT OF THERE!" screamed a woman.

The voice shocked me back to reality. I looked over to see my Aunt Robena aghast, looking simultaneously angry and scared.

"You can't swim by yourself like that! You're just a child!"

I obediently swam back to the corner and climbed up out of the pool.

"Come with me," she said. The two of us walked down the stairs to the ground level and around the corner toward room 128 where my parents were staying.

Look around! What's going on around the scene? There's more in your mind than you consciously realize.

Zooming out and up from Aunt Robena and me, I saw a teenager exit a room around the corner, near the parking alley, carrying a large white bundle that looked like a sheet bunched up under his arm. I zoomed in to see an ill-kept teenager with reddish-brown, somewhat long hair and a five-day scraggly shadow of a beard. His expression was one of anger and fear yet also resolve.

The bunched-up sheet was soaked with blood, as if in

the aftermath of a murder.

The teenager walked up to the large dumpster at the edge of the parking alley, opened the lid and dumped the bundle into the garbage. As he turned around and walked back toward the room, I saw his face clearly for the first time.

It was my brother, Hollis.

Zooming out and up again revealed Aunt Robena and me arriving at my parents' room. "I want you to know I found him swimming all by himself in the pool," she said in a very agitated tone. "He shouldn't have been up there. He's really just a child . . ."

Her voice faded as the resort came slowly into view with a dock, boat slips, and a shoreline adjacent to crystal-blue water. Zooming further out and panning to the right, I saw the clear blue water start to dominate the scene, dwarfing the compound.

CHAPTER FIFTY-EIGHT

Five Fucking Years

Over the course of the next few weeks, I began to piece together more of the trauma. I realized that the memory from the family reunion in Arkansas wasn't the totality of the abuse. Rather, it was just the beginning of it. The abuse continued over the next five years and the view I saw of the canopy of trees from the shack on Taaffe Road was near the end of it. And that the entire period was traumatic enough for me to repress it for the next fifty-five years.

The abuse changed me forever. It affected how I viewed power, men, and authority. And how I viewed myself: as dirty, wounded, unworthy. It made me doubt my own instincts and gut feel. It took away my belief in myself as a valuable human being. It caused me to dismiss my own thoughts and capabilities. A behavior that, in turn, would be mocked by my family and friends, and eventually some of my business colleagues.

And it changed how I viewed women, particularly those who helped enable men to wield raw power over other people, with no regard to the damage they inflicted.

One of those women was my mother.

* * *

I dropped by 12865 La Barranca to have the conversation. We made small talk as we cooked dinner together. My mother sipped on her second glass of Chardonnay while I drank ice water, searching my mind for an appropriate way to begin. My mother was relaxed and loose and I felt an opportunity had arisen. But instead of hitting the topic of abuse head-on, I decided to try a more indirect approach.

"You mentioned that Hollis and I roomed together at the reunion," I began in a calm, disarming tone.

"Well . . . I think so," she replied in a tone blending cautiousness with an air of casual indifference.

"I was just curious," I continued casually, "if you noticed he and I spending time together here at home." I purposely avoided any mention of abuse or bad behavior so as to keep her mind away from danger and avoid her shutting down.

She paused for a moment while she gazed out the window into the front garden, her eyes focussed softly in a peaceful moment of reminiscence. "Well," she began, her eyes drifting gently as she scanned her memory, "I do recall Nammie saying something."

My attention sharpened. Nammie was my grandmother, my mother's mother. She was a salt-of-the earth woman with a good soul and a clear sense of propriety. Whatever Nammie thought, well, in my opinion, that was worth its weight in gold.

"Nammie?" I asked, disguising my surprise. "What did she say?"

"Well, I remember her saying at one point that she was worried about you spending so much time behind closed doors with Holly."

The blood drained from my face. I stared over at her as her eyes gazed off in the distance. A faint quizzical expression slowly faded from her face.

"Would you like another glass?" she said, standing up abruptly, walking toward the refrigerator.

"Wait . . . Nammie said that?" I persisted. "I thought you said Hollis and I hadn't spent any time together?" At this point my tone shifted to genuine surprise. "Did you say Nammie was concerned that I was in Hollis' room too much behind closed doors?"

"I don't know," she said as she returned to the table, bottle in hand. Her voice had a faint warble in it, falling somewhere between an embarrassed sigh and an almost imperceptible chuckle. Then, suddenly, she pivoted.

"By the way, Phil, I noticed you are calling him Hollis now . . . when did that change? You always called him . . ." Just then, my mother's demeanor shifted. From inquisitive and matter-of-fact to slightly more defensive. "Oh, Phil . . . I keep hoping you'll move past all of this and just let it go," she said.

"Let . . . what go?" I protested.

"Well . . . I don't know exactly but you keep mentioning that you think something happened when you were younger. Whatever it is, it just seems like it's making you feel bad. I just don't want to see you get hurt."

"Well, if you don't want me to feel bad," I said after building up my resolve, "what I really need . . . is validation. Someone in the family to witness what happened to me."

"A witness for wha . . .?" my mother paused, staring across the kitchen table toward a blank wall. Her expression turned yet again, from combative to something else. It was as if she had stumbled upon a landmine and if she continued forward, it would kill her; yet a very small part of her wanted to know the exact nature of the object.

As she sat there, frozen, it occurred to me that now was time to break the news. No more waiting or questioning,

No more soft-pedaling. It was now or never.

"I just realized," I began soberly, "that Hollis sexually abused me."

"What . . .? Oh . . . no," she said. Her eyes grew wide—despite being somewhat glassy from the wine. "What makes you think that?"

"I realized it over the years. The dissociation starting in first grade, the reunion, some flashbacks . . . memories that I uncovered through therapy. All of the research I've done."

She continued to look at me with wide eyes, like she'd seen a ghost. I had thought about this moment, about how she would react. Even romanticized that once I broke the alibi, that she would just admit she'd witnessed it and corroborate my story. But there was none of that. Just shock . . . almost horror. As if the recounting of such cruel events—not necessarily the events themselves—had shattered her benign memory and the new, vivid truth was unbearable.

It was a very uncomfortable moment for me. Yet, I had to tell her the whole story, even though it might destroy her.

"And it went on for five years, from 1966 to 1971," I finally said.

"FIVE YEARS?" she gasped. "Oh my gosh . . ." Her face was white with shock. Her speech halted as her voice trailed off.

"Yes," I continued, filling in the silence with facts, thinking it might jog her memory or perhaps my recounting of the overwhelming evidence might make her understand. Or at least if I filled in the gaps, it would make more sense to her, be less shocking. "I know that mostly from how my memories are in dark gray from first to fifth grade and the length of time I dissociated in school. And the vivid, daunting images that are on either side of the abuse," I continued, unable to stop. "And my vivid memories of just before the reunion, and then at the shack. It's like my mind just redacted the whole time period. But then . . . the memories started to surface," I said as she stared at me in shock.

"Oh, Phil . . . Oh . . . no. Oh…that just makes me sick. For five years?" she repeated. Then as the reality sank in, her shock transitioned to something else.

"Oh, Phil," she lamented."I'm sorry . . ."

She was silent for a moment. I didn't interject a word or even a sound. I needed to hear her thoughts, whatever they would be. I couldn't unburden her or make her feel better, even though I wanted to. Then, moments later, her emotional journey came to a culmination.

"I guess I was a terrible mother," she finally said, her shock having transitioned to sadness, then finally to defeat, hopelessness.

She had run the full course of emotions yet did it without recounting so much as a single firsthand memory of abuse. The closest thing was a secondhand event that her mother had seen and relayed to her. Perhaps that was safe enough, being two parties removed. But anything closer, more direct than that, was forbidden. And I knew at that point that she would never act as a witness to my anguish.

"No . . . you weren't a terrible mother," I said finally in a consoling tone. "You did the best you could. You had no resources to help you. No doctors, no therapists, psychiatrists. . . . I don't blame you." I heard myself say these words and suddenly realized I was, again, taking ownership for someone else's emotion and dismissing my own experience, as though I was the parent and peacekeeper, keeping others safe.

It would be a trivialization to say that I was disappointed. It felt to me that I had not been valuable enough to be protected. As though in our family environment, back in the sixties, what I needed wasn't important—at least not as much as what others needed.

As though at my very core, I wasn't worthy of physical security and emotional safety.

I left her house feeling demoralized and defeated. I had braved the circumstances and confronted my mother with what I knew. I should have felt proud at that moment. But I didn't. All I felt was guilt, disappointment, and emptiness. Like I had taken an otherwise safe, happy childhood and destroyed it.

I needed to talk through the feelings I had about my mother. I'd gotten as far as I could with Joy. I knew I couldn't let these negative feelings about my mother just fester. It would destroy me. I reached out to someone I had connected with a month earlier at an AA meeting.

CHAPTER FIFTY-NINE

Matriarch

"She knew and let it continue. Why would she have allowed it to happen?" I said in a voice drowning in resentment.

My new sponsor stared back at me over the video call. Kevin had gone dark and I'd bumped into Jamie at the Friday night local AA meeting. He was a dark-haired, bearded man with a Jesus-like appearance. His hair was often up in a man-bun, but when he let it down it turned into shoulder-length rock-star hair. He always seemed kind of out of the box—almost like a caricature of a bohemian California surfer dude. Yet he had a profound way of nailing a moment, particularly when I least expected it.

"Maybe she was in denial," Jamie said. "Or maybe she was just trying to keep the family together. Wasn't Hollis her oldest son?"

"Yeah, but that means she chose him over me," I objected. "Why would she care more about him than me. . . . How could a mother do that?"

"Man . . . I don't think she chose him over you," Jamie

said. "From what you've told me she was just trying to hang on in a pretty messed-up family situation."

I stared at him, trying to take it all in, yet feeling resentment soak through my entire body. He must have sensed the disturbance.

"Phil, I want you to write up this resentment about your mom for next week."

* * *

The following Saturday morning we got back on a video call. I read the journal entry I had written as part of my Fourth Step: Making A Searching and Fearless Moral Inventory.

She knew and she let it continue. She gave Hollis the power as the dominant male in the family. He sexually abused me. He abused Sally as well. He may also have abused Pam—although I doubt she saw it that way, even if it did happen. There were women in my childhood years that sexualized me as well. It could have been Pam, Rachael, Anne. There was flirty, seductive behavior by the females around Chase and Hollis. My mother denied it, which helped enable all of it.

"OK, good. Now I want you to look at your part," he said.

"What?" This was confusing to me. It made me think I had done something to cause it. "So are you asking if I somehow helped cause it?"

"No, man," he said emphatically. "It has to do with your way of thinking about it that basically made it worse. It's how you've thought about it and held it over the years. How that might perpetuate it and cause you to feel disturbed. Think about what made it stick in your brain as a long-term resentment. Like, maybe there's something you're hanging onto?"

What was keeping me from moving through it? After the meeting I pulled out my notebook and wrote a few paragraphs. The words flowed easily as I thought back on the first few decades of my life.

The following week I read them to Jamie:

I was frightened. I was dishonest with myself thinking, at first, that it didn't happen at all. After that, once I realized what had happened, I felt like I had caused it and for that I felt dirty to my core.

I was afraid of who I was and that I was a bad, dirty person. I could not see the reality of what was going on. Rather than accept my mother as flawed and scared— even petrified that her eldest son was a deviant—I made her out to be a scheming and nefarious woman.

My part was viewing her as I wanted her to be, all knowing and all good, rather than who she really was: a scared, isolated, woman in denial who had no resources to cope with the reality of Hollis's condition, and who chose—whether or not consciously—to deny what was happening. I didn't accept her weakness as real. As a result, I chose to see her as nefarious and evil, as having hurt me on purpose. This allowed me to sit in the mindset of a victim and bear all the consequences—good or bad— of thinking that way.

After a long pause, Jamie looked up at me across the video conference. "Nice job, Phil. I think you definitely get it."

CHAPTER SIXTY

Athena

After hundreds of AA meetings I decided that I needed another fellowship to help me process what happened. Both therapy and AA had been useful for me, but I didn't feel the sense of connection that I had found my people yet. I needed a different kind of program—something that was more focussed, more to the point. I looked online and found an organization called Alliance of Resilience for Incest Survivors, or ARIS. The name was catchy and bold, especially for a survivors' group related to childhood sexual abuse. And I liked that it referenced the Greek god of war—kind of empowering, to say the least.

"I was abused by an older man after I started babysitting his kids. . . . I was eleven," she said.

Paula was the leader of the Wednesday night meeting that originated in Seattle. It had since become hybrid and was accessible to people around the world. Paula's coarse, straight brown hair and naturally rugged appearance gave her a weathered beauty. Her demeanor was parental and authoritative. She could maintain control, yet she was compassionate and kind at the same time. She would never, ever do harm.

She continued the story of how her perp had groomed her, initially striking up a friendship, almost as if he were a father figure. But then it turned sexual. She explained how her perpetrator had prepared her starting at age eleven. Around that time, she asked another boy who was eighteen to have sex with her.

"I have this other personality called Athena who gets triggered," she continued. "She is sexually overt and takes over these conversations when I need her. Athena is my alter ego. She comes out when I'm in a vulnerable place and drives the conversation toward being sexual."

This was confusing to me: a protector figure who would ramp up the sexual energy and act flirtatious. The story sat with me like a stomachache after a heavy meal and lingered for days. As I pondered it, I recalled the words of my therapist: Some people react to sexual trauma by being chaste and eliminating sex completely; others do the opposite by becoming very promiscuous.

I reflected on my own experience: my sexual dysfunction during my first encounter in high school, which traumatized me emotionally. Shortly thereafter, I chose to go to a Christian Science college that embodied a puritan view: no sex before marriage. I thought at the time that I made this choice in order to focus on my studies, which, technically, it allowed me to do. But the truth was more complicated. Ultimately, that choice shielded me from the immense amount of fear which—at that particular time in my life—accompanied sex. I was essentially avoiding intimacy. That four-year period in college comprised my chaste phase.

I finally lost my virginity to a woman during graduate school in Los Angeles. She was beautiful and shy and from a very wealthy San Marino family. Shortly after getting involved with her, however, I realized she wasn't right for me. But I was emotionally entangled, she having been my first. It was two years before I eventually extricated myself from that relationship.

After moving back to the Bay Area, I started dating again. It was chaotic and awkward. I was greatly conflicted. On one hand I wanted to be a Don Juan character and experience the love of many different women—the promiscuous version of me. On the other hand, it was traumatic every time I found myself in a new sexual situation. That part of me wanted to avoid the trauma—the chaste version of me. I stumbled into a few medium-term relationships (months to years). I became a serial monogamist.

Around this same time, though, I had unexpected reactions to male power and aggression. Whenever I was around men with power and authority who exhibited machismo, I would have what I can only describe as an antithetical reaction: homosexual sensations. As evidenced by my reaction to my aggressive male colleagues in Stowe, Vermont, as well as the bizarre evening at my neighbor Tony's house before my colonoscopy.

Then Hollis died. My primary relationship—my marriage—failed. I began dating and experienced some dysfunction again. Following that I entered my promiscuous phase in earnest. Almost like I had something to prove, like I was compensating.

After getting sober, I was celibate again for eighteen months. It was comfortable, if not exciting and full. Then I met Kathy, when I experienced sexual dysfunction yet again.

Then I entered a phase of sustained stability. In short, my own experience was an amalgamation of "all of the above"—an eerie Frankenstein version of my therapist's description. I had years of being chaste, months of promiscuity, and moments of homosexual tendencies dotting that chaotic landscape.

These two reactions, I realized, were two sides to the same coin. Chastity and promiscuity were both ways for a sexually traumatized person to cope. Paula's alter ego, Athena, was the promiscuous one. She was the protector.

Yet it was still an attempt by a child's brain to deal with a dangerous, objectified relationship and secure some semblance of control.

And I could also see the confusion that those around the issue would have. Confusion that perpetrators who wanted to change the narrative would exploit.

She wanted it, they would say.

No. She didn't want it. She was a child.

She was in survival mode. Her brain was trying to preserve her existence, and this was one of two ways to do it. It didn't mean she wanted it. A child can't even make that decision. And perpetrators know this even though they try hard to spin things. It simply meant that she was trying to survive. Her lizard brain was doing whatever it could to try to adapt and persist in a caustic, dangerous environment.

"Then, after he groomed me," she continued, "he raped me, twice. I was eleven. He was thirty-two."

As I pondered Paula's story, her final words reverberated in my mind. They served as both a testament to her resilience in the face of unspeakable trauma and a stark reminder of the depths of human cruelty. Her narrative left an indelible mark on me.

However, as I settled into my thoughts, my focus returned to my own trauma and the lingering void that remained. The absence of anyone to bear witness to my pain weighed heavily on me. Simply knowing what had happened didn't feel like enough. I needed someone else—someone who had been there—to validate and acknowledge my experience.

My entire family, including my mother, had denied my abuse. And with Bob gone, the only person I could think of who might have the capacity and the willingness to acknowledge my pain was Rachael.

CHAPTER SIXTY-ONE

Friedman Bails

"When my dad said 'Bye, I'm getting a divorce' we were all like 'What the fuck?'" Rachael recounted the episode when her dad left the family for another woman, her voice laced with bitterness. Little did I know then, it was the last time I would ever see or hear from her. Despite many subsequent calls and texts, I would get no response.

"One Thanksgiving he just didn't show up," she continued, her tone resigned yet colored with lingering hurt.

"Wait . . . what?" I interjected in disbelief. "He just didn't show up?"

"Yeah, we got a call from his answering service one day. They said he won't be home for a while."

"Jeez! From his answering service? That's how he broke the news?" I exclaimed, my shock mirroring Rachael's expression.

"Oh yeah, we knew what was going on. He had a young girl on the side. . . . He was a prick!" she spat out bitterly.

"Holy shit! That's absolutely terrible," I said, grasping for words of consolation.

"You have no idea," she murmured.

Then, my thoughts shifted to the money their dad had. Bob had mentioned he had been worth millions at one point. "So he was wealthy, right?" I asked, trying to steer the conversation in a different direction.

"Oh yeah, he had a shitload of money. He took care of his employees. Everything was a business. If you took care of him, he took care of you. If you worked for him for ten years, he'd buy you a car. Yeah . . . he took care of his employees. Us . . . no, he didn't give us shit!" Rachael replied, her words still saturated with resentment.

"Why would he do that?" I asked, my voice incredulous.

"Because he could." She said this last phrase in a different voice. Instead of bitterness, her tone had shifted over toward acceptance, finality. "He was . . . horrible; he was a mean, mean man."

There was a silence while it all sank in: the injustice. The selfishness her father had shown. The abandonment. Yet at the same time, perhaps Mr. Friedman had felt something else: fear. Perhaps even denial—not wanting to face what his family had become.

Gradually, my thoughts shifted toward Hollis and the parallels between our families." Well, I think when Hollis got into alcohol and drugs," I ventured, "things went south. My family started to break apart too. We were staunch Christian Scientists."

"Oh yeah . . . I remember," she quickly confirmed.

"I remember Hollis hanging out with Chase and—"

"Oh Chase . . . ohhhhh . . . he was the worst influence," she interrupted suddenly. Rachael's bluntness caught me off guard. This was something I didn't expect her to admit. She had soft-pedaled much of the neighborhood history up to that point, especially the deviant activities.

Protecting herself and the other older teenagers each step of the way.

"The worst influence? What do you mean?" I asked, keeping my voice as steady as possible, trying desperately to act as a tether for her rapid tonal shifts.

"Chase never got along with anybody," Rachael responded, her tone matter-of-fact. "He and my dad fought constantly. I remember one evening Chase got home late and my dad asked where he'd been. Chase said 'None of your business,' and my dad slammed him up against his bedroom wall—broke his ribs."

"Oh my God!" I reacted with shock combined with sympathy. "That sounds incredibly traumatic."

"It was," Rachael continued, her tone more animated, yet still detached. "Chase was born with a demon in him. Everything was hateful . . . even to this day. He was always unhappy. The way he treated people—it was awful."

She paused, just for an instant. I glanced over at her to see her thinking, contemplating for a brief moment. Her cadence shifted, just enough to be noticeable. Then, she continued her story but in a decidedly more solemn tone.

"Chase was the one that liked to go down to the pipe, where the creek was," she continued. "He and the Welty boys would get high. They were all down there sniffing glue and smoking and drinking—they drank so much—the whiskey . . . oh my God!"

Her description of the elder kids in the neighborhood was starting to fall in line with the dreams and memories I had from the sixties. During one of the EMDR sessions, I experienced the sounds of water trickling superimposed with teenagers laughing mockingly. While her recollections were not ostensibly about abuse, they did have the dystopian tone that matched my own memories. The substance abuse that might have led to other types of abusive behavior.

But it wasn't enough. I needed to cut to the chase, to ask the big question. I had strategized ahead of time: what is the best way to broach the subject of sexual abuse? Using those very words wouldn't work as they were loaded. Yet, to others, they were vague. People often dismissed the concept of sexual abuse as fantasy—the mental fabrication of psychotic people steeped in victimization. And some would just avoid the words altogether. Sexual abuse was bad; they were not bad people; ergo, they did not engage in sexual abuse. I had mentally prepared for weeks how to approach the subject and finally get the truth.

"My mom used to tell me," I continued, knowing full well I was broaching the taboo topic, "about how, at a certain point, Hollis kind of got a little deviant. He started drinking and using drugs." I began, stammering slightly as I tried to frame up the topic of abuse.

"I kn-h-h-h-h-o-w," she said, laughing through her words. "Yeah, everybody there did. EVERYBODY."

"Did you ever . . . feel unsafe around him? I mean . . . did you ever see any kids in the neighborhood . . . naked?" The words tumbled from my lips, heavy with the weight of unspoken stories.

Rachael froze. Her eyes widened, glassy and distant, as if peering back through decades. For a long moment her body was rigid, tension etching her features, her gaze locked on the worn photo album spread between us. Slowly, her hand rose to cover her mouth, a barrier against the ghosts of memories that might lead to words.

Her head bobbed, a tiny, almost imperceptible nod. Once, twice. It was as if she were confirming an inner dialogue only she could hear. It seemed to me a buried memory had clawed its way to the surface. I knew she was finally ready to shatter the silence that had obscured the neighborhood's dark secrets.

The air between us thickened, charged with the electricity of impending revelation. Decades of questions, of clawing through murky suspicions, were on the cusp of finally being validated. At that moment I felt something beyond anything I have ever experienced. In an instant, twenty years of desperately searching combined with self-doubt began to dissolve away, replaced by the solid, tangible underlying wireframe of truth.

I leaned forward, breath held, heart pounding against my ribs like a drum of war. The truth, no matter how grisly or devastating, had arrived. A witness to the shadows of the sixties was finally going to speak.

Then, Rachael leaned back, her movements slow, deliberate. The distance she put between herself and the photo album seemed like a chasm suddenly too wide to cross. Her head shook, a gentle, dismissive gesture that unraveled the tense thread of hope I had been clinging to.

Her demeanor lightened, a brittle facade of cheerfulness overlaying the solemnity of moments before. She chuckled—a sound that struck a dissonant chord in the heavy air. Glancing over toward me, her eyes dodged mine.

"Oh . . . God . . . no," she exhaled with a feigned laugh. "Nooo . . . everybody protected everybody. We were always joking around. When we wore two-piece bathing suits the boys would tease us, 'You're showing your belly button.' Yeah, it was the best neighborhood. It was great."

Her words struck me like a blow to the chest, a crushing realization that my hopes for closure were slipping away. I felt the weight of disappointment bear down on me, a bitter reminder that sometimes, the truth is buried too deep to ever be uncovered.

Rachael looked away, her gaze drifting toward the window where the late afternoon sun cast long shadows across the floor. The shift was palpable, as if she needed to escape the conversation as much as the room itself.

Yet at the same time, the incongruity of the transition left me reeling in disbelief. One moment we were tiptoeing around the dark underbelly of our shared past and the next, Rachael was painting a picture of an idyllic, innocent neighborhood. The rapid shift in mood was disorienting, leaving me struggling to make sense of it all.

Shock was beginning to set in. It was as if I had been through a war, which had exhausted me both physically and emotionally. I decided it was time to call it a day. With a heavy sigh, I pushed my chair back in preparation to leave. But then—

"You know," she began, her tone shifting towards nostalgia, "I remember when we got interviewed for security . . . for your dad. He needed his class A clearance." Her words seemed to come from a place of relief, as if retreating to a safer, more sanitized memory could cleanse the air.

"What . . .?" I was caught off guard, not just by the change in topic, but by the timing. It felt like an evasion, a skilled deflection from a master of preserving appearances.

"Yeah, the security team came to interview us. I guess your dad had put us down as a reference. He needed his clearance for the stuff he was doing at Lockheed. It was really secretive," she continued, a smile touching the corners of her mouth as she recounted the formality of those days. "Yeah, my parents all sat on the sofa with these guys in suits—super formal. We said oh yes, he's trustworthy...he's a great person."

Listening to Rachael, I realized this was more than just a change of subject. It was a window into how she managed pain—redirecting, reshaping it into something bearable, something mundane. It was a survival tactic, and perhaps, in her narrative, the only way to deal with the ghosts of the past without confronting them head-on.

Still, her narrative about my father drew me in. Over the years, my image of my father had become tainted with feelings of his inadequacy—as projected by my mother who was very critical of him. He had grown sad and depressed, starting in the late seventies. He would attempt to do things around the house but could never finish them. It seemed as if he had fallen into a deep hole. And my own feelings about myself as a man were closely connected to who he was. If he was weak, if he was a family reject, then so was I.

But Rachael's story reshaped my recollection of my father. She had gone back to a very different time in the neighborhood, a time before I could remember, and one that was simpler, more pure. When my father was at the rise of his career at Lockheed Missiles and Space Corporation. It was like a surprise gift from the past—a token of what had been good and virtuous. Back when my dad's career meant something to our family. And when people, even if it was only neighbors, realized the good in him. My dad was in the upswing of his career and the Friedmans, somehow, managed to help him get his clearance.

I excused myself and thanked her for her time, leaving with mixed feelings. Grateful for the glimpse of a happier past, yet troubled by the unresolved shadows that still lurked beneath Rachael's polished recollections.

CHAPTER SIXTY-TWO

Cain's Exile

As I drove away from the house and down Skyline Boulevard, turning right at Alice's Restaurant, Rachael's story about her father leaving the family weighed heavily on my mind. It seemed to me he had run away from a very painful situation, abandoning his family in the process. Rachael's contrast to my own father connecting more closely with the neighborhood community at that same time seemed more than incidental. It made me think about how my dad had responded to his chaotic family environment with a son exhibiting deviant behavior and a wife steeped in denial.

I knew that my father had, at the very least, remained in our home instead of deserting us as Mr. Friedman had. He had endured—though perhaps not very gracefully or heroically—the pain that comes from living in close quarters with a rebellious son. But how had my father responded to the realization that his eldest son had veered onto the wrong path?

In the deep recesses of my mind I recalled, vaguely at first, the angry voices in the kitchen. There had been many arguments between my mom and my dad. But this was a different kind of argument, one between my father and Hollis.

The circumstances had never been clear to me when Hollis left home to live on his own. It had always seemed to me a sad moment when we lost part of our family. Yet I had never fully understood the nature of his departure. As my brain began to piece together the clues—the drugs and alcohol, the rebellious behavior, Chase fighting with his father, Hollis and my dad fighting—a different interpretation started to condense in my consciousness.

I was ten years old, sitting on the floor of our entryway, leaning against the wall. I could see Hollis leaning against the frame of the pocket door that led into our kitchen. My father was talking sternly to him from inside the kitchen, though I couldn't see him. I was struck by the uncharacteristic firmness in my father's voice, which even bordered on menacing.

And I saw the impact of my father's words on Hollis's face—the disappointment creeping in. His jaw cocked sideways, tongue against the side of his cheek, trying to appear bold, still in control. But then his lips started to quiver, betraying his emotion. At some point he began weeping involuntarily, tears streaming down his face. He was eighteen, basically a grown man. But he was not the bold, brazen version of himself anymore. He was smaller, less formidable.

My father said a few last stern words. Hollis tried to object. But then over the course of maybe thirty seconds he gave up and slowly walked away, shoulders slumped. Beaten.

A short time later—I don't know if it was minutes or weeks, but to me it felt like an instant—he was gone. He moved out of the house and went to live in exile in an old freestanding structure above the freeway on Taaffe Road. My parents had rented a room for him until he could support himself.

At the time I felt a huge sense of loss. Like part of my life was disappearing—the part of me that Hollis represented. He couldn't leave . . . it would be the end. The end of . . . something, though I didn't know exactly what. I would go to visit that shack a few times after that, not knowing any better.

I didn't realize exactly what my dad was doing at that moment. I had, in some ways, always resented him for sending my brother away. Yet, what I began to realize was this: If it hadn't been for my dad's moral clarity, the clear consequences he enforced over my brother's bad behavior, things would have turned out much differently for me. If it weren't for his decisive action—as radical as it may have been—I would probably be dead.

What I realized driving down Highway 84, fifty years later, was that in that moment my dad was saving me. Just as when he kept me at the dinner table for hours talking about cosmology. Just as when he and I worked shoulder to shoulder building a drainage system above the barn. It was all he knew to do in an environment in which his wife fought his efforts every step of the way, yet he knew with every ounce of his being that something needed to be done. He had made a different decision than Mr. Friedman. One that changed my life forever. One that made my life worth living. And were it not for that decision, I might have followed the same tragic course as Budweiser Bob.

CHAPTER SIXTY-THREE

Tower of Babel

"My uncle abused me when I was seven," Talia said. "He was fifteen."

The following week, I again attended the ARIS Wednesday video call. I was struck by the similarities in our stories. Talia was raised Mormon, while I was raised in Christian Science—not identical but similar in their cultlike nature. Her family consisted of five kids as did mine, although she was raised in Seattle while I grew up in the Bay Area. And the age difference between her and her uncle was the same as between my brother and me. As she told her story I found myself both triggered and, at the same time, comforted that there was someone else in the world that had been through what I had.

She had refined features and wore glasses that gave her a slightly intellectual appearance. Yet despite her presentation, she was shy and soft-spoken. Often she would pause for tens of seconds while sharing. She seemed, at first, to be somewhat disinterested in her own story. But after a few meetings, I realized that what appeared as lack of interest was really a form of dissociation stemming from trauma.

"I blamed it on my own body," she said. "I developed early as a young teenager and was teased constantly." Talia paused for a moment and stared off into space. She contemplated for about twenty seconds. Then, as if coming back from a dream, she said, "I wasn't able to talk when traumatized. Words got caught in my throat."

It made me think about my own story and the shame I felt about not articulating what was happening to me as a child while my sister, Sally, seemed to have full agency over her voice and body.

Talia explained that when she was seven, she had told her mother about what had happened. When she finally spoke out about the torment she had endured, her mother's response was an icy silence—a denial that felt like a second betrayal. It was yet another similarity to my story.

Then she shifted her tack.

"I confronted my family this week." She talked about reaching out to her siblings telling of the abuse and explaining how it had impacted her life for years afterward. "After that, my next eldest sister came forward and said she had also been abused by the same uncle in almost an identical way."

It reminded me of my own family and my own mother. My abuse lasted for five years while my mother's denial, along with other family dysfunction, enabled it to continue.

How are mothers able to stand by and deny these things? In my mind's eye there are only two reasons I can think of: either they are evil—and in my heart of hearts, I know most mothers aren't evil—or it's a coping mechanism developed during hundreds of thousands of years of evolution that enables the family unit to survive. I recall the words of my sponsor: "It's not about choosing," he'd said. "It's about practicality and doing what she's capable of. It's about survival."

I believe it continues in many families today. It happened to Talia. It happened to me. And if the FBI is right, millions of people go through this every year, though you rarely hear about it, save for a few high-profile cases. How is it that, despite its prevalence (i.e. twenty to twenty-five percent of people go through it in this country alone) so few people talk about it?

"I approached my uncle about it as an adult," Talia continued. She explained that, determined to confront him in her need for closure, he exploited the moment, turning it into another act of betrayal that left her feeling more isolated than ever. Her words sent a shockwave through me, that this twisted power dynamic had perpetuated into her adulthood.

Despite being rattled to my core, I couldn't keep my mind from drifting back to something broader and more pervasive about the survivor community as a whole. This ARIS group typically had between three and six people in it. The total number of participants in ARIS is estimated at a few thousand people. Yet one in four women and one in six men are abused as minors, which means that well over thirty million people in the US have been through this traumatic experience. This means that one hundredth of one percent of abuse victims—or more simply put, *one in ten thousand people*—participate in ARIS. Where are the rest of them? And what is keeping people away? Is it that phrase that they say at the top of every meeting: "The sense of taboo has not been in committing incest, but rather in talking about incest, especially by those who have experienced it." This feels to me like a huge societal failure. That the very people who need the help can't—

"Phil, what are you doing?"

Talia's voice shattered the calm of the video call, her words sharp and accusing.

"What . . .?" I replied, caught off guard.

"You better not be writing any of this down," she continued before I could utter a sentence.

I blinked, surprised by the sudden hostility in her tone. "I . . . I'm just journaling," I stammered, my mind racing. "It helps me process my own recovery."

"You're exploiting us!" she snapped, her eyes blazing through the screen. Her typically soft, calm demeanor had been replaced by an aggressive, harsh tone. Her accusation felt like a physical blow, unexpected and disorienting.

"No, Talia, you've got it wrong. I'm not—"

"You're using our stories for your book, aren't you? You fucking opportunist," she continued, cutting me off. The sudden shift in Talia's demeanor was shocking. Each word was a dagger, and her aggressive tone left me scrambling for a response. I felt my face heat up, the confusion morphing into embarrassment and then into a creeping dread.

"I'm not writing your story, Talia. I swear. It's just about my own experiences."

"Bullshit, Phil," she scoffed, her tone cold and dismissive. "You're a parasite, feeding off everyone else's trauma. This isn't your therapy session; it's a safe space for us to tell our stories in private, away from voyeurs like you."

The room went silent. I glanced at the other faces on the screen, searching for some support or at least a hint of doubt in their eyes. But one by one, they looked down or turned away.

Talia's voice cut back in, firmer this time. "I want a group vote—now. All in favor of removing Phil from the group, say 'aye.'"

The chorus of "ayes" that followed felt like a verdict not just on my presence in the group, but on my integrity as a human being.

"Why are you doing this?" I managed to ask, my voice barely above a whisper.

"You don't belong here, Phil. You're unsafe for

everyone in this group, or *any* recovery group," Talia declared, her tone a mix of anger and conviction—brazen, even audacious, in her newfound boldness.

I had become the villain. All the rage, fear, and loss of control that had been buried deep inside was suddenly being focused on me.

"I'm in recovery myself, Talia! I need this as much as you," I said as firmly as I could manage, trying to conceal my trembling hands off-screen.

"You should have thought about that before recording our stories."

"Talia, you're making me out to be the bad guy. I didn't do anything to—"

"I'm not a victim," she interjected fiercely. "And I won't let you or anyone else turn my story into a spectacle."

Before I could respond, the screen flickered, and the faces disappeared, replaced by a chilling notification:

You have been removed from the meeting.

As I sat alone, staring at the blank screen, the silence was overwhelming. Talia's accusations replayed in my mind, her anger, her disdain. I was left to wonder: Had my intentions been misunderstood, or had I unknowingly crossed a line that I couldn't even see?

* * *

The shock of being rejected from the group reverberated through my psyche for the next three months. I tried to shake it at first, just pass it off as just redirected anger on the part of Talia.

Yet her words kept echoing through my mind: "You're unsafe for everyone in this group, or *any* recovery group." Was I truly a bad person? A menace to all in ARIS? A phrase percolated slowly into mind, a passage read at the beginning of each meeting that says abuse victims have a tendency to misdirect anger towards those we perceive as *safe*.

Was that part of the issue? That I was somehow safer to attack than her uncle?

This also underscores the delicate balance between honoring individual privacy and fostering a collective dialogue that could empower others. Each interaction, each attempt to share, has reinforced the critical need to approach this dialogue with compassion and respect for the boundaries others set, even while striving to confront and dismantle the broader culture of silence that allows abuse to persist.

As I grappled with the reality of my own abuse, all the while trying to process my recent exile, I turned to literature for understanding. In her work, Judith Lewis Herman poignantly captures the perpetrator's tactics:

In order to escape accountability for his crimes, the perpetrator does everything in his power to promote forgetting. If secrecy fails, the perpetrator attacks the credibility of his victim. If he cannot silence them absolutely, he tries to make sure no one listens.

This insight struck a chord with me, highlighting the complexity of abuse's aftermath—not just the act itself but the enduring struggle against imposed silence. It's no wonder victims of sexual abuse don't talk about it except in very small, controlled settings. And only a very small percentage of us ever tell anyone else, let alone confront our abuser. It's too terrifying. For a lot of people, the coercion exerted by the perpetrator carries well into adulthood. It happened to me. And I know of many other victims of abuse that have never been able to face their abuse because of the immense fear and shame involved.

Herman goes on to say that sexual abuse of a child isn't merely a violation; it's a theft of innocence, an entanglement of violence and arousal that spawns a confusing array of trauma responses. Through hours of reading and attending recovery meetings, I've come to understand that the secrecy surrounding abuse is often deeper than just the coercion by the perpetrators. It's a pervasive pressure that leads many victims to deny their own abuse outright, often resulting in repressed memories.

As I learned about these complexities of the human mind, a plethora of personal experiences from my own life flashed before me: Reactions to male power in Stowe, Vermont. Responses to coworkers and bosses that my traumatized psyche linked back to female enablement and manipulation. Even my constant escapism, chasing tumultuous wind and waves during risky windsurfing sessions. And the immense confusion I experienced in my adult years while in the throes of sexual passion as my younger traumatized child-self rewrote the script from ecstasy to tragedy.

CHAPTER SIXTY-FOUR

Beautifully Broken

As the reality of my childhood experiences settled within me, and I gradually came to terms with them, my anxiety began to lessen, and my urgency to find validation from a witness diminished. Eventually, I came to realize that I had all the answers within myself. Accepting this truth brought an emerging sense of peace and closure.

With this newfound clarity, I found myself spending more time at home, focusing on tangible projects. As the winds on the peninsula began to subside with the approach of fall, the tempest in my soul also quieted. This inner calm afforded me the mental capacity to undertake a series of home-improvement tasks. I demolished and rebuilt our old cinder block shed with help from Kathy and her father. I wired the new structure for electrical outlets and lighting. I poured concrete pavers in the backyard across the lawn and down the north side of our house. I put decorative rock around the pavers. I removed the hot tub and the pumps and old heater that were an unsightly mess just outside our bedroom window.

Then, I began working on a number of pieces of

furniture for our home. I rebuilt the bathroom vanity with a piece of marble that I cut and polished by hand. I refurbished our new workout room with a wood-paneled wall, a mirror with a custom handmade frame, electrical outlets to power the TV and satellite box, and a bench for weight training. I installed cubbies from Ikea. Soft-foam flooring. A rack to hold a training ball and elastic bands. And a wall plaque with the phrase: "You Got This!"

I've retained my dad's meticulous, thorough approach to projects over the years. Yet I'm careful to ensure that perfection doesn't stand in the way of good.

We'd been searching for a new kitchen table with a distinctive distressed appearance. But where could we get the material for it? Natural, weathered wood is not something you find at a store.

One day while driving out of the neighborhood I passed a picnic table that had been placed on the curb with a "free" sign on it. I went home, corralled Kathy, and the two of us walked back to the house rolling a dolly. We rolled the old, worn table constructed of six individual two-by-six planks back home.

I used my power planer to remove most of the old, damaged wood, but I left enough to give it a restoration feel, to embrace its history without dwelling on the past. I used epoxy to glue the planks together, then planed the whole surface flat. Then, I sanded the surface smooth using four different grits of sandpaper ensuring I still maintained the distressed history of the material through to the final project. By the time I got to four hundred grit, the wood was smooth and rich, yet had knots, a few termite holes, and a lush grain.

I gave it a coat of pre-stain conditioner, then stained it with my own custom mix of two stains to get just the color Kathy and I wanted. I gave it four coats of lacquer, rubbing it down with steel wool in between each coat. We ordered a set of trapezoidal legs from Amazon—black metal to contrast the natural wood. Our look had become the "Modern Farmhouse" motif.

The finish was something like baked peanut butter with a faint swirl of blueberry mixed in: ever-so-slightly glossy with an almost matte finish. Smooth, yet still hinting at the distress that comes over years of weathering the storm.

It is truly miraculous to take something damaged and distressed from being exposed, unprotected for years, then turn it into something beautiful.

* * *

"Are you done destroying the lawn?" Kathy said with a subtle wink. We sat on the back patio next to the lawn. I had smoked salmon and new potatoes on the grill, and she had sautéed asparagus. We were enjoying a balmy windless evening in late September on the peninsula.

"Baby, what do you take me for? Am I really that volatile?" I objected.

"I'm just saying, now that it's growing back in, are you going to leave it alone?"

I tried to form words but was overcome by feelings of guilt and embarrassment.

"I don't . . . mean that in an accusatory way," she added quickly, her tone taking on just a little more buoyancy.

"Look," I finally said, "I love our home, I love our yard." Then after a pause: "And I love you."

"You know what they say: you only hurt the ones you love." This time there was no wink.

"Do you feel like you don't know me anymore? Like at any moment I might rage and destroy something?"

She didn't answer. Instead, she stared out over the lawn.

"Babe, I don't want you to feel afraid at any moment I might rage and destroy part of our life," I consoled, wishing desperately to alleviate her fear.

Still nothing. My mind went back to the year before when I had dethatched the lawn very aggressively, so much so that I had created a dirt parking lot—a sparse, mangey combover of a lawn. I had passed it off as just aggressive gardening at the time; that combined with some unexpected effects from microdosing.

We had even had a laugh about it.

But now she seemed more serious, as if she was truly worried.

I felt perhaps it had been a bridge too far. As if she no longer thought I embraced the things she cared about. I had destroyed something important to both of us. And it had impacted her more than I knew. This was our home. Our love nest. And I wanted her to feel safe.

Yet something in that moment told me maybe she didn't. Maybe it was a bridge too far. Maybe . . .

Just then, her expression shifted, her face softening as she leaned forward in her chair. Drawing nearer . . . to something—ome unseen apparition. Her expression was less stern . . . more hopeful.

"You know," she said slowly, "it does look very different this year."

I looked over the lawn—this time more carefully, trying to see what she had seen. As we both stared out across the grass toward the new shed we had built that winter, the whole yard seemed different. It wasn't just that there was grass where there hadn't been. Not just that it was more even. It was something else.

"It does look different," I corroborated, my tone softening.

"It looks greener, more lush," she said in a more hopeful tone. "Even better than before last year's . . . episode," she continued, a faint smile coming across her lips.

"You know . . . It . . . really does," I said after a long pause, my voice laced with surprise.

What had been mostly dirt and a few wisps of grass had

since grown back into a lush, green lawn. It was thicker than before. The color was a darker, healthier green. There were virtually no gaps or brown spots left. It was far better than it had been, even before the previous year. Where there had been ugliness, there was beauty. Where there had been stunted growth there was vitality.

"How is that possible?" I said rhetorically.

"Well, as bad as it looked last summer, it's definitely rebounded," she said. "Better than before."

"Yeah . . . it has," I said. "I guess you have to pull out the old overgrown stuff to let the new grass grow."

"Hmmm, maybe it's a metaphor," she said. "You have to pull out the old dead stuff to make way for new growth."

As much as my obsessiveness—and even rage—had destroyed the lawn, as painful and destructive as that was, the lawn had grown back stronger.

"The end doesn't necessarily justify the means—I get that," I said after a long pause. "But I want you to know I really was doing what I thought was right. Do you . . . do you trust me?"

She continued staring out at the lawn. Then her gaze drifted back to me. Her expression gradually transformed into the kind, benevolent, tolerant version of Kathy. The one I remembered from before. An expression of quiet confidence.

"I trust you."

CHAPTER SIXTY-FIVE

Phil Would Go

It was billed as the Storm of the Century by newscasters. An atmospheric river the size of the Mississippi barreling toward the coast of California. It would arrive on New Year's Eve, 2022.

As winter set in, the weather shifted from a mild fall to one of the most violent winters California has ever seen. The forecast was for thirty-knot winds starting early on Saturday, December 31ˢᵗ. The Third Avenue WhatsApp channel was lighting up with kiteboarders planning on heading to Half Moon Bay first thing in the morning. While I was hesitant at first, thinking about the freezing temperatures combined with strong winds along the coast, at the same time I felt this was something I couldn't miss.

A rite of passage.

My stomach fluttered with the anticipation of screaming across the water being pulled by a seven-meter kite, feeling the sting of tiny raindrops carried by strong winds hitting my face. Of launching twenty-five feet in the air and seeing the land drop rapidly away below me as the kite lifted me upward to a breathtaking scene. Being able to see the shore from a bird's eye view. Seeing up and over the levee to the ocean, with its turbulence and white foam blowing across the water.

As Friday evening approached, my excitement level grew. I loaded up the car with gear. A second wetsuit to stave off the cold. Three kites: a seven-meter, nine-meter, and eleven-meter just in case. I told Kathy my plan.

"Be careful," she said.

Planning to wake up at around 5:00 the following morning, I decided to go to bed early. However, I found it challenging to fall asleep due to the overwhelming sense of excitement and anticipation coursing through me.

At 4:59 a.m. I woke up spontaneously and grabbed my phone. Was the wind building as the forecast had predicted? Or was this storm a false alarm? The iWindsurf app showed Half Moon Bay was already clocking in at twenty-seven knots and building. Thirty minutes later after a cup of coffee and donning an old pair of sweats, I again looked at my phone to see the wind sensor reading thirty-one knots.

I kissed Kathy goodbye and headed out the door, settling quickly into the driver's seat of my Subaru. Another wave of nervous energy came over me like a shot of whiskey spreading heat through my body. It was exciting.

But also . . . daunting.

I had faced frightening situations in the past, yet most of those were prior to becoming sober. I had little recent experience to go on. Moving back to the Bay Area after getting sober had filled me with fear, yet I'd succeeded. Mastering kiteboarding had electrified my senses.

But this new challenge presented a unique form of intimidation. The prevailing conditions beckoned me, compelling a response unlike anything before. It was akin to the irresistible pull of a flame drawing a moth.

I stopped for a moment and wondered why I was impelled to go in these extreme conditions. Why did I need to chase these high winds, to ride in the most extreme of conditions? It was as if I were coerced to go, forced to put myself in these conditions, and conquer them at all costs.

After all, Eddie would go.

It reminded me of the big wave surfers, the great titans of Hawaii who would brave even the most brutal conditions. If the waves were huge, they would go. I was no Eddie Aikau, yet I pushed myself in these situations, toward risk. I moved into danger, near the edge of annihilation.

Why?

It felt like, perhaps, I wouldn't be brave if I didn't go. Like I wouldn't feel fully alive. Like maybe . . . I wouldn't be as much of a man.

Yet something inside me whispered: *a man doesn't have to chase danger*. A real man makes good decisions and invokes good judgment. A real man contemplates whether or not to go instead of feeling compelled to go because of the opportunity.

Who forces themselves into risky situations? A traumatized boy, trying to relive the trauma, hoping for a different outcome?

Why did I feel I needed this? Was it to conquer some fear? To overcome?

I sat in the driver's seat of my car, thinking about the waves crashing against the levee sending stinging salt spray across the harbor at thirty knots. About launching off the sandy beach on a tiny seven-meter kite. About jumping high into the air, screaming across the glassy, buttery water with raindrops stinging my face, feeling like a demented sea captain.

Would that somehow make me whole? Would it somehow rinse the stain of abuse off my body? For a moment, I opened up my heart and let myself feel—something I had avoided for years. And there I sensed a feeling I hadn't in a long, long time. Something I had almost forgotten. A feeling of calm.

* * *

For the next two weeks, I wrestled with the decision I'd made. It was uncharacteristic of me not to go. Yet I had made the decision not to ride during the Storm of the Century and that seemed a wise choice. Some progress, perhaps?

At the same time, I struggled to discern if I was giving up kiteboarding altogether or just making a prudent decision in the face of dangerous conditions. My inner turmoil was a tempest of conflicting emotions.

It dawned on me that I could choose not to ride when the danger level was too high without abandoning my cherished outlet altogether. Exercising caution didn't necessarily mean giving up this exciting activity entirely.

While the temptation to chase the Storm of the Century hadn't compelled me to go on that particular day, I recognized a profound yearning within me to embrace the tumultuous wind and water. It wasn't merely about seeking thrills; it was about forging a connection with nature, feeling its raw power, and surrendering to the exhilarating chaos it offered. In those moments, I found a sense of completeness, a harmony with the elements that transcended mere adrenaline.

As successive storms of more moderate temperament swept through the Bay Area with strong southerly winds, I felt an inexorable pull toward Half Moon Bay. It beckoned to me, promising communion with the elements, an opportunity to confront my inner demons without the risk of annihilation.

This time, I embraced the journey.

A fluttery feeling arose in my chest as I arrived at Princeton Harbor and contemplated what was about to happen. The sensor was reading in the high twenties. Not the strongest winds I'd ever experienced kiteboarding, but intense, nevertheless.

The sun poked through the clouds, illuminating strips of frothy water. I walked up onto the south levee to see the ocean on my left, turbulent with wind waves mixed with ground swell breaking in every direction. Every few seconds a wave would crash against the levee, sending salt spray and foam up and over, stinging the side of my face.

I set up my nine-meter kite. In my excitement to get on the water I forwent my usual safety review and asked another kiter to launch me—a chiseled man standing about six feet with dark hair, a perfect masculine build, and a mesmerizing GQ smile.

As GQ held up my kite in preparation for the launch, it became clear that I had tangled a steering line during setup. And the cap to my inflater valve was off. This could have caused the kite to deflate halfway through the session; and the tangle was a nonstarter.

The combination of a new site and stronger winds than I was used to had created in me some nervous energy, causing me to rush my setup. And I'd made two mistakes in the process. They weren't as egregious as not knowing where the safety release was, but they were careless oversights, nonetheless.

My second launch attempt was successful. "Have fun," GQ shouted as I walked past him toward the launch.

As I stepped into the straps of my kiteboard and leaned back, diving the kite, I simultaneously sensed a strong gust of wind and felt the power of the kite accelerate me forward as my board began skipping across the water. It was both exhilarating and a little daunting as I headed westward toward the afternoon sun.

I transitioned and headed eastward on a starboard tack. As I coaxed my shoulders and calves to relax, feeling the tension slowly drain out of my body, I began to notice the pull of the kite and the skipping vibration of the board as it planed over the small wind ripples.

After making eight or ten tacks, continuing upwind toward the entrance to the harbor, I began to execute a few jumps—small ones at first. I was just thirty feet from the levee itself. Although the wind ripples had been dampened out by the levee, the long-wave groundswell was noticeable. As I crossed the entrance I felt the ocean rise under my board: up for three seconds . . . pause . . . then down. Feeling both the power of the wind and the undulating wave motion simultaneously was elating.

After crossing the entrance, I rode parallel to the levee back toward the launch. Being just twenty feet downwind of the levee I could sense the glassy look of the water that was shielded. Like butter. Or whipped cream. The wind overhead was twenty-five knots, yet the water was glassy and smooth, without a ripple. It was reminiscent of skiing fresh powder. Or carving down the glassy face of a wave on a surfboard.

As I headed back toward shore I raised the kite abruptly and carved the board sharply into the wind, jumping twenty feet into the air. A celebratory jump. Like a dolphin jumping off a wave, or a breaching whale.

Just as I began to drift back down toward the water, the sun shone through the clouds, illuminating light rain near the beach and creating a perfect double rainbow. It was absolutely breathtaking. I was overwhelmed in that moment with the most intense feeling of pure joy!

As I soaked up the moment, I couldn't help but think about how daunting it had been learning the sport. How, amid the intense discomfort and lack of control, I'd come very close to quitting. And were it not for my strongly developed characteristics of persistence and willingness to endure hardship, I would have missed this unforgettable moment.

And the person in my life most responsible for instilling this quality of persistence in me was my mother.

CHAPTER SIXTY-SIX

Succumb

When I was young and struggling with something, my mother had a way of snapping me out of the paralysis that can come from fearing that a task was too hard or that I might not be capable of completing it. She would lightheartedly say, "Just start it—do it for a few minutes— you don't have to finish the whole thing." She'd even go as far as to say "sometimes you have to trick yourself into just getting started. It'll get easier."

She always made it sound simple, as if the act of initiating a task—even one that seemed insurmountable— would somehow endow me with the skills and knowledge needed to see it through. Yet, for some uncanny reason, it worked. I would start a task that I was sure I would never finish, employing her lighthearted "just give it a try" attitude. And before I knew it, I was far enough through the task that I could see the end in sight. And that vision of the endgame would increase my motivation tenfold. At that point I'd begin to *believe* I could do it. And that, in turn, would bolster me to push through to the end.

My mother and I did a number of projects when I was in my teens. We worked well together. When I was sixteen and my '61 bug blew its engine, we rebuilt it together. I recall lying on our backs, tugging the 250-pound motor this way and that, trying to extricate it from the car. She would hand me tools when I asked for them. She would offer encouragement when we hit a rough spot. All of this gave me the mistaken impression I understood her.

Then later, after I realized the abuse had happened, I harbored resentment toward her, for letting it happen at first, then for letting it go on for years. But thinking back to my teenage years, I realized I could live with someone, spending hours each day with them, yet not actually *see* them. I thought I knew my mother because we were close and she had always wanted me to be happy and encouraged me to do my best. And for the most part I listened to her advice and followed it.

But I didn't know her.

Thinking about her life in the sixties and seventies, I realized the level of isolation and emotional pressure she must have felt, taking care of five kids as the sole parent while my dad was away at work all day. She was also involved in a cult religion that shunned doctors and therapists. She had struggled to do the best she could with five kids, two of whom who had already gone off the rails with drugs and alcohol, and a middle daughter who was attention-seeking, obsessive, and often combative. Again, all without doctors, medicine, or psychiatrists. The only mental-health assistance she got was through Christian Science practitioners, which were basically the metaphysical equivalent of witch doctors.

She was ultimately alone.

I remember she used to say around that time, "Let's move to a deserted island." She wanted to go to a place where life was simpler, maybe even innocent. I was young enough to believe her at the time. To think she really meant it. When I was about nine years old, I remember coming home from school one day and asking: "So when are we going to move to the island?"

She looked at me with a startled expression on her face, her eyes wide in shock. Then, once it dawned on her just exactly what I was saying, she quickly glanced away, changing the subject. Those words were just her own musings. Fantasies about a simpler, happier life. She hadn't meant them for me.

Just after our confrontational meeting, my mom was diagnosed with myelofibrosis, a blood disease that is often a precursor to leukemia. She began drinking less alcohol and tried to take better care of herself. Months later, her condition transitioned into full-blown leukemia.

She lay on her deathbed at 12865 La Barranca, weak and barely able to move. Her white blood cells were skyrocketing exponentially. And her red blood cells were rapidly decreasing. Her weight had dropped over the course of a couple of weeks to about ninety-five pounds. We'd made the difficult decision to put her in hospice care.

She had only a short time left.

I sat in a chair facing her bed where she lay propped up against pillows. There she rested, calmly, a serene expression on her face. It wasn't even the meds. She was just like that most of the time. She almost never held a grudge, at least not against friends, neighbors, or her kids. Her husband and sister-in-law were a different story, but you do what you can.

I was trying to convince her of something while she sat in bed. I don't remember exactly what it was. Maybe to get her to use the restroom to keep her bowels moving just to survive another day or two. Or drink more water. I had to solve it. I always had a difficult time with these kinds of moments. I had to be doing something to help. I needed to solve the problem and reduce the suffering.

But to sit there and do nothing but be in the moment was impossible. It felt like pushing a boulder up a mountain. Sensing that there was nothing I could do to improve her condition, I surrendered, feeling futility wash over me.

I sat back in my chair, facing her, and let out a sigh of frustration. Then I took another breath, letting the tension drain from my body. I saw her childlike, innocent expression, as if she were sixteen years old again. No anger on her face. No resentment. No judgment.

I looked into her eyes. She looked back into mine.

"I . . . love you," I said.

She giggled, a lighthearted laugh.

"I love you too, honey."

Two hours later she was gone.

Thinking now about the isolation she felt and the strength she had to muster to run a family of five on her own, I view her differently than I used to. She didn't have malice. She wasn't filled with apathy for me. She didn't sacrifice me for someone more important. She needed to survive, so her family could survive. At that moment, I sensed, profoundly, the struggle she had been through in her life: The mayhem of five kids, during the sixties, the bad behavior of the older two. The lack of emotional connection with her husband.

And I realized in that moment as she lay on her deathbed that she had done her best. And for me, that was enough.

CHAPTER SIXTY-SEVEN

Her

"We've tried that before," I said. "He doesn't want to hear it."

After my mom passed, and I came to accept who she was at the very center of her being, I began to think about my own struggle. I wondered if I'd really take the time to understand—and more importantly, accept—who I was deep down inside.

Although I'd sworn off therapy for good, Kathy convinced me over dinner one night that it might be worth trying again. Perhaps she sensed the inner struggle I was having as I came to grips with the abuse.

I began meeting with a new therapist in San Mateo. Dr. Paul was a tall, barrel-chested man with long-ish dark hair that gave something of a rock-star impression. He'd brought up more than once that I had a disconnect with my six-year-old self that he felt wasn't healthy. We'd done some EMDR work but after two months there was no tangible movement. Every time I got into a mindful state and approached that younger me—that six-year-old wounded kid who was victimized and reclusive—I got nothing but rejection. That child would say: "No, I don't need you."

"Let's approach it differently this time," Dr. Paul suggested. "You had an image from an EMDR session a while ago that you told me about," he continued. "Trees? A canopy?"

"Yeah . . . the trees were essentially before and after the five-year period of abuse," I responded. "One vision of them was on the approach zone of the Tulsa Airport in 1966 when we were on our way to Table Rock Lake. The other was the canopy of trees near the shack up on Taaffe Road where Hollis lived after he was kicked out of the house for good."

Dr. Paul gave me some instructions on getting into a mindful state: long, slow breaths, visualization, focusing on sensations in my body, articulating the feeling in words. I knew the drill. I had done it a dozen times.

Suddenly I was there, above the canopy of trees, moving slowly—as if perched atop a drone—as I panned across the scene. In my mind's eye I zoomed in to see gaps in the trees and some glimpses of grass and earth. I panned sideways and zoomed closer, between the branches, sliding down to the trunk. There, I saw a figure dressed in white lying under one of the trees. He was broken, bandaged, with a cast on one leg.

Battered as if he'd endured a war.

I came in closer.

He stared back at me with a defiant expression.

What should I say? What could possibly make this right. How can I possibly say anything that would help? He was bruised and broken. Adults, even his parents, had let him down woefully. There's not a reason to trust anyone, including my own adult self.

Dr. Paul must have sensed my bewilderment and immediately offered some coaching words. "I want you to tell him: I understand why you wouldn't trust me. But . .

. I'm here to help," he directed in a tone that was much more assertive than usual.

I repeated the words to my younger self.

Nothing.

I came in closer.

"I understand why you wouldn't trust me, but I'm here to help." Suddenly the little boy—this six-year-old version of myself—turned toward me and made a flirtatious gesture. A sudden physical advance. Then, as fluidly as one might change clothes at bedtime, he turned into a young girl.

At first, I didn't know what to think of the gender transition. Yet this wasn't something brand-new for me. I'd seen myself as feminine: in dreams, visions. I'd even become aware of feminine aspects in my own actions and demeanor.

And the sexual advance? Well, I understood the nature of it: a child immersed in a world of inappropriate sexual activities by older powerful people.

And I was there as the adult to my child. Not to judge, but to know and accept. To see.

She came closer to me; the wall was down. She was now accepting of my help and friendship. I'd finally gotten through. I'd reached the young version of me, the wounded, traumatized child. The pressure in my chest subsided. I felt a sense of calmness, even relaxation permeate my shoulders and chest. My body felt lighter.

I slowly opened my eyes to see Dr. Paul facing me. The trees and the vivid image of my younger self were gone. I felt slightly stunned, trying to sort out what just happened. I stared at Dr. Paul, elated about the connection, yet grasping for an explanation of the entire vision.

He contemplated for a moment, looking through me. I could see the wheels turning. Then he surprised me with an unexpected turn. "In a lot of ways, this is about acceptance of that younger you," he began. "It's about reparenting. If your parents didn't accept who you were and what was happening to you at the time, then it stands to reason that you wouldn't accept your own younger self, even today. So the question really is: can you accept your younger self unconditionally?"

I tried to grasp what he was saying. I had thought the problem was that the little boy didn't accept me. But it wasn't that. In fact, it was the exact opposite. The problem was that I, as the adult, didn't accept my younger self. I disapproved, like a judgmental father seeing his promiscuous teenage daughter gallivant around town, frowning with disdain.

It helped immensely that my parents had loved me. But that wasn't enough. At the end of the day, what mattered was that I loved and cared about myself. Even the wounded, damaged young part of me that seemed weird or inappropriate.

* * *

The following Monday, I stood in front of a row of twenty-one tiny bicycles. I walked over to one and adjusted the seat downward.

Kathy had enlisted me to help with her All Kids Bike program for the young class. She walked toward me with a row of twenty-one kindergarteners behind her, a mamma duck with her little ducklings.

As they passed by, I heard them say in unison: "Hi, Mister Jones." I glanced over at Kathy as she grinned back with a sheepish smile. Kathy and I didn't share a last name. She was Jones, I was March. But apparently to a group of kindergarteners, any partner of Kathy's was "Mr. Jones."

One by one I helped them get their helmets on, cinch up the fit system, and fasten the chin straps. Many of them glanced at me out of the side of their eyes as I bent down to help. One part curious, one part amusement—because, let's face it, putting on helmets is inherently funny—and two parts trust.

I was there for two reasons: one, to shuttle the bikes out to the playground and back. And two, to keep them safe.

As a friend once characterized me back in the boating days when I taught kids wakeboarding: I was making the scary safe. I never wanted anyone to go through what I went through as a child. Not just the abuse, but even being placed in daunting situations, feeling exposed and unprotected.

In short, I was there as a safety net for that six-year-old version of me; as a parent to that terrified child. I was to ensure these kids were safe as they tried something new and out of their comfort zones.

With one confident verbal command, Kathy sent the kids around the cones. It was Lesson Three: no pedals yet, but their speed was increasing. They could coast with their feet off the ground for seconds and could slalom through cones. They whirled by me, expressions of excitement, exhilaration on their faces. Kathy whizzed past me also on her adult-sized bike, showing the way.

They moved faster, around in a circle, blurring out my peripheral vision, like tigers chasing each other's tails as they turned to butter. Out of the blur I saw an image form in front of me. A small child came into view, coasting tranquilly toward me. The child was of slight build and had light-brown hair and fair skin.

He wasn't dressed like the other kids. His attire was unusual, with a bright bandana and a suede leather vest with tassels hanging down.

I stared at the kindergartener as he coasted to a stop in front of me. This six-year-old child. The one who pre-invented the weed wacker. The one who survived the gauntlet of dangers that were thrown at him by drunken, unscrupulous teenagers. The one who tuned out during elementary school for self-preservation, but then became a bright student in junior high and high school, excelling on the Advanced Placement tests in math and physics.

That part was easy to like.

But the other parts were harder. This small, frail, effeminate child, a mix of boy and girl. There were moments, even as recent as a year ago, when I wished he/she just didn't exist. I wanted to send that younger part of me away. I even hated what they stood for: effeminate, sexually ambiguous, timid, grossly out of touch with social norms.

I looked into the child's eyes, trying to understand. Trying to see but not judge. To see him. To see her.

In this moment, amid the blur of pedaling children, I began to view that young child differently. For the first time since I could remember, I actually liked him. For all the quirkiness and social ineptness, I saw a child who had emerged out of the chaos to be unusual, even kind of weird. Yet unique. Able to understand the plight of others suffering in the world. OK as he is. As she is. I began, in that instant, to love this androgynous child like a son. A daughter.

I approached him. Got down on my knees, arms out wide. I surrounded them in a warm embrace. They were the child. I was the parent. I would keep them safe. They didn't have to be on the lookout for nefarious power. They could go about the business of being a curious young child.

And, as if this newfound kinship with my younger self opened up some inner portal to another relationship I had struggled to understand, that night I was visited by the spirit of my father.

CHAPTER SIXTY-EIGHT

Who Art in Heaven

"Dude, you gotta hear about this dream I had" I said excitedly, sliding onto a barstool. Jared and I were back at Marufuku in Redwood City. This time on a Monday following a day's work. The soft lounge lighting contrasted with the loud voices of the restaurant. Every now and then, when a new customer entered the establishment, the wait staff would welcome them by shouting, "Irasshaimase."

"This one's deep," I continued. "You up for some serious symbolism?"

"Absolutely," Jared said in his characteristically encouraging tone. "I live for these kinds of subliminal journeys. Let's see what your subconscious is up to these days."

"OK . . . so picture this: I'm walking up this path with my dad, and it's the one leading up to Coit Tower. The sun's setting, casting this surreal glow over everything."

"Really? Coit Tower?" Jared said in disbelief. "So, was Freud your tour guide?"

"Yeah, I get the reference. But, hey, I didn't write the dream. Just dreamt it. Anyway, just then my dad walks up the path ahead of me and turns around." I paused for a moment to recollect the specific image in my dream. "And . . . his face, man, it's like nothing I've seen before. There's this calmness, this understanding in his eyes that I never noticed when he was alive."

"Wow! Dude, that's profound."

"Yeah, it hit me deep. And then he gives me this smile, not the usual dad grin, but something deeper. Like he's saying, 'I get you, Phil.' And the sun is behind him, giving almost a halolike heavenly effect." I paused again, allowing the complete experience to permeate me. "And then . . . he winks at me."

"Holy shit!" Jared burst out. "A cosmic wink?"

"Yeah," I responded, trying to piece it all together; to find the right words to describe the incredible vision I'd seen. "His expression was much more confident than usual. Like all the uncertainty and doubt that our dysfunctional family had drilled into him over the years . . . it had all dissipated, replaced by this contented smile."

"Wow! So, did he resemble the older version of your father," Jared asked, ever the psychological detective, "or was he more reminiscent of your childhood?"

"That's an intriguing question," I replied, my curiosity piqued. "I mean he looked mostly like his older, wiser self, with his gray beard and compassionate, warm eyes. He had on that hat he used to wear when he hiked—kind of a gray denim fedora. He even had that taupe jacket that he loved so much." I sank into the vision in my mind until I felt its full effect. "But in this dream, he was somehow . . . Stronger . . . more confident. And it seemed as though he was passing on some kind of wisdom, you know? Like he was telling me it's gonna be OK."

"That's . . . actually pretty moving, man," Jared said, his eyes growing cloudy as he brought a bar napkin up to his cheek.

"You're an old softy," I said, sensing the intensity of Jared's emotion. Then, anxious to maintain the continuity of our discussion, I continued. "So then, my dad turns and continues walking toward the setting sun and disappears as if he's ascending to some higher plane or something."

"Wow . . . that's a beautiful image! So…angelic!" Jared offered, always able to put my randomized thoughts into perspective. "So . . . what do you think it means?"

"Well, thing is, Jared, it felt real. I woke up feeling like I'd had this profound connection with my dad, like I finally understood him in a way I never did when he was alive. And," I glanced up at the row of bottles above the bar, trying to find the words, "it also felt like he understood me like he hadn't before. Like he understood the pain I was going through, and he'd found a way to help move me to safety, even from beyond the grave."

"Whoa . . . that is intense. So, Phil, we've known each other for, what, thirty years?" Jared mused, taking in the magnitude of our longstanding friendship. "In all those years I've never heard you say *anything* that positive about him . . . let alone heroic."

"Yeah . . . weird, huh?" I pondered.

"So let me ask you this," Jared continued, always one to seek the deeper, hidden symbolism. "Does this fundamentally change how you feel about your dad?"

I contemplated for a moment, watching the bartender wipe down goblets with a dishrag. Another couple entered the restaurant to the chant of "Irasshaimase." I sensed inside me a feeling about my father that I hadn't felt for a very long time.

"You know . . . it does," I said, finishing the sentence more conclusively than I expected. "It's been a couple of weeks since I had the dream. And, since then, I've felt like I had a completely different relationship with him. Like, despite our friction, I now know deep down that he loved me . . . enough to do everything he could to keep me safe."

As I finished recounting the dream, a sense of calm settled over me, like a warm blanket on a chilly evening. For the first time in a long while, I felt a weight lift from my shoulders, replaced by a newfound understanding and acceptance.

"So, what's the takeaway here?" Jared asked, leaning in with genuine curiosity.

I took a moment to ponder his question, letting the significance of the dream sink in. Then, a smile spread across my face as I found the perfect quip to fit the moment.

"Well, I guess the takeaway is this," I said, raising my cup of green tea in a toast. "Even in the afterlife, my old man still knows how to give one hell of a wink."

Jared chuckled, lifting his own glass to join mine. "To cosmic winks," he declared, clinking our glasses together.

And as we laughed together, surrounded by the comforting bustle of Marufuku Ramen, I knew that no matter where life took me, the memory of that dream would stay with me, reminding me of the enduring bond between my father and me, even beyond the confines of this world.

Epilogue

I drove down the rebuilt eastern span of the Bay Bridge from Yerba Buena Island toward Oakland on a beautiful spring day. The plan was to meet my friend Peter for some kiteboarding at the Albany Bulb.

Just past the suspension tower, I glanced to my right to see the Oakland shoreline and the estuary that separates the mainland from Alameda Island.

Not the most auspicious location.

I had passed by this place many times since. In those moments I always felt a very dark, foreboding sensation. Just as when I would run across some belonging of Hollis's like a beach towel or one of his old tools.

Alameda had always felt to me to be Hollis's domain. It's where he lived during his last years. Where he moored his sailboat. It was the last place I had seen him, in the dark cabin of his boat on an evening in January 2004. One month before the tragedy. Alameda was where most of his friends lived. Where we had his funeral. And it was ultimately where he died.

He'd been hit by another boat in the waterway separating two pieces of land. The border. Not the solid, unmovable mainland. Yet not the isolated purity of the island either. But the fluctuating, constantly evolving, constantly changing, volatile waterway that moved up and down with the tides and rippled with the bay winds.

As had happened many times in his life, he found himself in a fray—friction with another boat captain— some kind of competition, or maybe a lingering resentment from an infraction minutes earlier. Perhaps the other captain had usurped his authority or encroached on his territory, threatening his power. Regardless of the reason, the two boats had gotten into a skirmish, and it had killed him.

This estuary was his ending. Yet, in some sense, it was my beginning. I had endured trauma. Parts of me were damaged. But those years didn't define who I was. I was moving on.

I remembered Hollis as a broken man who did some terrible acts. Yet he had a faint semblance of goodness inside him. He was ultimately himself, in whatever version—good or bad—he could muster at the time.

And yet as an adult, during his short-lived grown-up phase in the nineties, he had apologized. Perhaps it was overwhelming guilt, or he just needed to set the record straight. Yet he had stopped well short of rigorous honesty. His apology, I concluded as I drove along the bridge adjacent to the estuary, wasn't really about the go-kart. Nor was it about putting me in physical danger.

It was really about his greater transgression—his remorse for breaching my boundaries and objectifying my body.

As I drove toward Oakland, I saw the wind rippling on the water leading into the Alameda estuary. Cranes unloaded cargo from freighters onto the docks. In contrast to previous times when I had passed this location, today felt different. It didn't hold the same fear that it used to for me. He no longer held the same power.

I felt in my heart of hearts something more than dismissal, though less than forgiveness. This was just another place in the Bay Area. Yet another scenic waterway. One that I was passing to get to a better one.

He was my brother and my abuser. Yet, I had endured. For all the domination and aggressive behavior he had embodied, he was gone and I remained. Even though he had been the more physically powerful one—eight years older, three times my size—somehow I had managed, ultimately, to survive when he didn't.

* * *

I pulled into the parking lot at the Albany Bulb and saw Peter standing along the fence facing me. I got out of the car and walked toward him.

"Hey Phil, good to see you," he said cheerfully in his mostly Americanized Swedish accent.

"Likewise, Peter." He gave me a hug in his quintessential European fashion. "It looks good out there . . ." I added. "The sensor is reading nineteen knots."

"It's perfect!" he said.

It was his first time at the Albany Bulb. I coached him through the sequence. "Head on a short tack to the north, then transition and come back to the south. Repeat that until you clear the broken pier just south of the beach. Don't cut it too close in case you drop your kite."

We launched. Minutes later we'd worked our way to the upwind end of the Bulb. The wind was strong, and the three-foot waves rolled through, perfect for launching into the air. Pure freedom. Downtown San Francisco and the Golden Gate Bridge were just over my right shoulder, like a gorgeous painting. Bright sun. Wind. Waves. And there, adjacent to the downtown skyline, stood Coit Tower, its silhouette a silent reminder of the momentous dream I'd had just weeks before.

Was I still chasing trauma? Did I need to get close to violent wind and waves, and survive, just to feel alive? Did I need to bring myself close to death? Or was there something else going on?

I remained astride the huge elephant that comprised my subconscious, its massive form ever present in my mind. Yet, instead of battling against its will, I found myself synchronizing with its rhythm, harmonizing with its powerful gait, no longer shying away from it or ignoring its existence. Instead, I embraced it fully, acknowledging its intent.

To me this felt different from my windsurfing experiences three decades earlier. Getting into the elements yet thriving. Not just surviving but rising above. Skimming across waves, using the power of the wind and harnessing it.

Dancing on the head of a pin.

Things had changed since the nineties. Instead of being out in the channel, two miles offshore, I was half a mile upwind from the launch. Any equipment failure or drastic change in wind conditions would send me drifting safely back to the sandy beach where I'd started. A margin for error. A second chance.

And ultimately, that was what I got in this life: a second chance. I had endured everything he had sent my way. Now, fifty-five years later, I was forging my own direction, sometimes immersing myself in wind and waves and occasionally confronting those violent conditions. I placed myself in the middle of the turmoil—the eye of the hurricane—where I felt the untempered anger and the brutality of his wrath, yet somehow wrestled back control.

Seeing what the tempest was like—something few others had seen and lived to tell about it—I could glimpse, if just for a moment, what it had been like with him. To accept what had happened to me. Then make the choice to leave it.

And ultimately glide back to land upon solid ground.

Afterword

When I gave an early draft of this manuscript to my longtime friend and high-school buddy, Bill, for feedback, he surprised me with a story from decades earlier.

We'd made a date to talk over the manuscript. Sitting in the kitchen of his Los Altos home he gave both positive and negative feedback about the storyline. Toward the end of the meeting, as he stood up from the table, he told me that reading this memoir had jogged his memory about something my father had said to him in the late eighties.

Bill had been visiting me at 12865 La Barranca when my dad approached him. "I want to thank you for being a good friend to Phil," my father had said.

At the time Bill hadn't made too much of it. Just a kind comment from my father. Maybe a basic show of gratitude.

But after reading the manuscript, Bill thought differently about it.

"Maybe he was saying something else," Bill conjectured. "As if he appreciated me for being a decent, positive force in your life as opposed to others in your life who were bad, even violent, to you. I'm wondering if he was thanking me for balancing out the negative forces inside the family. When those closest to you were doing some really bad things."

In many ways the process of writing this book has been just like that. A memory would come into focus after writing a particular chapter and it would put things just a little more in perspective. Or a family member or friend would read a scene I'd written and then recount an event I had forgotten. Something which, at the time, seemed insignificant, even routine. But in light of my story, as it was finally revealed, the event took on greater meaning.

Yet another clue uncovered in a decades-long journey to unravel the mystery of my life.

Resources for Recovery

- National Institute of Mental Health (NIMH)
  Website: www.nimh.nih.gov
  Provides comprehensive information on mental health disorders and treatments.
- RAINN (Rape, Abuse & Incest National Network)
  Website: www.rainn.org
  Offers support for survivors of sexual violence and operates the National Sexual Assault Hotline.
- Substance Abuse and Mental Health Services Administration (SAMHSA)
  Website: https://www.samhsa.gov/find-help/national-helpline

Support Groups

- Alcoholics Anonymous (AA)
  Website: www.aa.org
  Helpline: 650.577.1310 (San Mateo County)
  Helpline: 408.374.8511 (Santa Clara County)
  A fellowship of men and women who share their experiences to solve their common problem and help others recover from alcoholism.
- Survivors of Incest Anonymous (SIA)
  Website: www.siawso.org
  A 12-step program for survivors of childhood sexual abuse.
- Al-Anon Family Groups
  Website: https://al-anon.org/

- Voices of Recovery (San Mateo County)
  Website: https://www.vorsmc.org/
- Sex Addicts Anonymous
  Website: https://saa-recovery.org/

Hotlines

- National Suicide Prevention Lifeline
  Phone: 1-800-273-TALK (8255)
  Provides 24/7, free, and confidential support for people in distress, prevention and crisis resources.
- National Domestic Violence Hotline
  Phone: 1-800-799-SAFE (7233)
  Offers support for victims of domestic violence.

Books

- *The Body Keeps the Score* by Bessel van der Kolk, M.D.
  A seminal book on trauma and its impact on the body, offering insights and strategies for healing.
- *Healing the Child Within* by Charles L. Whitfield, M.D.
  This book addresses the concept of the inner child and provides guidance for healing past traumas.

Acknowledgments

First and foremost, I want to thank my good friend, Bill Prescott, who saw the vision of this story long before it became a book. Your support and insight were instrumental in transforming an idea into a tangible reality.

I am deeply grateful to my friend of many decades, Jared Smith, for his profound guidance, both in my life and in the creation of this book. Your wisdom, patience, and unwavering support have been a steady anchor throughout this process. You have been a mentor and a friend, and this book would not exist without your influence and encouragement.

I would also like to extend my deepest gratitude to my brother, Peter March, for his unwavering encouragement and energy that helped me push forward through the toughest parts of this journey. Your belief in me has been a guiding light.

My heartfelt thanks go out to Abby Bailon. Thank you for your insight and encouragement during the final beta reading phase. Your feedback was crucial in the final stages of refinement. Thanks also to Kate Daly and Katy March; your feedback during the early beta phase was invaluable in shaping the narrative and refining the story.

Special thanks to Lisa Manterfield for her deep editing prowess. Your keen eye and thoughtful suggestions helped turn a very rough idea into a compelling story.

Molly Spain, your meticulous copy editing ensured that the final manuscript was polished and professional. Thank you for your attention to detail and dedication.

My sincere appreciation goes to Christina Holloway for her insight and encouragement on the publishing and marketing process. Your expertise and advice have been invaluable. And to Steve Latner, thank you for sharing your insight and publishing experience, which has been a tremendous help. I also want to extend my thanks to other beta readers, Lauren and Summer. Your input was vital in honing the story to its final form.

And finally, Kathy, words cannot express my gratitude for your love and support. Thank you for enduring my many moments of frustration and moodiness, and for helping me stay grounded through the entire process. Your unwavering presence has been my rock. Your love and patience gave me the strength to keep going, and your faith in me and this project kept me inspired and motivated. This book is as much yours as it is mine.

Each of you has played a significant role in the creation of this book, and for that, I am eternally grateful.

Thank you for taking the time to read this memoir! If you enjoyed the book, please consider leaving an honest review on Amazon. Your feedback helps other readers discover the story, and I greatly appreciate your support.

About the Author

Philip March is a seasoned technology entrepreneur, writer, and adventurer who has spent over three decades navigating the dynamic landscape of Silicon Valley. Born and raised in a Christian Science family, Philip's journey from his childhood in Los Altos Hills to his professional success in marketing for leading technology companies like Cisco, KLA, and Oracle has been marked by resilience, curiosity, and an unwavering quest for understanding.

Philip's academic background in physics, crowned with an MBA from Santa Clara University, laid the foundation for his extensive career in the technology sector. His work spanned various roles in marketing and strategic development, including influential positions in several cybersecurity startups. His ability to blend technical expertise with creative marketing strategies made him a respected figure in the industry.

Beyond his professional achievements, Philip is a passionate kiteboarder, cyclist, and skier. He is a regular participant in the Noon Ride group out of Palo Alto, where he enjoys the camaraderie and challenge of cycling with like-minded enthusiasts. His love for the outdoors is matched only by his dedication to personal growth and healing.

Philip's memoir, *Riding the Elephant: Unraveling the Mystery of My Childhood Trauma*, is a deeply personal narrative that explores the profound impact of his brother Hollis's untimely death and the subsequent flashbacks that revealed repressed memories of childhood abuse. Through candid reflection and unflinching honesty, Philip shares his journey of confronting these painful memories, grappling with substance abuse, and seeking recovery through therapy, a twelve-step program, and a transformative psychedelic retreat. His story is one of courage, resilience, and the quest for truth, offering hope and inspiration to others facing similar battles.

Philip lives with his soulmate, Kathy Jones, in the serene hills of Silicon Valley. Their relationship, marked by mutual support and understanding, has been a cornerstone of his healing journey. Together, they share a love for adventure, a commitment to personal growth, and a deep appreciation for the simple joys of life.

Riding the Elephant is Philip's first book, but his passion for storytelling and helping others through his experiences promises more to come. As he continues to write and explore new ventures, Philip remains dedicated to living authentically and encouraging others to do the same.

To learn more about Philip Arthur March and stay updated on his latest projects, visit his website at www.philipmarchbooks.com.

www.ingramcontent.com/pod-product-compliance
Lightning Source LLC
Chambersburg PA
CBHW071703120626
46550CB00001B/83